THE
GREAT INFLATION
1939–1951

THE
GREAT INFLATION
1939–1951

BY

A. J. BROWN, M.A., D.Phil.

Sometime Fellow of All Souls College, Oxford
Professor of Economics in the
University of Leeds

Issued under the auspices of the
Royal Institute of International Affairs

OXFORD UNIVERSITY PRESS
LONDON   NEW YORK   TORONTO

Oxford University Press, Amen House, London E.C.4

GLASGOW   NEW YORK   TORONTO   MELBOURNE   WELLINGTON
BOMBAY   CALCUTTA   MADRAS   KARACHI
CAPE TOWN   IBADAN   NAIROBI   ACCRA   SINGAPORE

FIRST PUBLISHED 1955
SECOND IMPRESSION 1956

PRINTED IN GREAT BRITAIN

PREFACE

THE inflation of 1939–51, in any sense one of the greatest, if not the greatest, in the history of the world economy, is clearly a large enough theme for one of the rare masterpieces of broad economic interpretation, or for several lesser works with more modest pretensions. I have no illusion as to the class into which this book falls. If it is pretentious in its scope, that is only because it seemed useful to compare, contrast, and, in part, analyse a number of different kinds of inflationary experience, even while the processes in question were still going on, and before more than a few of the detailed studies had appeared upon which some future writer will be able, no doubt, to base more considered and better documented judgements about this episode in history as a whole.

One of the main difficulties encountered by anyone trying in the last five or six years to understand the inflationary processes which had been going on since 1939, and were still very much in progress, arose from the unsatisfactory and rapidly changing nature of the theoretical framework at his disposal. Modern dynamic economics is a young subject, and the process of price increase under the pressure of excess demand or under the influence of expectations, after having attracted very little interest in the fifteen years before 1939, has been discussed in considerable detail since then and especially since the end of the war. Moreover, the institutional machinery by which prices and wages have been determined and changed has been quite largely different during the period of inflation from what had been assumed in most theoretical formulations; most of the theorists have not caught up with actuality.

This book, therefore, contains a certain amount of exposition of theory, not as a solid body of doctrine, but rather as separate introductions or frames of reference for each of the aspects of inflation which are discussed, the main object of the discussion being to find how well the facts of experience fit the framework. The first chapter is wholly theoretical, but has been kept as general and simple as possible, its main object (apart from mere definition) being to bring out the extent to which the economist seeking to give a theoretical explanation of inflation must choose, on the basis of observation, between rival possibilities. This is followed, in Chapter 2, by a broad, if superficial, chronological account intended to give the reader his bearings for the more particular discussions which follow.

At the beginning of the war the process of income expansion which goes on in the recovery and boom phases of the trade cycle had been studied with some success, and the apparatus developed for this purpose was that which it seemed most natural to apply to the process of inflation. The results of doing so are discussed in Chapter 3. While this approach, with some modifications, has its uses, the fact emerges that it is designed essentially to deal with a situation in which real income can expand, and cannot be transferred to conditions of full employment with success unless prices in general are flexible. This was, of course, very far from being the case in most economies of the world in the period under discussion, and the consequences of this fact, and of the ways in which prices actually moved in the main economies, fall to be discussed in Chapters 4, 5, and 6. In Chapter 7 the purposes, problems, and lessons of official price control are briefly treated.

The following four chapters—8 to 11—deal with some rather special aspects of the inflation: first the relatively rare and highly spectacular phenomenon of hyper-inflation, which has loss of confidence in money as its essential feature, then the inter-relation between inflation and interest rates, then the direct effects upon output and expenditure of the high levels of liquidity which characterized most economies during the greater part of the period, and finally a group of somewhat varied international aspects of inflation—the processes by which it spread, its relation with the foreign exchanges, and its relation with the post-war international disequilibrium.

The last chapter in the book makes some attempt by way of summary and conclusion to identify and to assess the main processes of inflation in the world economy as a whole, and to state—but not to solve—the outstanding problems of policy which seem to emerge from the inflations of these twelve troubled years. If the reader finds the resulting sketch of the working of the present world economy rather commonplace, he is asked to remember that the analyses which are currently put forward by economists and taught to students are still quite largely based upon the very different world economy which existed (or was supposed to exist) before 1939, and that to set out even the obvious may be a service to those who happen to be looking at something else.

Like most writers, I owe more debts than it is practicable to acknowledge. First, I am indebted to the Royal Institute of International Affairs, which encouraged me to undertake this study, and especially to Mrs. J. M. Fleming, who assisted me by bringing together an enormous quantity of the most relevant data from almost every country during the first two years of the work on it. To the Royal Institute also I owe a profound apology for the slowness with which the work proceeded, in competition with the rival claims of academic administration and teaching. Secondly I am indebted to Professors R. G. Hawtrey and R. S. Sayers, who were good enough to read the book in typescript at different stages in its evolution. To Professor Hawtrey, who made detailed comments upon it in its earlier stages, very special thanks are due, as much for those of his suggestions which I did not feel able to accept as for those which I endeavoured to follow out with, I think, very great profit. Finally, I am indebted to my colleagues in the University of Leeds, with whom I had the benefit of much discussion, and in particular to Mr. W. T. Newlyn and Mr. H. C. Hillmann, who made most useful comments upon drafts of many of the chapters. My debts to some of my research students, particularly Dr. A. M. Khusro and Mr. Z. Kubinski, will become clear at particular points in the text, and I am also indebted to Mr. Kubinski and to Mr. J. F. Brothwell for the diagrams and to Mrs. J. F. Brothwell for the final typing.

A. J. BROWN

May 1954

CONTENTS

DIAGRAMS

TABLES

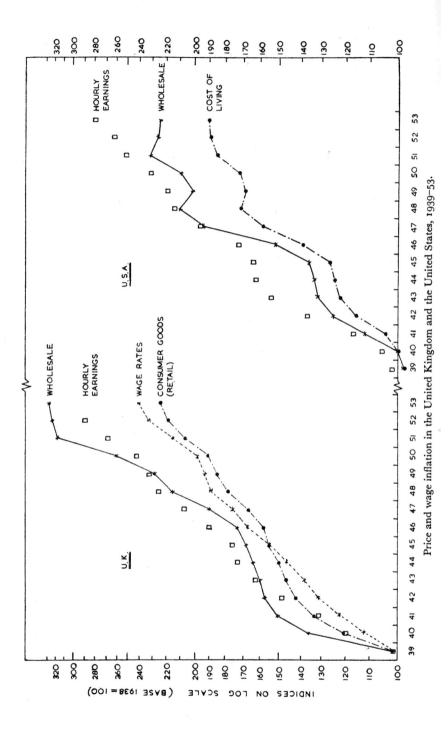

Price and wage inflation in the United Kingdom and the United States, 1939–53.

I

The Nature and Sources of Inflation

What is Inflation?

IN two world wars and their aftermaths inflation has become familiar to the people of most countries as a threat or an actuality. Yet, despite the volume of experience so accumulated and the amount of attention so directed to it, one cannot say that there is general agreement as to how it can best be defined, how the threat of it can be assessed, or how the extent to which it has proceeded can be measured. For, despite its painful familiarity, inflation is, from the economist's point of view, an elusive phenomenon—or, perhaps more correctly, an elusive and bewildering variety of phenomena. The word itself is used to describe several different processes, or states, sometimes with prefixes which help to identify what is referred to, sometimes without. Thus, people speak of price inflation, meaning an inordinate rise of the general level of prices; of income inflation (or of the inflation of some section of total income, such as wages or profits); of currency inflation, meaning simply an excessive increase in the supply of money, without any necessary reference to what has happened to prices; of cost inflation, meaning that the prices of factors of production have risen; or of suppressed inflation, meaning that, in all the circumstances, certain specific controls are the only bulwark against an inordinate increase of costs, prices, incomes, or of all three.

These things do not necessarily go together. Income (or a part of income) can be increased without any increase in prices provided that unused resources can be brought into production; one section of income can be inflated at the expense of another, leaving total income, and perhaps the general level of prices, unchanged; in the event of a catastrophe, such as severe crop failure, or invasion, it is possible for prices to rise alarmingly without total money incomes being increased; prices of factors of production (costs) and of finished goods can sometimes show an appreciable degree of independence of one another in their movements; the quantity of money can certainly increase at times without any increase in money income—even in the absence of controls tending to hold income down—and income or prices can rise spectacularly without any increase in the supply of money.

Despite this variety of independent, or partly independent, happenings to which the name can be applied, however, inflation as ordinarily understood has something to do with an inordinate rise of prices. An increase of income, or part of income, without any substantial increase of prices in general, may be described by the economist as an inflation, but the word so used will fail to rouse in the ordinary man's mind the alarming associations that it generally carries. Those associations include everything that goes with a general increase of prices, as frequently experienced in the past. For instance, distortion of the distribution of income arises because the rise of prices, though general, is not uniform; consequently there is distortion of the composition of the economy's output, probably in the direction of more luxury goods at the expense of necessities. The purchasing power of savings held in money or in bonds is lost, and ultimately there is the danger that the inflationary process may gather strength from its own effect on the economy and explode into a hyper-inflation in which money may cease altogether to fulfil its normal functions. It is with these unpleasant things, or the danger of them, that the word inflation is now firmly associated. They stem from an inordinate rise of prices; and it is with this, or a situation which contains the danger of it, that people are concerned when they talk about inflation.

This statement requires one qualification. Although an inordinate rise of prices is what people mainly fear—with good reason—from a situation that can be described as inflationary, experience of effective administrative control of prices during and since the Second World War has shown that a situation that contains the potentiality of great price increase has severe disadvantages even though the realization of that possibility may be repressed—even though confidence may be established that it will continue to be repressed. The essential quality of money—its acceptability in exchange for any good or service whatever—can be just as effectively destroyed by making it virtually impossible to spend more than a very limited amount of it—the amount sanctioned by a system of rationing and price control—as by creating a belief that its purchasing power will melt away in the holder's hands, as happens in a hyper-inflation. Suppressed inflation has, therefore, come to be feared for its own sake, not only for the danger it may hold if suppression fails.

The two practical questions therefore which arise in connexion with the causation of inflation are: first, what makes prices rise; second, how, if prices are prevented from rising, may a plethora of money come into existence?

The Raising of Prices in a Free Market

So far as the former of these two questions is concerned, the more orthodox and traditional answers are based upon the assumption that whatever price (or set of prices) is ruling can be explained as being a condition of market equilibrium. That is to say, it is assumed that the price of each commodity is such that the amount the market as a whole wants to hold at that price is the amount that is actually available. If, at the price in question, all the participators in the market, taken together, had wanted to hold more than is actually available, the attempt of some or all of them to increase their holdings would, it is assumed, very quickly have raised the price to a higher level; if they had wanted to hold less than is in the market their attempts to sell would equally quickly have lowered the price. The basic supposition here, of course, is that price is determined by bargaining in the market and is perfectly flexible. So long as this is so, the price must, at every moment, be that which reconciles the market as a whole to holding just as much of the commodity as it happens to have.

When one applies this principle to the general level of prices of goods, one is, of course, ignoring relative changes which take place in the prices of different commodities, and considering, as it were, the price of a bundle composed in such a way as to be representative of all the goods which are in fact sold. The price of a bundle is then such as to reconcile the market (or perhaps one might say the community) to holding the number of bundles actually available. What it is will, clearly, depend upon the quantity of goods to be had; equally, it will depend upon the quantity of money. A price is simply a rate of exchange between two kinds of commodity, and is bound to depend in general upon supplies of both of them; if one is therefore considering the general price level of goods, one is concerned with the rate of exchange between units of money and hypothetical bundles representative of goods in general; and the relative price of the two will depend upon the quantities available of both.

If it were adequate to think of the price level at any moment as depending in this way merely upon the quantity of money and the quantity of goods in existence, all would be very simple; one could then say that a rise in the general price level might be attributed either to an increase in the supply of money in existence or to a diminution in the amount of goods. This, indeed, does correspond to one of the popular descriptions of inflation—'too much money chasing too few goods'. But even if one assumes that the ruling price is always an equilibrium price, it has still to be admitted that the relation connecting price with the available quantities of goods and of money is not likely to be a constant one; people will not always want to hold the same stocks of goods at some specified price and with some specified quantity of money in existence, or (to put the same thing in another way) people will not always be reconciled by the same price level to any specified level of stocks and of money.

Perhaps the most general reason for variations in their attitude in this matter is change in their general view about the level of prices in the somewhat longer run. A given level of commodity stocks and of money holdings will be reconcilable at very different price levels according to whether it seems that consumption is outstripping production or that production is outstripping consumption. In some commodity markets it seems that the current rates of production and consumption (which are presumably projected into the future) are more directly relevant to price formation than are the current levels of stocks. From time to time, too, the relation of price to production, consumption, and the monetary position is disturbed by the market's receiving news which leads it to believe that the current rate of production or of consumption (or perhaps the current policy of the monetary authorities) is likely to change in the near future.

This suggests that, by virtue of the way in which expectations about price in the future enter into the formation of current price, the price which comes to rule in a market may be a sort of collective estimate of the long-run equilibrium price—the price which could persist indefinitely, because it is the one which makes the rates of production and of consumption of the commodity equal. This may be so; though even if it is, there is no guarantee that the collective estimate will be even approximately correct during most of the time—that market price will not in fact vary widely and frequently from the long-run equilibrium price. On the other hand, in a market where much of the business is done by dealers who are not committed to hold their stocks for more than a short time, it is possible that little or no attempt to estimate the long-run equilibrium price may be made, the majority of dealers (or the more important of them) acting in accordance with their views of what the market as a whole will expect in the short run rather than any views they may have about what will actually happen in the longer run. There is, no doubt, very great variety of behaviour between different markets in this regard, and it is clear that there can be very wide temporary movements of price which have little or nothing to do with the current rates of production and consumption, with the level of stocks, or with the supply of money.

Upward movements based upon expectations in many or all markets simultaneously are an essential feature of hyperinflation. Once prices have been given a sufficiently strong upward push by any cause whatever, it is possible that further increases may be expected, and the automatic fulfilment of this expectation, in advance of the time at which the further increase was anticipated, may then cause a further upward revision of prices expected to rule in the future. A mechanism of this kind can, clearly, produce an indefinitely accelerating price increase, provided that certain requirements are fulfilled. In the first place, all or most prices must be flexible—that is, to say, capable of being changed very quickly as a result of changed expectations about their future course. Secondly, the supply of money must be sufficient to enable stocks to be carried and transactions performed at the higher and higher price levels which result from the process.

The latter condition—the sufficiency of the money supply—demands a word of explanation. It is plain that, if the total amount of money (including credit money) in existence were fully used to finance the carrying of commodity stocks, the payment of wages and salaries, and the other transactions connected with the working of the economy, either all the time or at the peak season of the year, then an increase in those payments could take place only if the supply of money were increased equi-proportionately. It is not, however, normally the case that the stock of money in existence is as fully employed as this. At all ordinary times (even peak seasons) there are large amounts of money which it suits their owners to keep idle, either to meet possible emergencies or because it does not seem worth while to invest them for the period expected to elapse before they may be wanted for spending. If these sums can be borrowed (perhaps at an enhanced rate of interest) by those who require working capital, there is normally scope for a very large increase in the latter without any increase in the actual supply of money. Moreover, if prices are expected to rise, the inducement to hold money idle is very much reduced. Those who entertain such expectations will want to hold goods or claims to goods instead of money, and the existing stocks of money and of goods will accordingly come to be in equilibrium with one another at a much higher price of goods (in terms of money) than before.

There is thus a considerable degree of independence between the supply of money and the total value of transactions, even in an economy where all prices are flexible. A great deal of inflation of prices is generally possible without any increase in the quantity of money—a revision of expectations may bring it about. Nevertheless, large inflationary movements in such economies are usually associated with great increases in the supply of money, partly because they go with budget deficits which involve the creation of money by the government, or by the banks for the government, and partly because, in a time of rising commodity prices, banks are apt to extend increased credit to customers to meet the needs of trade. The causal connexion between such inflations and budget deficits is frequently a double one—the deficit, by its direct creation of new purchasing power, is often, in practice, the main initiating cause of the inflation, but, once price inflation begins, it tends also to raise government expenditure ahead of revenue, and thus to generate further deficits.

Looking therefore at the price level in the simplest possible way, one may say that, in so far as it is flexible, it is determined at any moment by the quantities of money and of goods in existence, and by the preferences of the community in regard to their holdings of money and of goods. Any of these elements in the situation may change in such a way as to bring about increases in the price level. The quantity of goods may be diminished by harvest failure or enemy action. The quantity of money may be increased by the direct action of the government in printing more, or of banks in creating more credit, or (for a particular country or region) by a net inflow from outside in payment for a net sale of goods or services. The attitude of the public may change in favour of holding goods and against holding money because they expect prices to rise in the future; an expectation which may be based upon observation that demand is currently outrunning supply, or upon a piece of news which suggests a future operation of one of the other inflationary factors just mentioned, or perhaps upon projection of recent changes into the future.

Contractual and Administered Prices

This simple way of looking at things provides a fairly adequate analysis of inflation in an economy where prices are, as we have so far assumed, determined by bargaining in the market. That, however, is manifestly not the way in which most prices are fixed (immediately, at any rate) in advanced modern economies. It is true that the prices of many primary commodities appear to be so fixed in the great world markets, but this is not true of most manufactured or semi-manufactured goods or even foodstuffs as sold at retail. In all these cases the manufacturer or the seller sets the price as he thinks fit in view of the circumstances known to him, and the price so set is often changed only with reluctance. Moreover, the prices of the hired factors of production, especially labour, are very imperfectly sensitive to market conditions. In all but times of very rapid inflation wage rates in any one trade tend to be changed after elaborate bargaining, only every two or three years, or even less frequently. In some instances in many countries, and universally in some countries, they are subject to automatic adjustment to changes in the cost of living, which itself depends largely upon prices fixed at not very frequent intervals by the manufacturers rather than upon sensitive adjustments to supply and demand. The picture, therefore, of inflation which represents all prices as equilibrium prices reached by bargaining in the markets requires modification, even if price control is absent; still more if it is present.

It may be objected that the modification which it requires is not radical. If prices are very rigid because of control or some other institutional cause, then price inflation will not arise; if they rise in spite of the various institutional factors which have just been mentioned, then (it may be argued) they must do so within the limits set by the possibilities which would exist in free, flexible markets. The effects of stickiness, in fact, will merely be to delay the achievement of the result which would follow in such a free, flexible market, or to render it incomplete.

In a formal sense this may be correct, especially if one is concerned with a considerable inflation taking place over a not very short period. If one compares the situation in, say, the United Kingdom in 1952 with that in 1939, it is no doubt correct to say that the rise in prices can be accounted for by the rise in the quantity of money, the much smaller rise in the quantity of goods, and the change in the public's preferences as between money and goods, apart from the fact that some prices were, in 1952, restrained from rising to their full equilibrium level by official controls or by the cautious pricing policies of firms, and others (especially, perhaps, factor prices) had not caught up to their true equilibrium position because of the cumbersome nature of the machinery of adjustment. There might also be some satisfaction in knowing (if that were possible) what is the equilibrium level towards which prices would move in the existing state of preferences and of supplies of money and of goods, if official controls were removed, and if time were allowed for the slow mechanism of adjustment to work.

The practical interest of such an analysis and of such knowledge, however, clearly diminishes in proportion as the hypothetical circumstances of freedom and equilibrium to which they apply are remote from reality. What it is practically important to know is not simply what forces have operated to permit price inflation, perhaps to a very much greater extent than has actually been experienced, but what forces, acting together or in part against each other, have caused price inflation to occur to the precise extent to which it has occurred. We want to know, not merely what was the nature of the forces that made the balloon rise (and how far it would have risen if it had not been tethered), but, since it was in fact a captive balloon, how far the rope was paid out, and why neither more nor less.

There is another argument of perhaps even greater cogency which works in the same direction. The changes in quantities of money and of goods and the changes in preferences cannot properly be treated as if they were independent of the amount of price inflation which the controls or the stickiness of the market have permitted. It has already been mentioned that the public's preference for goods rather than money may be stimulated simply by their projection into the future of price movements which have been going on in the immediate past—a vitally important part of the mechanism of hyper-inflation. The movement of prices which is actually permitted thus affects the strength of the pressure working for further price increase. Again, the quantity of money in existence can hardly be regarded as given independently of prices. In many economies, during most of the inflationary period, the monetary authorities have been largely passive, creating as much money as the public wanted, or, at least, wanted for a generous number of approved purposes. In these circumstances it is hardly satisfactory to give increases in the quantity of money as a main part of the cause of price inflation; the actual order of events was that some contractual prices (such as wage rates) or the controlled prices of finished goods were raised, and that the extra demand for credit to finance wage payments or the holding of stocks then resulted in the creation of more money. Or, again, the quantity of goods cannot be taken as independent of prices. During the greater part of the inflationary period, no doubt, with resources fully employed, output was largely independent of prices, but stocks (and the location of stocks) certainly were not. Control of prices, or their maintenance by institutional rigidity at a level below equilibrium, will reduce the level of stocks, thus making the immediate short-run equilibrium level of prices much higher than it would have been if prices had not been restrained. Alternatively, if it comes to be expected that price control will break down, producers and dealers will withhold stocks from sale—a phenomenon which was clearly revealed when such stocks in Germany were released after the currency reform of 1948. In the most extreme cases, too, the volume of output itself becomes dependent upon price in an inflationary situation, the holding down of prices when money holdings are very large acting as a strong deterrent to earning and so to production.

The formation of the price level may thus, in practice, take place in many ways, and, so far as modern economies are concerned, at least, it is not to be satisfactorily explained on the assumption that it will generally be in, or near to, the short-term equilibrium position, determined in some simple way from the amounts of money and of goods available. It has been pointed out above that over large portions of a modern economy prices are fixed by manufacturers or other sellers. How are they so fixed?

Practice no doubt varies a great deal, but there is much evidence that, even in ordinary times (not of inflation and price control) they are very widely fixed in some sort of relation to cost of production—probably to the average total cost of production calculated on the assumption that plant is being utilized to some standard extent. The reasons for some such procedure are not hard to guess. In most markets, whether they are highly competitive or not, the individual producer must have regard to the policy of his competitors, whether they compete with him directly, indirectly, or even only potentially. Once he finds a price for his product which enables him to survive or to prosper (according to his luck), he may or may not vary it according to what he estimates to be the state of demand; the evidence is that this is done only sparingly, probably because changes in demand are often thought to be temporary, and because any such change in price both raises the danger of price war and conflicts with the widespread belief that consumers like price stability. On the other hand, a rise in direct costs of production is very likely indeed (unless it is thought to be temporary) to lead him to raise his selling price. Not only is this a common-sense method of preserving profit margins, and unlikely to be thought aggressive by competitors, but in many industries it is expected that all or most firms will adjust themselves to it in much the same way, so that to adjust one's selling price to changes (or, at any rate, increases) in cost of production is likely to leave one's competitive position roughly unchanged. Whether this is a correct picture of price formation in ordinary times or not, however, it is certain that most systems of price control, which have been so widespread during much of the inflationary period, have the effect of causing prices of finished goods to vary with costs of production.

In so far as selling prices of manufactures, and other retail prices, are adjusted in this way to changes in cost of production, the question, what makes prices rise? leads straight on to: what makes costs (that is, principally factor prices) rise? So far as raw materials are concerned, it seems that we arrive, at last, in a region where market price is generally a short-term equilibrium price, so that the simple analysis of the formation of such prices, given earlier in this chapter, provides one with, at any rate, a good approach to the understanding of them. With wage rates the position is not so simple. In some countries, and at some times, the variations in wage rates seem to have been fairly closely related, though mainly with some delay, to the ebbing and flowing of the demand for labour, which in turn has corresponded in the main (though not precisely) to the ebbing and flowing of general demand for goods and services. Elsewhere, however, changes in wage rates have borne a less direct, or more complicated, relation to changes in demand; they are dependent in a high degree upon the nature of the negotiating machinery which exists and the general social and political position of organized labour.

It thus seems possible that, in a largely industrial community, the most direct and powerful price-raising influence in a time of inflation may be either the rising price of raw materials and foodstuffs (which depends upon world-wide market forces) or the rising price of labour within the community. In so far as the community is self-sufficient its own labour costs will tend to be the major of these two factors; in so far as it depends upon imports of raw materials and foodstuffs, their prices will predominate. If prices of finished goods are moved up, in general, in accordance with rises in costs, it is obvious that these factor prices are the main immediate determinants of the general price level. Monetary factors can impinge upon the price level of finished goods in these circumstances only in so far as they affect factor prices. How effectively they can do this is a large question: in an economy as large and self-contained as the United States monetary policy can doubtless affect the markets for primary commodities; in more open economies, such as the United Kingdom, it has far less chance of doing so, since the prices of the commodities in question depend upon monetary demand in all the main consuming countries taken together. Monetary policy, also, can certainly influence the demand for labour, but how it thus affects the wage level is more problematic. Certainly it seems to be the case in more than one of the most advanced economies that monetary stringency cannot halt the advance of the wage level, especially in the face of a rising cost of living, except by producing a deep depression with heavy unemployment. In any case, however, during the inflationary period studied here money was generally either superabundant or freely supplied in response to the needs of trade. In these circumstances price levels in the main economies of the world tended to be determined by wage rates and by the prices (generally the world market prices, modified by subsidies and other local circumstances) of foodstuffs and raw materials, without hindrance from monetary stringency.

Forced Saving and the Accumulation of Money

This is, perhaps, all that need be said by way of introduction about the first of the two questions posed earlier in this chapter: what makes prices rise? The second question, which now demands a little attention, is: how, if prices are prevented from rising, may a plethora of money come into existence? The importance of this question has perhaps been emphasized by the foregoing discussion, in which attention has been drawn to the frequency with which, because either of official price control or of firms' pricing policies, prices have been below the equilibrium level which the quantities of goods and of money and the state of the public's preferences would appear to justify.

The way in which this state of affairs comes about is simple enough—there either are not in existence as many goods (of the desired kinds) as consumers and firms would like to buy at the ruling prices out of the incomes which they have available, or, if the goods exist, they are prevented by rationing or licensing systems from buying them. Part of the income received during the period in question is, therefore, retained in the form of money instead of being spent on goods and services.

It is worth reflecting, however, on how it comes about that the supply of goods does not match the purchasing power which the community would like to direct towards them. Looked at from a very general point of view, this state of affairs may, indeed, appear a little paradoxical. By a drastic, but useful, simplification of the real world, one may think of the income received in any given week as being the money (including profits at some usual level) paid out for the production of the goods made in the previous week, which are becoming available in the shops in the week in question. In this simplified picture, the income available in the week in question is exactly sufficient to buy the goods which are coming forward. It is plain that the money received by purchasers will be exactly spent up by them, so that there will be no net accumulation of money in any quarter, *if the goods produced were of the kinds that purchasers wanted to buy.*

Suppose, however, that they were not; suppose, for instance, that the government has diverted a large part of the productive capacity of the country from normal peacetime goods to armaments. When the last week's production comes forward for delivery, the government will have to find money to buy the armaments, and the rest of the community will be receiving a much larger income than is necessary to purchase the non-armament component of output at its cost of production. Their income, in fact, equals the total cost of production of *all* output, including armaments. How does the government find the money to purchase the armaments which it has ordered and which are now delivered? It may levy taxation on current incomes to the necessary extent. In this case, the disposable incomes of the rest of the community (after tax) will be reduced to precisely the amount necessary to buy the non-armament goods, so that, since the government has enough revenue to buy the armaments, the whole of output can again be purchased at its cost of production without any net accumulation of money anywhere in the economy. Or, the government may borrow the money it needs. If the lending is done by the rest of the community out of the excess income it has in hand after buying the non-armament portion of output, then the result is broadly the same as before. It will again be broadly the same if the government borrows from the banks, provided that the rest of the community uses its surplus income either for repaying its existing debts to the banks, or (in a slightly more complicated model than that so far described) for purposes for which it would otherwise have borrowed from them. It is plain, however, that to the extent to which the non-government part of the community retains some of its surplus income in the form of an increased holding of money, the government, in order to buy the armaments which have been produced for it, will have to create new money, or to get the banking system to do so.

This exposition may seem to imply that the responsibility for an increase in the amount of money in existence, when the level of transactions (expressed either in real or in money terms) is constant, rests with those who choose to accumulate increased holdings rather than to lend the money they cannot spend to the government or to use it to repay debt to the banks. To maintain this, simply and literally, would be misleading. The extent to which the public has an opportunity to get rid of the money which it is unable to spend, in exchange for assets which it can regard as equally trustworthy, depends upon the skill with which the government conducts its financial policy, and in this as in most other matters perfection is not, in practice, attainable. People hold large parts of their unspendable surplus income in money form because they are unaccustomed to holding securities, because they do not trust them, because the advantage of holding them, with taxation on their interest yield at wartime levels, is low, and, no doubt, from sheer inertia. Moreover, in the Second World War in particular, governments were sensible of the advantage to themselves, as very large borrowers, in keeping interest rates down. This limited the incentive to invest savings, or, to put the same thing in another way, meant that the public had to be fed with money as well as with securities if it was to be persuaded to go on buying the latter at the interest rates offered. It was for these reasons, in a situation in which governments did not find it practicable to cover the whole of their expenditure by revenue from taxes, that very large accumulations of money arose.

The General Character of Inflation and its Particular Causes

The situation in which prices are actually rising and that in which money holdings are accumulating because prices are prevented from rising are both, as was noted earlier, said to be inflationary, and it will now be seen that they have something in common. Their common element may be described as a disposition on the part of the community, as a whole, to spend more than its income on internally-produced goods and services. The income of the community, for this purpose, must be thought of as what is paid out in the current period (this week) for the services rendered in the previous period (last week) in producing the goods now available for purchase, the profit which is thus paid out being calculated on the assumption that the goods will sell at the same prices this week as last. Expenditure of the whole of current income and no more will thus result in the goods on offer being bought at the same prices (or, at least, at the same average price level) as ruled last week. If the community as a whole spends more than its current income, the price level will be raised. If the community would like to spend more than its current income, but is prevented from doing so by the fact that prices and supplies of goods are limited, then there is an accumulation of money over and above the amount that the community as a whole wants to hold at the present level of income, or, to put it in another way, expenditure (which becomes next week's income) is less than the community in general would like it to be, given this week's income and their present money holdings. The propensity to spend more than its income in this or a similar sense has come to be described or assessed as an 'inflationary gap' in the market for finished goods and services. (For some analytical purposes it is useful to speak of a similar gap in the market for factors of production.) This gap in the goods and services market may be defined as the excess of the sum which the community as a whole would spend on finished goods and services in the coming expenditure period if they were in unlimited supply at their present prices, over the value (at present prices) of the goods and services which will come forward for purchase in that period. It will be seen that, even if there are no restraints on prices, this gap does not correspond precisely to the amount by which expenditure in the next period will exceed income in the present one, because when prices begin to rise people may not spend the same amounts as they would have done had prices remained constant—in other words changes in prices may make people change their minds about the amount of money they want to accumulate or to release. Nevertheless, the 'inflationary gap', so defined, is in principle a good measure of the pressure making for inflation in the market or set of markets in question.

Accurate though it may be, however, to describe inflationary processes in this way as characterized by a propensity of the community to spend more than its current income, or in other words, by the existence of an 'inflationary gap', it appears from the discussion in this chapter that such a description does not necessarily throw much light upon the causes of inflation. One wants to know the reason for this propensity. The possibilities here are numerous. The community may want to spend more than its income because it has an urgent demand for armaments or for materials for reconstruction, and because the government or the banks have created new purchasing power to implement this demand. Or the raising of prices by events abroad or by administrative action or political agreement at home, may be the initiating factor, the supply of purchasing power responding in a passive manner. Not only may prices go up because people want to overspend, but people may want to overspend because prices have gone up. Or expectations concerning price movements may change and with them the preferences of the community as between liquid purchasing power and goods. In extreme cases the propensity to overspend income may arise from and feed upon price inflation which is already happening. And, apart from these ways in which the propensity to overspend income may arise, one must take account, once it has arisen, of the various ways in which suppressed inflation may pass into open inflation—ways which may themselves bear upon the propensity to overspend.

In other words, though it may be possible to give a generally valid formal description of what constitutes inflation, the causal mechanisms by which it happens are various and their roots may go deep into the market institutions and the social and political structures of the communities concerned. For this reason it is not profitable to approach the events of the inflationary period treated in this book with a single theoretical scheme into which they must be fitted. The mechanisms of inflation in the world, or in the principal countries, may have been basically simple and similar, or they may have been complex and diverse. One cannot know the mechanism without examining the events. It will be useful, therefore, to begin with a short chronological account of the superficial appearance of those events before trying to analyse them in their various separate aspects and, finally, trying to reach broad conclusions about the main ways in which, predominantly, the machinery worked.

2

The Inflationary Years

The Variety and Content of Inflationary Experience

THE decade and more following the outbreak of war in 1939 constitutes one of the four great periods of virtually world-wide inflation of modern times. The first was the long period—amounting to something like a century—during which the treasure of the Spanish Indies served to raise prices throughout western Europe, quintupling them in Spain, trebling them in England, and more than doubling them in France. This, however, was a long drawn-out inflation, and it is unlikely that it was continuous. The other three great modern inflations have all been associated with general wars, and have been by comparison short and sharp.

In the Revolutionary and Napoleonic period, between 1790 and 1809–12, British wholesale prices were more than doubled, and United States prices almost doubled—precisely what happened to French prices it is hard to say, but they certainly rose drastically. Between 1913 and 1920, United States, Dutch, and Swiss wholesale prices more than doubled, British nearly trebled, French quintupled, Italian sextupled, German increased fourteen-fold, and Austrian fifty-fold. German and Austrian prices were, of course, to rise further to fabulous heights; but for most of the world, a doubling or a trebling of prices having come about in those seven years, there followed deflation.

The general magnitude of the price increases during 1939–48 was not dissimilar from that during 1913–20—or, for that matter, during 1790–1812, so far as those are known. Table III (p. 302) shows (column 6) the level of the wholesale price indices in thirty-three countries in August 1948, the base period (= 100) being the first half of 1939. Wholesale indices are chosen here on account of their general availability and because they are not subject to the extreme distortion from subsidies which in some cases renders official cost of living indices deceptive from certain points of view. August 1948 is chosen as being the first halting-place in the inflation that may be associated with the war and its immediate aftermath. If these indices are arranged in ascending order of magnitude, the result can conveniently be represented as in Diagram I (p. 50) which shows them measured logarithmically, so that a given length on the horizontal scale indicates the same *percentage* change on any part of the diagram. From this, the following facts emerge.

First come five countries—Australia, Venezuela, New Zealand, South Africa, and Norway—with increases of between 70 and 86 per cent. To judge from the indices of cost of living, Uruguay might perhaps also fall into this group, while Western German prices had probably risen less than those of any other country—cost of living had risen only by some 44 per cent. These countries in which prices had risen relatively little are a mixed bag; three of them were belligerents in which price control during the war had been particularly rigid, two were (until later on) neutrals in which rigorous monetary policies were pursued, South Africa was less fully mobilized than most belligerents, and Norway pursued a successful policy of monetary reform after an enemy occupation which had been less damaging than in some other countries.

Sweden, with a price rise of 98 per cent., falls midway between this lower group and another one of six countries in which the price increases had been remarkably similar to each other, lying between 116 and 130 per cent.—namely Canada, Switzerland, Costa Rica, the United States, the United Kingdom, and Eire. This group clearly consists of the two great trading countries which set the pace for world-wide price movements plus others which were particularly sensitive to these world movements. Sweden and (at the other end of the range) Denmark (with a price increase of 137 per cent.) are countries which, from the importance of their connexions with the Anglo-American world, had hardly less reason to conform to its price changes. To judge by its cost of living index, much the same may be true of Colombia. Next comes a group of countries with price increases between 150 and 200 per cent.; Portugal, Mexico, Argentina, Peru, the Netherlands, and (if one can trust a

c

cost of living index in this context) Cuba. These were essentially countries closely connected with and swept along by the currents flowing from the great trading countries, but undergoing somewhat greater degrees of price inflation either because of less rigorous internal policies, or because their exports were primary products whose prices rose particularly high, or for both reasons. After this, the price increases become considerably more widely dispersed. Between 220 and 400 per cent. there falls a mixed collection of countries—Czechoslovakia, Spain, Egypt, India, Chile, Palestine, Belgium, Turkey, Iran, and probably Brazil and Bolivia—in which the Middle Eastern group takes the lead through the wartime expenditure of the Allied armies coupled with relatively ineffective internal controls. In the Lebanon, indeed, the price increase was much greater (674 per cent.), bringing that country into a further group, of which it may be said that inflation has at some point been thoroughly out of hand, but had been arrested before true hyper-inflation set in to render the currency virtually valueless. Bulgaria, Finland, France, Italy, Japan, and Poland, the last two with hundred-fold price increases, may be regarded as the main members of this group. Beyond them come the four countries which have experienced hyper-inflation proper—Greece, Hungary, Rumania, and China.

One important omission will already have been noted, and will, indeed, continue to be noted throughout much of the remainder of this book. The data available for the Union of Soviet Socialist Republics are scanty—there is a complete absence of official data on general price levels and quantities of money in circulation—and, where they exist, generally in forms which make direct comparison with other countries difficult. The most comprehensive source at present available from which a broad generalization about the course of Russian prices might be made is the table of prices of consumers' goods published in the *Economic Survey of Europe in 1951*.[1] From this it may be calculated that the general price level of consumers' goods in State retail shops in Moscow rose by about 150 per cent. between 1940 and December 1947. It is not possible to judge whether at the end of 1947 (the time of the

---

[1] U.N. Department of Economic Affairs, *Economic Survey of Europe in 1951* (Geneva, 1952), ch. 5, table xxxv.

monetary reform) prices were at their peak, though it may well have been so. It seems clear, however, that from that time onwards these prices, unlike those in any other country, showed a declining trend which by the spring of 1951 had brought them to a level only some 70 or 75 per cent. above that of 1940. The inflation of the price of consumers' goods thus ended in the Soviet Union much sooner than in most countries, just as it had commenced earlier—there is evidence of something like a five-fold increase of the price level of non-food goods between 1928 and 1934, and of increases of about 16 per cent. in food prices and 26 per cent. in clothing prices in Moscow between 1936 and 1939. The mechanism of inflation was probably different in the Soviet Union from what it was in most other countries, except, perhaps, during the war years themselves. On the other hand, a further calculation published in the same *Economic Survey of Europe in 1951* suggests that prices of investment goods in the Soviet Union remained steady during the war, but rose by some 40 per cent. between 1946 and 1949 and subsequently fell half way back to the 1940 level by 1951.[1]

It is hardly necessary to point out that such classification as can be attempted by studying the net price increases of various countries in this way is exceedingly rough—not so much a classification as an indication of some vague tendencies. Degrees of price inflation do not display a neat regional distribution; western Europe and Latin America, for instance, both show extremely wide diversities of experience. Nor can one easily generalize about either the countries occupied by the Germans or the countries finally defeated by the Allies. Generalization

[1] The rather odd course of the prices of certain industrial products could probably be matched in other countries; in regard to munitions in particular it seems clear that, though prices may have risen sharply in the early years of the war, they rose little or even fell in the later years in the United States and the United Kingdom owing to increased efficiency in production. In the United Kingdom the volume of output of the main classes of munitions, warships, and aircraft nearly doubled between 1941 and 1943, while the total money cost of the war (excluding cost of pay and allowances of the armed forces) rose by only 15 or 20 per cent., and the numbers employed on war contracts in the engineering, metal, vehicle, shipbuilding, and aircraft industries (an indicator of real costs of production) rose by only 25 or 30 per cent. In the United States the course of events was similar. Between the beginning of 1943 and the end of 1944, the ratio of employment in the munitions industries to their output fell by about 30 per cent. Since this was very much more than the proportion by which hourly rates of earning rose, the presumption is that money costs per unit were reduced.

can scarcely begin until the various phases of the inflationary decade have been distinguished.

One generalization, however, may perhaps be attempted on the basis of the net price increases over the decade as a whole, without reference to geographical or political characteristics of the countries concerned. The relative frequency of the various degrees of inflation is itself the clearest possible evidence for the self-reinforcing nature—beyond a certain point—of the inflationary process. If inflation were simply a tendency to which all countries were exposed, some more than others, and which some resisted better than others, one would expect the degrees of inflation actually undergone to be distributed more or less normally—a few cases of relatively slight inflation balancing a not too dissimilar number of severe cases, with a large number of medium cases in between. In fact, the most frequent price increases in the years under survey were only some 50 per cent. greater than the smallest recorded increase, while the largest increases were thousands or millions of times as great as those most frequently met with. Inflation is not simply an accident, which may be mild or severe; it is a disease which (beyond a point, at least) feeds upon itself in such a way as to produce a large number of very severe cases relatively to the number of very mild ones.

Stress must, however, be placed upon the qualification 'beyond a point'. If those cases are eliminated in which prices have risen by more than 240 per cent. the remaining price increases are found to be distributed in something very like the normal way. These increases are grouped round a geometric mean value (coinciding with the median) of 126 per cent. which is almost exactly the increase experienced in the United Kingdom, and only slightly more than that in the United States. The price increase in these two countries may thus be regarded as constituting the increase in the world price level, not merely in the sense that they are the countries of greatest importance in world trade, but in the sense that the increases experienced by a large group of other countries are grouped symmetrically about the Anglo-American norm. These facts also suggest that the inflationary process experienced by the Middle Eastern countries, by France, Italy, Belgium, Bulgaria, Poland, Austria, Finland, Japan and by Brazil, Bolivia, and Chile (not to mention the four countries of real hyper-inflation) was somehow different in kind from that undergone by the economies which showed smaller price increases; that it contained a self-reinforcing element which was lacking in the more fortunate countries. The average annual rate of price increase (over the nine-year period 1939–48), which seems to constitute the upper limit of the group in which the increases are normally distributed, is about 15 per cent. which might therefore appear, from this very speculative survey, to be the highest rate of price increase which can be sustained over a considerable period of years without serious danger that the inflation will develop a momentum of its own. It is perhaps more likely, however, as will be argued in a later chapter, that what constitutes a dangerous rate of price inflation can be diagnosed better from the maximum rate of increase of prices over a shorter period rather than from the average rate over as long a period as nine years.

The Phases of Inflation

(i) *Economic Mobilization, 1939 to December 1942.* After these generalizations, it is necessary to remember, once again, that inflation since 1939 has been far from a smooth and continuous process. Its phases must be distinguished with some care if a reasonably accurate impression is to be formed of the nature of the processes at work.

The Second World War, like that of 1914–18, began at a time when prices and economic activity in general were below a peak level attained a year or two previously. In most countries of the world, except Germany, Japan, and the Soviet Union, the level of economic activity fell during the later months of 1937 and the early months of 1938; the League of Nations world index of industrial production fell some 20 per cent. in nine months. From mid-1938 there came a recovery, which had made good more than half the loss in the world as a whole by the end of the year, but which was not generally maintained in the early months of 1939. Only shortly before the outbreak of war did economic activity begin its steady climb.

Wholesale prices, in the main, fell fairly continuously from their 1937 peak until the outbreak of war; the first decisive increase came in September 1939. In China and Japan, which had been at war for two years, prices were already rising. In

Shanghai, indeed, wholesale prices doubled in 1939, more than doubled in 1940 and again in 1941 and trebled in 1942. In the United States the general wholesale index leapt some 5 per cent. in a month, thereafter remaining steady until early 1941. In the United Kingdom—owing to the 14 per cent. devaluation of sterling on the outbreak of war, the effects of subsequent heavy purchases of raw materials on special terms, and the rise of transport costs—the wholesale price rise was both steeper and more prolonged. The Board of Trade index rose by 20 per cent. in the first four months of the war (corresponding roughly to the United States increase plus the effect of sterling devaluation) and a further 22 per cent. during 1940. This further increase can be explained largely by the great rise of shipping costs. Thereafter, the rate of increase of wholesale prices in the United Kingdom steadily declined; it was 5 per cent. in 1941 and less than 4 per cent. in 1942. In the United States, on the other hand, the great price increase consequent upon the growth of military demand in the absence of price control came in 1941, when the wholesale index rose by 17 per cent. In the following year, largely owing to the increasing degree of government control both of prices and of the allocation of factors of production, the rate of increase slowed down to 8 per cent. Thereafter, however, it slowed down still more. The period from the outbreak of war to the end of 1942 is, therefore, a useful one to distinguish; it covers the economic mobilizations of the two economies which have the greatest effects upon world economic conditions generally. Changes in wholesale price indices during this time are shown in Diagram 2 (p. 51) as well as in Table III (p. 302).

The United Kingdom and the United States had experienced considerably different increases in their price levels; in the United States wholesale prices had risen in all by only 32 per cent., in the United Kingdom by 66 per cent., which is considerably more even than the United States increase plus the effects of sterling devaluation. Some commodities were obtained by the United Kingdom at f.o.b. prices less than the United States price, but transport costs had become very heavy. Other countries' wholesale price levels had risen variously, but mostly to a greater extent than in either the United States or the United Kingdom. Indeed, the only countries whose prices had risen substantially less than those of the United States were Germany (where rigid control had kept the increase to negligible proportions), and some Latin American countries—including Mexico, Venezuela, and probably Uruguay and Colombia—which had pursued relatively cautious monetary policies, and whose products were not yet really scarce. The rise of shipping costs had interposed a large gap between prices of many overseas products in their countries of origin and their prices in Europe or (in some cases) the United States. The most frequent price increases were between 70 and just over 100 per cent.; they were experienced mainly by countries which were still neutral—with the relatively loose government control of the economy which characterized most pre-war economies—by many European occupied or neutral countries on which German (and in a few cases Allied) demands pressed heavily, and by those Latin American countries whose goods were in heavier demand or which pursued less cautious monetary policies. Beyond this group came Finland, which had already suffered one military defeat, and the Middle Eastern countries, on whose relatively primitive and small economies the pressure of Allied military expenditure had fallen with such effect that prices in the Lebanon were already increased more than seven-fold. Beyond these again came Greece, where the economy had been on the verge of hyper-inflation at the time of the German occupation, and where prices had risen more than eighty-fold. In the main therefore in this phase, neutral and occupied countries had already begun to experience a greater measure of price inflation than the main belligerents.

To some extent this was, of course, due to the greater effectiveness of the controls in the main belligerent countries, to which reference has already been made; in some important instances, however, these main belligerents avoided drastic price inflation in this phase partly by virtue of the high elasticity of supply of goods and services—either because of pre-existing unemployment or because of a very rapid increase in productivity. Thus, Japan, Canada, and the United States almost doubled their money incomes in this period; their real income increasing by something like 50 per cent. On the other hand, the fall of real incomes in certain occupied countries was a powerful factor making for price inflation. In the Netherlands, for instance, even money income fell, despite a rise of about 50 per cent. in prices (both wholesale and retail). In Norway, likewise, real income must have fallen by some 20 per cent., and still more drastic falls occurred in Finland and Greece. In fact, apart from certain east European countries, it seems likely that real income fell throughout continental Europe outside Greater Germany, whereas the real output of the world as a whole probably increased by a quarter or a third.

In the United Kingdom prices of vegetable foods, textile materials, petroleum, and timber were among those which rose most in this period. Home agricultural prices—especially of grain crops—were sharply raised; the fact that continental Europe was no longer a competitor in the purchase of certain imported commodities, such as wheat, kept down their prices, despite the increased freights. The sensational rise in the price of timber—it increased more than three-fold—is hardly surprising in view of the high freight costs in relation to the f.o.b. value of this commodity, and the cutting off of the European sources normally responsible for so high a proportion of the timber entering into international trade, which both produced great scarcity and increased the average length of haul. In the United States also, once prices began to climb in 1941-2, it was the prices of farm products that rose most, with textiles next in order. This reflects, no doubt, the low short-term elasticity of supply of foodstuffs and textile raw materials in the face of rising demand. Supplies of metals and chemicals, on the other hand, were relatively elastic, on account of the existence of excess productive capacity, which was not eliminated until the end of the period in question (or later) when price control had become effective. The relative cheapness of most of the ferrous and non-ferrous metals in the main world markets throughout this period is related, like the relative cheapness of most internationally traded grains, to the fact that some of the most important users were forced into self-sufficiency.

This first phase of inflation was, quantitatively, by far the most important for most countries in that it brought them by far the largest increases in both price levels and money incomes. Still more strikingly, however, it resulted in vastly increased liquidity in most parts of the world—a large increase in monetary stocks even relatively to money income. This flood of liquid funds was

pronounced both in certain countries in which real income fell
—Finland, France, Norway, and the Netherlands (in all of
which money stocks more than trebled in relation to money
income)—and in certain countries where output expanded—
Mexico, Canada, Japan, Italy, and the United Kingdom. The
only countries, indeed, in which money income seems to have
outrun the supply of money in this period were Greece, Turkey,
and the Lebanon, in which price inflation reached dangerous
proportions, causing a 'flight from cash', which will have to be
discussed in detail in a later chapter.

(ii) *The War Economy*. The second of the phases of inflation,
which may be regarded as lasting from late 1942 or early 1943
to the end of the war, was that in which the principal belligerents
had got their resources fully transferred to the purposes of war,
and had achieved satisfactory methods both of allocating those
resources and of controlling prices by direct administrative
action. It was a phase during which the increase of real output
was much smaller than during the preceding period; it was also
a period in which prices were relatively stable. The world's war
economy had become a going concern (see Diagram 3, p. 52).

In this phase, as in the first, the principal belligerents experienced smaller price increases than most other countries.
Wholesale prices rose by only 4 per cent. in the United States,
about the same amount in Germany, and 6 per cent. in the
United Kingdom. Other countries with effective price control,
such as Australia, New Zealand, and Canada also kept their
prices down. In many countries which were heavily involved
in supplying the main belligerents—Spain, Portugal, the Latin
American countries—price increases were greater, owing to the
absence of rigorous control; but there were few of them in which
increases of more than 30 per cent. were experienced. The
movement of the tide of war, first away from the Middle East
and then, increasingly, to the Far East, had, however, important
effects in this economic field. The price increase in Palestine and
Turkey almost, or quite, ceased during this time; it continued
in Egypt, the Lebanon, and Iran at a much reduced rate; but
increasing military expenditure and famine produced an increase of more than 50 per cent. in wholesale prices in India,
while the final war effort and the disorganization of defeat
brought about a trebling of prices in Japan. Chinese wholesale

prices continued to treble each year—they increased more than thirty-fold between the end of 1942 and the end of the war.

Some of the German-occupied countries in Europe brought their prices under effective administrative control in this later part of the war (German price control holding with amazing efficiency to the end), though, largely because of the great burden of occupation costs, French prices again doubled. Defeat, disorganization, and military occupation had their most powerful effects in southern and eastern Europe, where administration was traditionally weakest. In Italy prices rose twenty-fold; in Hungary eighty-fold (a prelude to hyper-inflation). Rumania also started on the hyper-inflationary road, and Greece had already experienced full hyper-inflation and established a new currency in November 1944. Lack of effective price control and sudden falls in physical output were at the root of these drastic inflations.

Although wholesale prices in the main belligerent countries were, as a general rule, fairly steady in this period, there were certain important commodities which rose markedly in price. Thus, the relatively easy position which had ruled in the main world grain markets (in so far as there still were world markets) in the earlier years of the war was drastically changed. The United States, with the enormous growth of its consumption and production of meat, became a large importer of grain for animal feeding; much grain was used for industrial purposes (especially the production of alcohol for synthetic rubber manufacture); the requirements of the liberated territories after the end of the European war began to be anticipated; rice supplies were cut off by the war in the Far East; failure to maintain and develop food production in India caused the great Bengal famine, and a substantial demand for wheat from the Western Hemisphere. For these reasons world grain prices rose. The Far Eastern war was the main reason for a further rise in prices of oils and fats. Prices of coal and ferrous metals also rose substantially, owing in the main to the continued rise of wage rates, especially those of miners. These and other price increases were, however, insufficient to embarrass the main belligerent economies; the system of price control (with subsidies) which had been perfected was able to insulate these economies from them generally without excessive strain.

In every country for which sufficient data exist, except those in which prices almost or more than doubled, this phase brought a further increase in liquidity. In many countries the supply of money increased relatively to money income by something between 20 and 40 per cent. For the main belligerents, indeed, this increased liquidity was an essential concomitant of the 'disequilibrium system' (as Professor Galbraith has aptly called it)[1] by which so large a proportion of the national resources was pushed into the war effort. Governments created new purchasing power. In the earlier stages—especially in the United States—this had simply drawn new factors of production into employment. With the approach to full employment, however, this was no longer possible. At the same time, since most prices were rigidly controlled, they could not rise to the equilibrium levels which would have absorbed the new purchasing power. Inertia and the satiation of the desire to take up the floods of new government securities which were offered naturally prevented the whole of this extra purchasing power from finding its way back to the State, and the residue was added to liquid stocks. Moreover, prices were stabilized in most countries, and, in the later part of the period, began to decline in some. This reduced the fears which had lowered the propensity to hold cash in certain of the countries concerned (in the Middle East for instance) in the earlier phase. In Japan and Italy, on the contrary, and probably in Bulgaria, Finland, and France also, the continued or accelerated price inflation brought about the beginning of a 'flight from cash'.

(iii) *Demobilization, August 1945 to June 1946.* The period from the end of hostilities in August 1945 to the first important relaxation of price control in the United States in June 1946 was that in which the most drastic part of the re-direction of resources to peacetime uses took place. It was also one in which, as a consequence of the sudden cancellation of war contracts before demand could flow effectively into normal channels, some measure of deflation was widely anticipated and, in some countries, experienced.

There was, indeed, a very widespread fall in both real and money incomes. In the United States money income fell by

[1] J. K. Galbraith, 'The Disequilibrium System', *American Economic Review*, June 1947.

13 per cent. between the second quarter of 1945 and the first of 1946; in the United Kingdom it was 3·5 per cent. lower in 1946 than in 1945. The national income of Germany fell by more than half in consequence of defeat.

Nevertheless, although prices fell in some countries, there was no fall in the most important ones; and the world price level— on any reasonable interpretation of that elusive term—continued to rise slightly. The nine-year course of inflation, though irregular, was never clearly interrupted.

Why was the fall of money income in the most important countries not accompanied by a fall in world prices? The reason is not really far to seek. Firstly, the real supply of goods and services in the world was reduced at this time, not through lack of purchasing power seeking them, but for physical and psychological reasons—the supply curve moved to the left. Secondly, although money incomes were reduced in the main countries, the propensities to save and to hold cash were also reduced, so that the demand for consumers' goods and services did not fall —or, at all events, did not fall *pari passu* with income.

The reduction of physical supplies in the world at large is most clearly seen in the case of foodstuffs. The harvests of 1945 and 1946 were abnormally small outside North America; world meat, fat, and sugar supplies were much reduced as a result of wartime slaughtering and post-war dislocation in Europe and the Far East. The world's grain stocks, abnormally high in the middle of the war, were approaching exhaustion. Moreover, with the shift of demand from materials of war to ordinary peacetime manufactures an almost universal shortage of the latter became apparent. Labour had been moved out of the industries concerned, and, in moving back, was slow to enter certain of them which, before the war, had been relatively underpaid. Coal, textiles, and certain building materials were at first almost universally scarce; timber was scarce in western Europe because of boundary changes and the enormous reconstruction demands of the Soviet Union, as well as because of shortage of coal in Scandinavia. Steel supplies were short in Europe as a whole because of the paralysis of Germany. These shortages, together with the sub-normal efficiency of labour which had not settled down to its new occupations, and (for a time) the battle-damage to transport facilities in certain areas, reduced the world's physical output considerably below what it had been at the peak of the war effort; indeed, below the pre-war level.

The reduction in the propensity to save on the conclusion of the war will have to be discussed more fully in another chapter. It is sufficient to remark here that the American public's expenditure of somewhat more on consumers' goods than was forecast on the basis of the pre-war relation of such expenditure to income, was one of the factors responsible for the incorrectness of the widespread expectations of substantial unemployment in the spring of 1946.

These two factors—reduced supplies and reduced saving—resulted in the generation of a very considerable inflationary pressure in the world economy as a whole, despite some reduction of money incomes. This pressure was, however, still held in check by price control in the principal ex-belligerents (except Japan), so that prices in the United Kingdom, the United States, and many of the countries closely connected with them rose only very little (United States wholesale prices rose by 7 per cent. in this period; United Kingdom by 1 per cent.). Relative movements of the prices of different commodities were not very important, but it is worth noting that it was the prices of minerals and textile materials, rather than of foodstuffs, that rose at this time. In some overseas countries in which the food and other shortages exerted a powerful effect—India and Argentina, for instance—the rise was slightly, but not much, greater. It was only locally, where powerful effects were exerted by budget deficits, the reduction of real income, and the release of purchasing power accumulated in wartime, that substantial price increases occurred. The Netherlands, Poland, Finland, and France for these reasons experienced increases of some 50 per cent., Japanese prices nearly trebled, and Greek prices (in terms of the reformed currency) rose more than ten-fold. Hungarian hyper-inflation, which may be said to have begun with the Russian occupation at the end of 1944, finally exploded in the summer of 1946 in the most spectacular manner ever seen. In China, however, the first year of peace brought a slight reduction in the rate of price increase (see Diagram 4, p. 53).

Locally, too, the deflationary forces of the time gained the upper hand. Italy, Switzerland, Sweden, Turkey, Egypt, Iran, and the Lebanon all felt the effects of the cessation of the war expenditure of the main belligerents. In some countries, such as Norway and Denmark, deflationary policy measures, combined with these forces, had some effect in reducing prices. Nowhere, however, except perhaps in the Middle East, does there appear to have been an income deflation of any great magnitude. In Italy, where wholesale prices fell by some 20 per cent., real income increased by something like a corresponding amount, so that money income probably did not fall at all.

Norway, Sweden, and Denmark were almost the only countries, among those for which money incomes are reliably estimated for this period, where liquidity diminished—where money holdings increased less than money incomes. There seems little doubt, however, that the same happened in Czechoslovakia and Belgium, where there were drastic currency reforms aiming to produce precisely this result, as well as in France, Japan, Finland, and the Netherlands, where prices increased markedly more than the stocks of money. In most other countries— including the United Kingdom, the United States, Germany, Australia, and New Zealand—liquidity, already abnormally high, continued to increase in the period of demobilization. In Germany and Austria the position was most remarkable. German money supplies had quadrupled during the war; at the end of it real income was halved, price control meanwhile remaining effective over a considerable part of the economy. The result was that money largely ceased to fulfil its normal function—it lost its acceptability hardly less than in the countries where its exchange value evaporated in hyper-inflation. This was the period when a large part of continental Europe, because either of hyper-inflation or of fantastically excessive liquidity, was for the purpose of many every day transactions on the 'cigarette standard'. In general the 'disequilibrium system' remained in being; opportunities for expenditure either on consumers' goods or on capital goods were restricted, while entrepreneurs in particular had reason to save up liquid funds against the day when long-overdue replacements and extensions of plant and stocks could be undertaken. The absence of serious price inflation had, again, the effect of preventing any speculative anticipations from forbidding the holding of money.

In the particular case of the United Kingdom, too, the cheap money policy of the time swelled stocks of cash, since it was implemented through the encashment of substantial quantities of privately-held government securities. This general continuation of the increase in liquidity naturally fed the succeeding boom.

(iv) *The Post-War Boom, June 1946 to August 1948.* From mid-1946 to mid-1948 both real and money incomes in almost every country expanded. For this, three main reasons may be assigned. The first is that the physical process of reconversion from war to peace economy was nearing completion, or was actually completed, so that the supply curve of goods and services, which moved to the left at the end of the war, was moving once more to the right. The second is that there were everywhere both eagerness and accumulated purchasing power to buy the increased supply of goods—both capital goods to remedy the enormous depletion of the war years and consumers' goods to repair wartime wastage and to indulge desires long repressed by the necessities of war and the claims of patriotism. In most countries, however, the increased eagerness to purchase consumers' goods was more important in this phase than the pressure of capital re-equipment. The third reason for the inflation is that the restraint of price control was largely removed, most notably in the United States, so that the 'disequilibrium system' which had been so important in the war economies of the chief belligerents, began to melt away, and the rise of prices—mainly of necessities—set in motion the price–wage spiral.

Apart from certain countries—Finland, Hungary, Italy, France, and Japan—where inflation was still proceeding under the pressure of exceptionally strong domestic forces, North America led the world-wide inflationary movement in this phase, largely because prices there were most completely freed from control. Money incomes in Canada and the United States must, indeed, have risen by more than a third in this period, though the increase in real income was relatively small —industrial production in both countries rose by about 13 per cent. and total real income probably by considerably less than 10 per cent. Price increases were responsible for the greater part of the income inflation.

In Europe, on the other hand, the increase even in total

money incomes was in most countries less than in North America, and what increase there was is to be attributed more to increases in the real supplies of goods and services and less to increases in price. Between 1947 and 1948, according to the Economic Commission for Europe,[1] the value of the output of commodities, measured at 1938 prices, increased by some 14 per cent. in Europe as a whole (including the United Kingdom, where it increased by 11·5 per cent.) and by only about 3 per cent. in the United States. Wholesale prices, correspondingly, increased only by 27 per cent. in the United Kingdom, 17 per cent. in Sweden, and 12 per cent. in the Netherlands between June 1946 and August 1948, as compared with nearly 50 per cent. in the United States. The greater expansibility of supply in Europe, where reconstruction was a so much longer and heavier task, combined with the maintenance of price controls to prevent (in all but a few exceptional countries) the large price increase which occurred in the already fully-reconverted and relatively uncontrolled economy of North America. It is noteworthy that in Belgium, where there was little central control and where the physical task of reconversion was light, the price increase was much the same as in the United States.

The rise in United States prices was of very considerable importance as an inflationary factor in the Old World (see Diagram 5, p. 54). Dollar prices of United States exports (to all destinations) rose by 31 per cent. during the period under discussion; dollar prices of European imports from outside Europe rose by about 40 per cent. in this period. In the conditions of full employment prevailing in Europe at the time, it was clearly difficult to prevent these price increases from being passed on throughout the economy. This was done to some extent in the United Kingdom by subsidizing the cost of living; but even that —entailing as it did, increases in taxation which were partly indirect, and leaving raw material costs free to rise—could not be entirely effective in neutralizing the inflationary effect of dearer imports. The price–wage spiral would doubtless have operated in the United Kingdom and other European countries in any case under full employment and with the restraints of wartime patriotism removed; but it operated far more powerfully in consequence of the price increases imposed from without.

[1] *Economic Survey of Europe in 1948* (Geneva, 1949).

Those European countries in which prices rose more than in the United States were affected, mainly, by a more powerful operation of the price–wage spiral. In some cases the continued existence of budget deficits made some contribution. In the financial years beginning in 1946, Belgium, France, Italy, the United Kingdom, and probably the Netherlands and Czechoslovakia had budget deficits exceeding 7 per cent. of the national income. In the following year only Czechoslovakia and the Netherlands had such large deficits and in the year beginning 1948 only Italy still had such a large inflationary pressure emanating from internal public finance (and this was, indeed, almost entirely offset by United States aid), while the United Kingdom had achieved a large surplus. Thus, the correlation between budgetary policy and inflation in this period is very far from close; in Italy and perhaps in Greece, however, budget deficits were probably major factors in producing unusually heavy inflation, though it should be noted that the Italian deficit was offset by another factor, namely foreign aid.

In most of the world outside Europe and North America the increase of prices in this period was nearer to European than to the United States size. In the Lebanon, indeed, a deflationary tendency still persisted, and there was little price inflation in the other Middle Eastern countries; nothing took the place of the abnormal inflationary factors which had ceased to operate by the end of the war. In India, however, the persistence of the threat of famine during, at least, the earlier part of the period was probably the main factor responsible for a price increase of almost the United States scale. In China the continuance of a huge budget deficit rendered the currency reform of 1948 ineffective; and hyper-inflation was accelerated when the civil war flared up in 1949. In Japan, too, where prices increased eleven-fold, the fundamental conditions of stabilization were not established in this period.

The price movements of this period reflected the fact that it was outstandingly one of industrial recovery and boom. The demand for industrial raw materials rose greatly, and so, in the face of inelastic supplies, did their prices. The price index of raw material imports into the United Kingdom rose twice as much as that of food, drink, and tobacco imports. In the United States non-ferrous metals, timber, and petroleum were among the commodities which rose most in price; much the same was true of the United Kingdom except that timber, having been exceedingly dear during the war for reasons connected partly with freight rates and the cutting off of the customary European supplies, did not rise in price very much further. Wool trebled in price in the face of increased manufacturing demand and the call for a replenishing of European stocks, despite the placing upon the market of large stocks held by the Joint Organization, which in the first six years after the war supplemented current production by as much as one-third. Nevertheless, though industrial raw materials in general led the price rise, the increase of foodstuff prices—apart from those of grains—in the United States was also above general average, meat in particular rising in price more than two-fold. This was in sharp contrast with United Kingdom experience; the technique of purchasing by long-term contract in a rising world market kept prices of British food imports below those prevailing in the United States, and by increasing subsidies the price to the consumer was kept fairly stable.

The inflation of this post-war boom period was, nearly everywhere, marked (and, in most cases, assisted) by a reduction in liquidity. There were probably only a few countries—China, Japan, and, in the earlier part, France—in which this was mainly a speculative 'flight from cash', motivated by fear of a continuing fall in the value of money. In the main it was probably a consequence of the movement away from the 'disequilibrium system' towards a general equilibrium of prices and money holdings. With the removal of price controls and the increased availability of the goods which the public had long wanted to buy, money was no longer added to liquid stocks because there was nothing upon which to spend it, but, on the contrary, taken out of those stocks (which were of unprecedented size in relation to income) and spent. In two notable cases, however—the Soviet Union at the end of 1947 and Germany in mid-1948—liquidity was reduced by a complete currency reform, as had been done earlier (with less spectacular success) in Belgium and Czechoslovakia.

In the United States money holdings hardly increased at all in this period, although money income grew by some 30 per cent.; in Canada the ratio of money holdings to income fell by nearly 30 per cent., in the United Kingdom by about 15 per cent., in Sweden by nearly 20 per cent. Nevertheless, the ratio of total money stocks to national income at the end of 1948 stood higher than in 1938 for every country for which the relevant data are available, with the significant exceptions of Greece and Japan. For a number of countries—the United States, Belgium, France, Finland, and the Netherlands—the ratio was no more than 12 per cent. higher than pre-war; but for others it was substantially higher—24 per cent. higher in Sweden and Canada, 50 per cent. higher in the United Kingdom, 56 per cent. higher in Denmark, 69 per cent. in Czechoslovakia, twice as high in Australia and more than three times as high in Norway.

To some extent, it is clear, this increase in liquidity over the inflationary decade as a whole is a measure of the persistence of price control—the persistence, that is, of the 'disequilibrium system'—at the end of it. The generally increased liquidity at what appears to have been the summit of a boom, as compared with a pre-war period of relatively slack activity is, nevertheless, a phenomenon to be accounted for. Habits with regard to the holding of money are, like other habits, subject to considerable secular changes, and a decade of super-liquidity could hardly be expected to pass without establishing some change in what people regard as normal relations between money holdings and income. Moreover, in most countries the long-term trend seems to be towards ever-greater liquidity. Professor Alvin Hansen has pointed out,[1] for instance, that in the United States the stock of money increased from 5 per cent. of the national income in 1880 to 57 per cent. in 1920, and 86 per cent. in 1935. Furthermore, there had been an enormous increase in security holdings in many countries, which would be likely to increase the equilibrium money holdings at any given rate of interest. Until, however, one has seen how the monetary habits of mankind adjust themselves in a subsequent period not marked by price controls and inflationary pressure it will hardly be possible to place the net wartime and post-war increase in liquidity in perspective.

(v) *The Recession of August 1948 to August 1949.* The recession

[1] A. H. Hansen, *Monetary Theory and Fiscal Policy* (New York, McGraw Hill, 1949), p. 4.

of business activity and income in the United States, which
started in the third quarter of 1948, may be held responsible for
the only considerable break in the process of virtually world-
wide price inflation between 1939 and the spring of 1951. What
was the nature of experience during this brief halt? Certainly it
cannot be said that anything like world-wide deflation took
place. Of forty-one countries for which indices of wholesale
prices are available for August 1948 to August 1949, twenty
experienced a fall in this index and the remaining twenty-one
a rise (see Diagram 6, p. 55). The distribution of these price
changes was not entirely symmetrical; if the indices for August
1949 (with August 1948 as 100) are classified in five-point
intervals, the numbers of countries in each of these intervals
prove to be:

57–79	80–84	85–89	90–94	95–99	100–4	105–9	110–14	115–19	120–4	125–9	130–4	135–9	140–4	145–9
1	1	2	5	11	6	6	3	1	1	0	2	0	1	1

The mode is slightly less than 98 and the median slightly less
than 102, while the arithmetic mean is somewhat higher still.
Nor were all the internationally traded goods similarly affected.
The recession affected industrial production more than total
consumption, and the commodities which fell in price were
largely industrial raw materials, other than the main textile
materials. Prices of foodstuffs also fell sharply in the United
States, but continued to rise in the United Kingdom, owing
mainly to time-lags and the method of purchasing imports.

It is perhaps useful to divide countries into three groups:
first, the United States and other economies where there were
internal deflationary forces, or where the internal inflationary
forces were well under control so that deflationary pressure
arising from recession of income in, and imports into, the
United States, turned the balance; secondly, countries which
were fairly well insulated against United States deflation, and
which maintained full employment with the small increase in
price levels which seems to be inseparable in the existing state
of economic statesmanship from that condition; thirdly, countries where there were still special inflationary factors similar to
those which had existed almost everywhere at some time since
the war.

In the first group of countries, Italy and Belgium are those
which most clearly owe deflationary pressure to internal factors

(notably credit policy); Canada, the Philippines, Venezuela, the Dominican Republic, New Zealand, and a number of Middle Eastern and west European countries, fairly heavily dependent on external trade, owe it mainly to the fall in the volume and price level of their exports for which the recession of United States income, and the partly speculative reduction of United States importing, were mainly responsible. The United States recession, in which money income fell some 5 per cent., value of imports by 15 per cent., and volume of imports by 9 per cent., is thus the central phenomenon of this period. How did it come about?

It would appear that the first important event was the slackening of the rate of growth of consumers' expenditure from about the beginning of 1948, associated with a return to something more like the pre-war relationship between this expenditure and the size of expendable income. At the end of 1947 consumers' expenditure had been somewhat above the level that might have been predicted from its pre-war relation to the consumers' disposable incomes; no doubt because of the process of wiping out wartime backlogs of purchasing, largely of goods officially classed as non-durable, such as clothing. Purchases of durable goods—motor-cars, radios, household equipment—remained considerably lower than might have been predicted from their pre-war relation to expendable income, presumably because supplies of these commodities had not been built up to the level appropriate to the very high aggregate income which had been attained.

This working off of backlog demand seems to have been responsible for a failure of purchases to grow as fast as had been expected, and thus for a largely involuntary accumulation of stocks—almost as great an accumulation as in the great deliberate re-stocking of 1946. As a consequence of this, orders to manufacturers were cut, and a deflationary process began. Stocks, which had been growing at an annual rate equal to about 3 per cent. of the national income in 1948, were shrinking at an almost equal rate by the third quarter of 1949; by that time expenditure in the private sector of the economy was some 6·5 per cent. below the 1948 level.

It is evident that this recession of total income was arithmetically almost exactly equal to the change in inventory investment. Long-term internal investment fell only slightly (less than 1 per cent. of national income) though there was a further fall of about the same amount in net foreign investment, traceable largely to European recovery. Consumers' expenditure remained almost constant at the 1948 level throughout 1949. How did it come about that total private investment could fall by no less than 15 thousand million dollars, or 5·5 per cent. of gross national product, without inducing a fall in consumers' outlay? How, indeed, could it happen that gross national product could fall by more than 5 per cent. without inducing a subsequent reduction of private fixed investments? These are the questions which must be answered if one is to understand why the recession of 1948–9 did not develop into a full-scale slump.

In the first place, the fall in total private investment was very largely offset by changes in the financial position of the public authorities, a surplus of $8½ thousand million in 1948 being succeeded by a deficit of $3 thousand million in 1949. The net reduction of all non-consumption expenditure thus amounted only to some $3 thousand million. It is perhaps worth trying to distinguish the changes in public finance which were 'automatic' consequences of the recession from those which were not. The chief 'automatic' changes were a fall of about $2 thousand million in receipts from corporation profits tax, and an increase of about $1 thousand million in transfer expenditure, mainly on relief. Some part of the fall in receipts from personal income tax was presumably 'automatic' also, but the major part of this change is stated to have been a delayed result of earlier alterations in the rate of tax. It seems, therefore, that substantially less than half of the most opportune change in the financial position of the public authorities was such as could be counted upon in any recession. The greater part must be attributed to rising expenditure, largely connected with defence, and, in a minor degree, to past reductions in the rates of taxation.

Given that total non-consumption expenditure fell even by as little as $3½ thousand million, it still, however, remains to be explained why consumers' expenditure did not fall to any appreciable extent. The reason for this is to be sought in the disequilibrium which still prevailed in the market for durable goods. From the end of 1948 the improved supply of these was readily taken up by consumers who, apparently, had been prevented by the previous shortage from buying as much as they could have afforded. During 1949 expenditure on consumers' durable goods reached a level at which, for the first time since the war, it bore much the same relation to total available income as in the years 1929–41. The failure of consumption to respond to a fall in non-consumption expenditure (and in total income) must, therefore, be regarded as due to exceptional circumstances connected with the aftermath of war.

This non-responsiveness of consumption to a change in income, together with changes in public expenditure, clearly saved the economy from an immediate recession which might otherwise have reduced income by 15 per cent. or more, instead of by five. Whatever the magnitude of the immediate recession, however, one would normally have expected some corresponding, later, reduction in private fixed investment, which would have carried depression a stage further. That this did not occur in 1948–9 is again, in all probability, to be attributed to the existence of backlogs of demand. Expenditure on producers' durable goods did, indeed, fall by a small amount between 1948 and the last quarter of 1949; but expenditure on building had risen somewhat to offset part of this. The inadequacy of United States housing in relation to the high current standards of living in general—the legacy of a decade and a half of stagnation and war—was still such as to keep the demand for residential building, in particular, fairly independent of minor fluctuations in income.

The European countries in which internal deflationary forces were most clearly at work in this period were (as mentioned above) Belgium, Italy, and (perhaps) Switzerland. In Belgium, a restrictive credit policy, which had enabled consumption to reach high levels in the earlier post-war years without creating too great inflationary pressure, tipped the balance strongly to the deflationary side when backlogs of consumers' demand disappeared. In the latter part of 1948, industrial employment began to fall, and continued to do so throughout 1949 and early 1950. In sharp contrast with experience in the United States, Belgian demand for industrial equipment never became effective on a large scale after the war, despite the high average age of the existing equipment. In the earlier post-war years, when the state of internal and external demand generally was favourable to industrial expansion, investment was discouraged by credit policy; when both internal and external demand slackened, there was in any case no incentive to invest.

In Italy the credit restriction of 1947, which effectively brought inflation to an end, inaugurated a period in which industrial employment and, indeed, employment generally remained steady at a level slightly below that of 1947, despite the continued rapid increase of population. The deflation which occurred was, in respect of its social effects (as well as in terms of the general price level) the most severe experienced in any of the principal countries since the war The reduction of the budget deficit, which had been the largest single factor behind the previous inflation, was at least as important in producing this result as the limitation of the supply of credit to private enterprise; indeed, as is generally the case, once deflation gets under way, the supply conditions of credit soon became relatively unimportant in view of the slight demand. The cause of the much slighter recession in Switzerland seems, most probably, to have been the glutting of wants, perhaps mainly in the field of producers' durable goods. Certainly, credit stringency was not there a factor, since liquidity was already high and became higher in the course of 1949.

That this period was in some degree one of recession is further confirmed by the fact that, in the course of it, liquidity increased in many countries, in contrast to the trend of the preceding two years. There is evidence of this, indeed, for nineteen out of thirty-five countries for which statistics of money supply are available; fourteen out of these nineteen being countries in which prices fell, including the United States, Canada, Belgium, Switzerland, Sweden, New Zealand, and Italy. On the other hand, there is fairly definite evidence of a reduction of liquidity in ten out of the sixteen countries, for which the requisite information is available, in which wholesale prices rose, including the United Kingdom, Norway, the Netherlands, India, South Africa, Austria, Peru, and Chile. The former countries are those in which deflationary forces were most clearly dominant, so that the circulation of money became more sluggish; the latter group consists of countries which were fairly effectively insulated from the deflationary forces at work in the world, and were still enjoying a post-war boom and/or getting back towards an equilibrium between the level of income and the supply of money. It can perhaps be said that, as the whole world approached nearer to this equilibrium, it was again becoming true that the supply of money fluctuated less in the short run than the volume of transactions which it was required to finance.

(vi) *The Impact of Devaluation, September 1949 to June 1950.* The course of world prices was sharply influenced by the devaluation on or shortly after 18 September 1949 of most of the other important currencies of the world in relation to the United States dollar and to gold. The inflationary or deflationary effects of such an event are two-fold. In the first place, the local currency prices of imports into the devaluing countries from non-devaluing countries are at once raised; so are those of some goods produced by devaluing countries of which part of the supply goes to other countries, where the demand for them is thought to be inelastic. Correspondingly, the local currency prices in the non-devaluing countries of imports from the devaluing countries are lowered, and so are the prices of goods produced by the non-devaluing countries, where the demand for them is thought to be elastic. Thus, the immediate effect should tend towards price inflation in the devaluing countries and to price deflation in those which do not devalue.

Secondly, the effect of devaluation should be to alter the balances of payments on current account; improving those of the devaluing countries, and causing those of the countries which do not devalue to deteriorate—unless the elasticities of demand for goods entering into international trade are so low that the effect of devaluation is opposite to this. Unless the effect is 'perverse', in this sense, the changes in external payments should tend to produce income inflation in the devaluing countries and income deflation in the others. This second effect therefore normally supports the first. Can the combined effect be traced in practice?

So far as general price levels—or even general wholesale price levels—are concerned, the effects of devaluation can be perceived only in a very broad way. In the first place, the period from just before devaluation to just before the invasion of

South Korea (August 1949 to May 1950) was one in which the general tendency was, again, mildly inflationary. The wholesale price index fell in only eight out of thirty-seven countries for which it is available, and, in particular, it rose by 2 per cent. (after having fallen by 10 per cent. in the preceding twelve months) in the United States—the heart and the main part of the non-devaluing territories. The divergent tendencies due to devaluation, which have been briefly discussed above, were therefore superimposed upon a gently rising trend. Secondly, many and various internal forces were at work in different countries, which were not connected with devaluation, or its absence, so that any systematic effect of devaluation is overlaid by random disturbances. (See Diagram 6, p. 55.)

The wholesale price changes of this period are, in fact, distributed in a remarkably symmetrical manner, the median change (for the thirty-seven countries) being a 5 per cent. increase. Of the countries which devalued to the same extent, or something approaching the same extent, as the Sterling Area, however, only four—India, Sweden, South Africa, and Ireland (all with price increases of 3 or 4 per cent.) fall below the median, while eleven—the Netherlands, Iraq, Norway, New Zealand, Finland, Chile, Australia, the United Kingdom, Denmark, Egypt, and Austria—are above it. All eight of the countries in which the wholesale price index fell—Iran, Tunisia, Switzerland, Italy, Lebanon, Venezuela, the Dominican Republic, and Guatemala—devalued not at all or only slightly, unless one takes account of the devaluation of the official (as opposed to the free) rate for the French monetary area, to which Tunisia belongs.

There is thus some correlation, though a very imperfect one, between devaluation and price inflation in this period. It is important to note, however, that general indices of wholesale prices had come, in the nine months under discussion, to reflect the rises in the prices of dollar imports into devaluing countries only very partially. In no case had the general wholesale index risen by more than half the percentage by which these local prices of dollar imports must have gone up; most generally the proportion was only a quarter or an eighth. In the United Kingdom, the rises of the relevant wholesale price indices over this period were as follows:

Per cent.

Raw materials.	23
Imports (general)	18
Finished products (mainly semi-manu- factured)	3
Exports	5

In this period of renascent inflation the general balance of experience swung once more away from increases in liquidity, though as yet there was no renewed general tendency for liquidity to decrease. The relevant data are available for twenty-nine countries, in only ten of which liquidity seems to have increased, while it decreased in seven and remained roughly the same in twelve. It still increased in all the countries where prices fell—Italy, Guatemala, Venezuela, the Dominican Republic, and (perhaps) Switzerland; it continued to fall in the United Kingdom, the Netherlands, and Norway, where the movement was still towards relaxation of direct controls. In the main, however, despite the effects of devaluation, the monetary changes of these months suggest that cash holdings were in most countries near to equilibrium. It was a condition which, in happier political circumstances, might have presaged a period of quiet economic progress.

(vii) *The Korean War Boom, June 1950 to May 1951*. The outbreak of war in Korea in June 1950 made a far greater impact on the world economy than any other political event (excluding, at any rate major acts of purely economic policy) since the beginning of the world war in 1939. Its economic effects were two-fold; in the first place, it brought about a rapid though short-lived rise in commodity prices, which was followed by the usual chain of consequences extending through the markets for finished products and labour; secondly, it led to decisions to rearm on a substantial scale in all the principal countries of the world. The commodity boom produced immediate inflationary effects which were exhausted in many countries within nine or twelve months; the selection of any date for the general closing of this phase must be in some degree arbitrary, but its end was a definite one in many countries, though it did not occur everywhere at the same time. The inflationary effects of rearmament—except in so far as they were speculative effects which fed the commodity boom—were, naturally, very much slower to develop. The maximum effect of the increased armament expenditure planned in the year after the invasion of South Korea was not expected to be exerted until 1953 or later, and the growth of this expenditure in the first two years was not generally sufficiently rapid to swamp entirely the effects of the collapse of the commodity boom in 1951.

Apart from the Soviet Union, the increase of wholesale prices in this period was general, as it had been in 1939-40, though in some countries whose own products were not in greatly increased demand and which are not heavy importers of raw materials, the increase was only moderate—it was small or moderate, for instance, in most of the Middle Eastern countries (except the Lebanon), but large in all the industrial countries which depend heavily on imported materials, in the timber and paper producing countries of northern Europe, and the overseas countries which export industrial raw materials. National indices of wholesale prices rose anything from 6 to 54 per cent., but in a large number of cases the increase was between one-sixth and one-third, with both the median and the arithmetic mean near to a quarter. Something like this average amount of increase was recorded in a number of the countries most dependent upon international trade—the United Kingdom, Western Germany, the Low Countries, and Norway—but Sweden and France, where the price-wage spiral worked particularly vigorously in this period, showed considerably greater increases, and Switzerland a considerably smaller one. The moderation of the increase in the United States (some 17 per cent.) may have been partly due to the imposition of comprehensive price controls in January 1951. It is to be remembered, however, that the world prices of different commodities diverged in this period to a remarkably large extent, so that relatively small differences in the weights assigned to them in the various national indices necessarily made large differences to the values which those indices assumed.

The course of commodity prices was affected very largely in this period by speculative or strategic accumulation—mainly by governments. It was, for instance, stockpiling encouraged by the United States Government which was largely responsible for the phenomenal rise in wool prices (about 170 per cent.)

in the eight months after the invasion of South Korea, as well as for the more than doubling of rubber and tin prices in the same period. The cessation of United States purchases of these commodities in early or middle 1951 was, similarly, largely responsible for the break of the boom. Stock accumulation by European countries and, indeed, in some instances by others (such as China) also made some contribution to the boom, though it was generally more evenly distributed through time than was United States stockpiling. Prices of foodstuffs were far less affected by these erratic influences, and although some of them (such as coffee and cocoa) rose to a peak in the spring of 1951, the majority rose gradually during both the boom and the subsequent slump in the more volatile raw material prices. Certain raw materials also—such as wood-pulp—continued to rise sharply in price after the spring of 1951, as well as before.

In view of the character of the boom, it is not surprising that it was very generally accompanied by a reduction in liquidity, in the sense of the ratio of total money supply to national income. This was particularly marked in the United Kingdom and the United States, in both of which money supply rose only by about 4 per cent., while money income rose by 20 per cent. in the latter, and must have risen by considerably more than 10 per cent. in the former. Other countries, however, had similar experiences, apart from certain exceptional cases, such as Israel, Turkey, and perhaps Chile and New Zealand, where there were relatively large increases in the amounts of currency and credit outstanding, and smaller increases in money incomes. The total supply of money (demand deposits and currency outside the banks) in the United States had, indeed, returned by 1951 to only a little more than its 1937 ratio to national income; in the United Kingdom this ratio was still about one-third greater than before the war, but had fallen by nearly one-quarter from its peak value of 1946.

It has already been mentioned that not all commodities fell in price in the world markets in the early part of 1951, and that the Korean War boom did not everywhere come to a well-defined end in that year. In some countries—the United Kingdom, South Africa, and Norway, for instance—the indices of wholesale prices continued to rise without any substantial interruption throughout that year. In some others—France, Germany, Austria, Sweden, Portugal, Japan, and Australia—there was a definite break of the boom in the spring, followed by a quickly renewed rise which carried the wholesale indices past their previous highest points. In yet others—perhaps most notably the United States and India—the price fall of the late spring was followed by some months of stability. The fall in commodity prices was followed in many countries by a decline in demand for consumers' goods—principally clothing and footwear—which caused considerable local unemployment, despite the mounting rate of expenditure on armaments. This slackening of consumers' demand perhaps marks the end of the Korean War boom more definitely than the far from universal downturn of wholesale prices.

The slackening—or apparent slackening—of demand for consumers' goods does not seem to have been due to any fall of aggregate real incomes, for there is little or no evidence that real income as a whole—even after deduction of taxes—had fallen in any of the countries in question, though it is certainly the case that in several of them it had ceased to grow as fast as in most of the post-war period. Changes in distribution may have had some effect, but this can only have been small. There seem to have been two substantial reasons for the consumers' goods slump: in the first place, there was a very considerable speculative stocking-up by consumers in the first seven or eight months of the war, which left them disinclined to buy further when it became apparent that goods of the kind in question were not getting scarcer, but seemed, on the other hand, not unlikely actually to fall in price, owing to the collapse of raw material prices. Secondly, the commodity-price boom worked through into the retail prices of certain goods (mainly clothing and footwear) with some delay, so that these retail prices reached their maximum well after the buying-fever had subsided, and so aggravated the tendency of buyers to hold off. It has been calculated, for instance, that the rise in the prices of clothing relatively to other consumers' goods was probably responsible for about a third of the reduction in clothing purchases in the United Kingdom at the depth of the slump (autumn 1951) in relation to the level just before the Korean War. The rest of the reduction, being about equal to the excess of sales in the

early months of the war above the pre-war level, may be attributed mainly to the inevitable reaction from such anticipatory
purchases.

It can hardly be said that, at any stage, these events seemed
likely to herald a substantial recession of total demand in any
of the main countries. The probability always seemed to be,
rather, that they marked a second minor setback in the process
of inflation which had gone on since 1939. In the United
States, to which the world mainly looks for signs of change in
the economic weather, there was little indication of general
recession, and it was not until 1953 that real apprehension of
such an event arose. The absence of any important rise in
American prices for three years after 1951 was, however, the
clearest evidence the world had yet received that the great
inflation might be over at last.

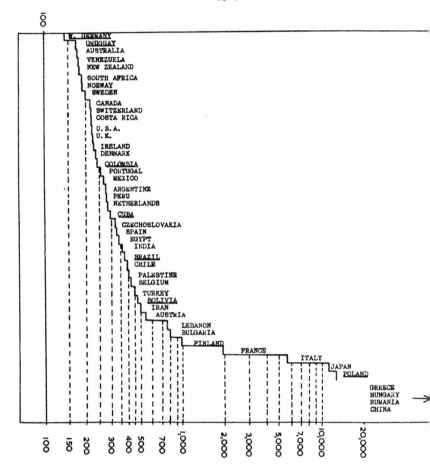

DIAGRAM I. Wholesale prices, August 1948 (July 1939 = 100)
(countries underlined = cost of living indices).

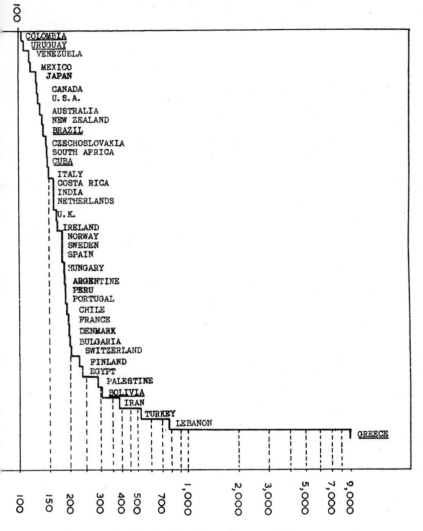

DIAGRAM 2. Wholesale prices, December 1942 (July 1939 = 100)
(countries underlined = cost of living indices).

E

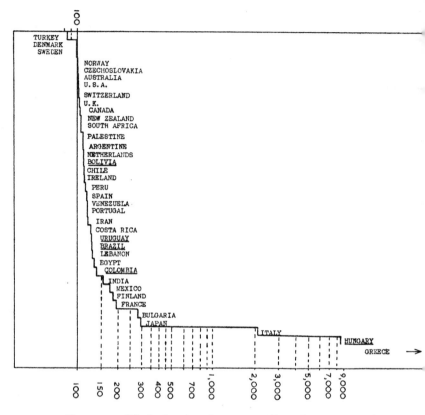

DIAGRAM 3. Wholesale prices, August 1945 (December 1942 = 100)
(countries underlined = cost of living indices).

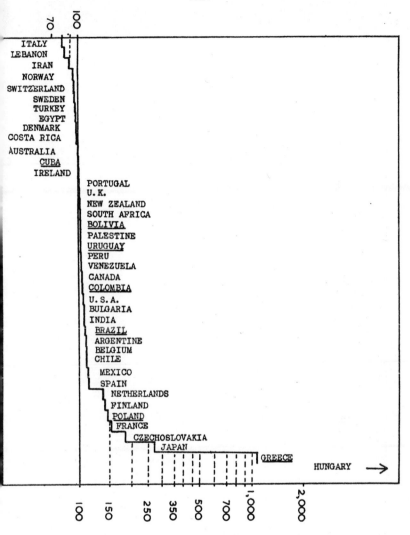

DIAGRAM 4. Wholesale prices, June 1946 (August 1945 = 100)
(countries underlined = cost of living indices).

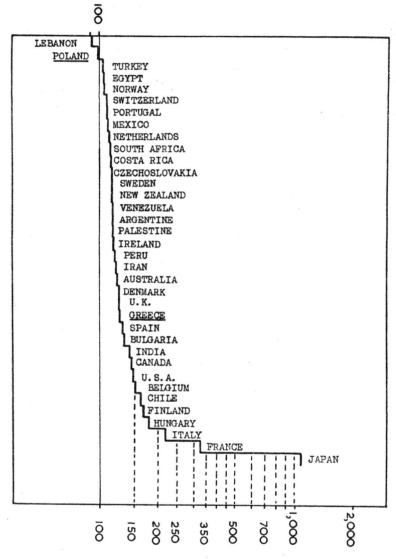

DIAGRAM 5. Wholesale prices, August 1948 (June 1946 = 100)
(countries underlined = cost of living indices).

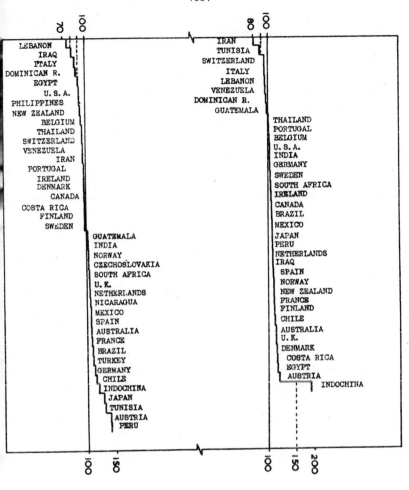

DIAGRAM 6. Wholesale prices. Left, August 1949 (August 1948 = 100);
Right, May 1950 (August 1949 = 100).

3

The Inflationary Effects of War Expenditure

The 'Multiplier'

NEEDLESS to say, public expenditure for the purpose of war was far the most important generator of inflation in the chief countries of the world during the first two of the phases distinguished in the last chapter. The way in which it results in an expansion of money income has already been hinted at in Chapter 1; now, however, it is necessary to examine the process rather more closely before endeavouring to trace its operation in practice in those countries for which adequate data are available.

The way in which expenditure generates income has become a main study of economists since the great depression of the nineteen-thirties. It is plain that any new act of expenditure must generate a convergent series of further expenditures as the income created by the original act is spent and re-spent. It is usual to simplify the matter by assuming that a known and constant proportion of each addition to income is spent within the country concerned. If this proportion is $\frac{3}{4}$, for instance, the original additional expenditure being £1 million, then the total additional income generated will be 1 plus $\frac{3}{4}$ plus ($\frac{3}{4} \times \frac{3}{4}$) plus ($\frac{3}{4} \times \frac{3}{4} \times \frac{3}{4}$) plus, &c. which is $1/(1-\frac{3}{4})$, or £4 million. The addition to income will in this case be four times as great as the expenditure which initiates it, and the factor 4 is termed, for obvious reasons, the 'multiplier'.

Any portion of the national income (or expenditure) which is subject to control by public policy, or is determined by some outside force, may be selected as the 'multiplicand', and an attempt made to trace a relation between changes in it and the immediately following (for practical purposes, often virtually simultaneous) changes in the magnitude of the national income as a whole. Two conditions clearly have to be fulfilled if there is to be hope of finding a clear and constant relation of this kind

—the effects of changes in other 'multiplicands' must be negligible (or must be eliminated), and the 'multiplier' itself must be constant over time.

The first of these conditions is fulfilled if we take as our 'multiplicand' the sum of all the expenditures which we regard as independently variable or autonomous, as opposed to those which depend on the size of the national income as a whole. These autonomous elements are generally taken to be the net expenditure of public authorities (i.e. the excess of their expenditure over their receipts from taxation and other current sources), the net receipts of the country from abroad, and the expenditures of private business on plant, equipment, buildings, and additions to stocks of working capital. The sum of these elements, often called net non-consumption expenditure, is most usually taken as the 'multiplicand' in analysing changes of income.[1]

The second condition—the constancy of the 'multiplier'—is fulfilled so long as a fixed proportion of any additional income

---

[1] Strictly speaking this is not a correct procedure unless not simply consumption expenditure, but that expenditure *plus* the revenue of the public authorities *minus* their transfer expenditure (i.e. their expenditure other than in return for current goods and services) is assumed to vary systematically with income as a whole. It is perhaps more plausible to assume that indirect tax revenue of public authorities and total private expenditure on consumption within the country both vary with the income disposable by the private part of the economy—that is to say, with total national income *minus* direct taxation, *plus* transfer expenditure of public authorities. This available private income will then be the aggregate whose magnitude should vary with variations in non-consumption expenditure. The above conclusion can be demonstrated thus:

If Y is a change in net national product at market value

C	,,	,,	consumption expenditure
V	,,	,,	net private investment
G	,,	,,	government expenditure on goods and services
D	,,	,,	the budget deficit
T	,,	,,	public transfer expenditure
R_D	,,	,,	direct tax revenue
R_I	,,	,,	indirect tax revenue
X	,,	,,	exports
M	,,	,,	imports

then: $Y = C+V+G+X-M$.

But: $G = R_D+R_I+D-T$;

so that: $Y = C+V+R_D+R_I+D-T+X-M$.

Thus: Y will not be proportional to $V+D+X-M$ unless it is also proportional to $C+R_I+R_D-T$.

If, however, we put $C = k_1 (Y-R_D+T)$ and $R_I = k_2 (Y-R_D+T)$, we have $(Y-R_D+T)(1-k_1-k_2) = V+D+X-M$.

The error which is likely to be made, however, in relating national income, instead of disposable private income, to non-consumption expenditure, is not very great.

is, in fact, re-spent on consumers' goods. This seems to be true for many countries over considerable periods in peacetime, since the ratio between changes in the 'multiplicand' (as defined in the last paragraph) and the concomitant changes in the total national income have been shown statistically to remain reasonably constant in these countries over a number of years.

Suppose, therefore, that the 'multiplier' remains constant in the early stages of a war, when the government is beginning to incur budget deficits. The increases in money income will be proportional to the increases in the deficit (if for the moment we may ignore any changes in the foreign balance and in private internal investment). If, initially, there was considerable unemployment of resources of all kinds, the total real income will increase in step with the budget deficit. Moreover, the increases in the amount of goods and services which the government obtains will be nearly, or quite, proportional to the increases in its expenditure. To put the matter in another way: an increase in the budget deficit will increase *real* income in the community to just such an extent as will involve the increase of savings required to cover the higher deficit. It was to analyse this process of increasing real income that the concept of the 'multiplier' was originally developed.

The 'Multiplier' in Full Employment

Before long, however, all the national resources will be drawn into employment. The effect of a further increase in the deficit will then be, not to increase real income further, but simply to raise prices. Two consequences follow: in the first place, the increments in the real resources obtained by the government through deficit financing will no longer be proportional to the increases in the budget deficits which it incurs, even if the 'multiplier' (in terms of money income) does remain constant; in the second place, it is very unlikely, with total real national income stationary and prices rising, that the 'multiplier' will be constant, or will be the same as it was when real and money incomes were increasing *pari passu*.

With regard to the first of these consequences, suppose that the government in some short period makes purchases, financed by deficit, which absorb, say, one-tenth of the national output in that period. The effect of this deficit expenditure is to increase the national money income by something more than one-tenth—say by one-fifth (the 'multiplier' thus being 2). Since real income is incapable of expanding appreciably in so short a time when there is already full employment, the price level must, therefore, have been raised by 20 per cent. Thus, if it wants to buy the same amount of goods and services as before, over and above what it can buy with its current revenue, the government will have to run a budget deficit in the next short period 20 per cent. greater than in the previous one. So long as the real value of the deficit remains constant, the national money income must expand by 20 per cent. in each of the periods which it takes for the 'multiplier' to operate. There are, of course, complications at this point; one should, strictly, substitute a more precise concept for the rather vague one of 'the period in which the "multiplier" operates'; but it is unnecessary to go into that here. The essential—and substantially valid—point remains that, once full employment is attained, the government's endeavour to secure a constant proportion of the national output by running budget deficits will result in an exponential growth of money income and prices, provided, always, that the 'multiplier' (and its speed of operation) remains constant.

It might, therefore, seem profitable to look for a wartime relation between the size of the budget deficit (or, more properly, total non-consumption expenditure) expressed as a proportion of the national income, and the rate of increase of the national income measured in money at current prices. For some countries such a relation can be found. In Hungary, for instance, over the years 1938–9 to 1942–3 there appears (from the rather inadequate data available) to have been a quite straightforward relation of this kind, the logarithm of the ratio of end-of-year to beginning-of-year rate of income flow being almost exactly proportionate to the ratio of non-consumption expenditure to income during the year (see Diagram 7, p. 72).

The search, however, is often disappointing. In Japan the ratio of non-consumption expenditure to income varied little over the years 1940–3, during which the rate of increase of income first fell, then rose; probably because of changes in the rate of operation of the 'multiplier'. The rise of non-consumption expenditure to some 40 per cent. of national income in 1944 set rapid inflation in motion; but thereafter the increase in the speed of operation of the 'multiplier' and the rise of the marginal propensity to consume kept this inflation going despite the very drastic reduction of non-consumption expenditure after the surrender.

In the United States a somewhat similar relation is clear enough in the four years 1938-41 (see Diagram 8, p. 73); it seems that the logarithm of the ratio in which money income increased over the year (measured by the ratio of the income in the first quarter of the next year to that in the first quarter of the year in question) varied in an almost exactly linear way with the ratio of non-consumption expenditure to national income.[1] From 1942 onwards, however, there is a most marked falling away from this relation. By 1945 money income was actually declining, with the ratio of non-consumption expenditure to income still considerably higher than it had been even in 1941. In the three succeeding years, too, though there was a return to something much nearer the old 1938-41 relation, one cannot say that this relation was resumed.

In the United Kingdom there is no sign of a simple relation between the two variables in the period 1938-47. Here, the rate of increase of income began to fall, despite an increasing ratio of non-consumption expenditure to income, as early as 1940; here, too, a fall of the rate of growth of money income occurred in 1941, despite the fact that this ratio was higher than it had been in the great income-expansion of 1939.

The Changing Relation between Income and Consumption

The reason for the absence of a simple relation between the two variables under discussion in the years when the countries concerned were belligerent is to be found, of course, in the non-fulfilment of the second of the conditions mentioned above—namely, the non-constancy of the 'multiplier' and, to some extent, change in its speed of operation. The magnitude of the 'multiplier' depends, as explained earlier, on the relation between an increment in the national income and the increment which it brings about in expenditure on consumers' goods. The main problems in this line of analysis arise, therefore, from

[1] The relation would be roughly: $\log X = -0.1 + 1.1R$, where X is the ratio of end-of-year to beginning-of-year income, and R the ratio of non-consumption expenditure to gross national product. This indicates that income is neither increasing nor decreasing when R is about 9 per cent.

the inconstancy of, or uncertainty about, the relation between the total income available for expenditure by consumers (after direct taxation) and the amount which they actually spend. This relation—the income–consumption schedule or consumption function—is probably the most important quantitative relation in the whole of modern economic discussion and analysis.

During the years 1946–9 an animated discussion took place, mainly in the pages of the *Review of Economics and Statistics*,[1] about methods of expressing the consumption function of the United States, and the validity of the expressions which have been derived. It is not necessary here to go into these controversies at all deeply, since the main point which is relevant to the present chapter emerges from any reasonably convincing formulation of the consumption function. No matter how this function is formulated, it is clear that the wartime levels of consumption do not fit in with it; consumption is far lower than it would have been if the peacetime relation between disposable income and expenditure had held good. In other words, the schedule moves downwards under war conditions.

Take, for instance, the simplest possible formulation of the function—that which relates consumers' expenditure, measured at current prices, to disposable personal income, similarly measured (see Diagram 9, pp. 74–75). For the years 1929–40 the relation between these two variables can be expressed with a high degree of accuracy by the formula:

$$\text{consumption} = 7.2 + 0.85 \text{ (disposable personal income)}.$$

(The units used are thousand millions of dollars.)

Assuming that this is the 'normal' relation between the variables, and that it continues valid at higher levels of consumption and income than were experienced in the years 1929–40, one finds that the consumption expenditures of the subsequent years departed from the 'normal' by the following percentages:

1941 −5.5 per cent.	1946 +4.2 per cent.
1942 −14.5 ,, ,,	1947 +9.2 ,, ,,
1943 −15.0 ,, ,,	1948 +5.9 ,, ,,
1944 −15.8 ,, ,,	1949 +6.2 ,, ,,
1945 −10.2 ,, ,,	1950 +6.3 ,, ,,

[1] *Review of Economics and Statistics, 1946–49* (Cambridge, Mass.).

That these are substantial movements is emphasized by the fact that, during 1929-40, no annual total consumption expenditure was above or below the value given by the schedule by more than some 3 per cent. It will be seen from this that the schedule moved downwards by a full 15 per cent. between 1941 and 1943-4, and then moved upwards again by 1947 to some 9 per cent. above its 'normal' position. During the next three years it remained at about 6 per cent. above its 'normal' position, though there was, of course, no guarantee that it would stay there.

Similar movements occurred in the United Kingdom. The following account relates, not to personal disposable incomes, as in the foregoing discussion of the American data, but to total private disposable income—i.e. the undistributed profits of businesses are included. This is necessary in the British case if one is to obtain a picture of the saving and spending habits of the country as a whole, since fully half the net savings of the United Kingdom before 1938 consisted of undistributed profits. Moreover, the totals both of private disposable income and of consumption are measured at the prices of 1938 throughout—not at current prices.

It seems that in the United Kingdom, during 1929-38, changes in consumption depended, not only on the *current* changes in disposable income, but also on changes of some little time previously. Consumption appears to have been most closely related to a weighted average of incomes in the current and the two previous years (the weights being 3, 2, and 1 respectively). Moreover, there appears in this period to have been an increase in consumption of some £25 million per year irrespectively of what happened to private disposable income. The relation is approximately:

consumption = 1290+0·61 (weighted average of disposable private income in current
and two previous years)
+25 (number of years since 1929).
(This is expressed in million £ of 1938 purchasing power.)

From this relation with disposable income consumption never deviated by much more than 1 per cent. in the period 1929-38.

It seems reasonable to regard the automatic and regular

increase in consumption of £25 million a year as having ceased after 1938: from then onwards, therefore, the 'normal' change in consumption may be taken to be 0·61 of the corresponding change in the (lagged) total of disposable private income. Taking this to be the case, the percentage deviations of actual expenditure on consumption from the 'normal' in succeeding years were as follows:

1939 −1·6 per cent.		1944 −19·0 per cent.	
1940 −12·0 ,, ,,		1945 −13·8 ,, ,,	
1941 −16·6 ,, ,,		1946 − 1·6 ,, ,,	
1942 −18·9 ,, ,,		1947 + 1·7 ,, ,,	
1943 −20·5 ,, ,,		1948 + 1·0 ,, ,,	

These changes are represented in Diagram 10 (p. 76).

By way of contrast it is interesting to consider the course of events in Hungary. There, the amount spent on consumption remained an almost perfect linear function of personal income throughout the period 1938–9 to 1943–4, every increase in the latter being accompanied by a change 0·89 times as great in the former. Although price control nominally existed in Hungary after 1939, it does not appear to have prevented the economy from behaving much as one would expect in the absence of all controls.

The percentage reductions of consumption below 'normal' may be regarded as measures of the extent to which spending habits were distorted by administrative action and social change during the war. What were the reasons for and the means of distortion? In the first place, it will be seen that the peacetime relation between income and consumption, in times of some unemployment, is the result of two processes. First, changes in average real income per head over the trade-cycle or in the course of technological progress cause people to alter correspondingly their real expenditure on consumption. Secondly, the peacetime fluctuations of income go with changes in its distribution between classes. In a boom, not only is more saved, for instance, because most families are better off, but (it is usually held) more is saved also because a higher proportion of the total income is going to profit receivers, who, being on the whole wealthier than wage earners, have less urgent needs to satisfy out of their increased income.

In war, once full employment is reached, and so long as it is maintained, real income will not change with money income as it does in the course of the trade-cycle. For that reason, one would expect increased money income in the hands of consumers no longer to cause them to spend a smaller proportion of the total, as they normally do if money income rises in peacetime. Their real income is not changed; there seems, therefore, to be no reason why they should change their spending habits. This fact would tend to steepen the income–consumption schedule and raise the 'multiplier'. On the other hand, an income inflation unaccompanied by increases in employment seems peculiarly likely to lead to changes in income distribution— usually supposed to be in favour of profit receivers. If taxation could be neglected, or bore equi-proportionately on incomes of all sizes, that would doubtless mean that the income–consumption schedule would become less steep, and the 'multiplier' smaller. If there is a steeply progressive system of taxation, however, the 'shift to profits' will be greatly reduced, and this effect may not be important.[1] In fact, what is commonly assumed in this matter does not seem to apply to all economies; in the United Kingdom, for instance, the share of wages in the national income, after deducting direct taxes, actually rose slightly during the war. In so far, therefore, as wage earners are less likely to save out of additions to their income than the rest of the community, the distributive changes of the war years would tend to steepen the schedule and increase the 'multiplier', rather than the reverse.

It seems plain, however, that one must look elsewhere for the sources of most of the wartime shifts of the consumption function in the United Kingdom and the United States. Indeed, it is in rationing, price control, and the savings campaigns that the main cause obviously lies. People could not spend more on the things on which they would most eagerly have spent more in the circumstances had rationing and price control been absent—in the United Kingdom most notably food and clothing; in the United States largely durable goods. To a large extent they spent on other things instead—tobacco, drink, travel, and

---

[1] For this purpose one may either regard taxes paid as a form of expenditure, or confine one's attention to what is left after payment of direct taxes. The latter is the course adopted in the above discussion of consumption functions.

entertainment—but shortages and price control became virtually universal, and also limited expenditure there. The result
was that they piled up government securities, bank deposits,
and currency.

The downward movement of the income-consumption schedule
in the years of conversion to full war economy may be usefully
thought of as involving a drastic slowing down in the operation of the 'multiplier', as well as a decrease in its magnitude.
If one studies the annual increases in private disposable income
and in consumers' expenditure (measured this time at current
prices) in the United Kingdom, this is strongly suggested (see
Diagram 11, p. 77). The increases in income fell continuously
from a sharp peak in 1940 till the end of the war: those in
expenditure rose with increasing slowness to a peak in 1942,
and then fell sharply, only to begin rising again in 1944. This
suggests that, in the war years (up to the time when some relaxation of the strain began), the lag between changes in income
and changes in consumption was greater than previously. It
has been explained that there is evidence of lag in the pre-war
relation between the two quantities—a distributed lag with a
mean length of some eight months. In the years 1939–43 an
unweighted distributed lag of 0 to 2 years (mean length one
year) seems to be suggested. Applying this lag, one finds that the
changes in consumption expenditure in this period tended to
be about one-third or one-quarter of the corresponding preceding changes in income—which would give a 'multiplier' of 1·33
or 1·5, as against 2·6 before the war. It is very understandable
that the 'multiplier' should be both reduced in magnitude and
slowed down in its operation in wartime; not only will an increase in disposable income lead ultimately to a relatively
smaller increase in expenditure than in peacetime, because of
the difficulty of finding goods and services to buy, but the
spenders, frustrated in their desire to spend more on the things
which would normally absorb most of their increased income,
take some time to adjust their spending habits and to change
their tastes in such a way that they spend more on other things.

In the United States the evidence of an increased lag between
increments in disposable income and increments in consumption is less convincing (see Diagram 12, p. 78). It is true that
the peak of wartime increments in expenditure on consumption

was reached in 1943, a year after the peak increment in disposable personal income, but the 1943 peak was not clearly marked; it is substantially true that consumers' spending increased at a steady rate from 1941 to 1945, despite the fact that their incomes increased very rapidly in 1941 and with rapidly decreasing speed thereafter. Americans did, in fact, find additional goods on which to spend some of their increased income; their real consumption increased during the war in nearly every class of goods and services except motor-cars and some other durable goods, whereas in the United Kingdom it increased only in drink, tobacco, public transport services, and amusements. It is not surprising that it took increments in British purchasing power longer to squeeze through the relatively narrow gaps in the structure of rationing and price control than it took similar increments in the United States to result in general, though moderate, increases in consumption. The surplus of United States purchasing power which remained over after this general improvement in the standard of living would, however, normally have flowed mainly into certain channels—motors, houses, and other durable goods—which were firmly blocked during the war, and there was not sufficient pressure of real demand to drive it to any great extent elsewhere. Hence consumption's virtual independence of income in the war years, in contrast with the limited and delayed but nevertheless definite dependence displayed in the United Kingdom.

Expenditure and Income outside the Main Belligerents

Inflationary pressure was thus generated in the principal belligerents on a vast scale by war expenditure, and was contained with considerable success by controls which both limited private expenditure and secured the transfer of resources without competitive bidding in the market. The United Kingdom, the United States, Canada, Australia, New Zealand, Japan, and Germany all had, at some stage in the war, budget deficits amounting to 30 per cent. or more of their respective national incomes. Most countries, however, were not obliged by the exigencies of war to finance military expenditure by deficits on so large a scale (in relation to their economies) as was the case with these main belligerents.

In some instances, however, inflation was produced by the

direct expenditure or the exactions of foreign military forces. The German-occupied countries of Europe were in this case. In some of them, indeed,—in Belgium, Norway, the Netherlands, and France, for instance—the exactions mainly took the form of occupation costs levied through governmental channels, so that enormous budget deficits (amounting in some years in Belgium and Norway to nearly half the national income) were the chief instruments of inflation. In Denmark, on the other hand, the chief demands of the occupiers did not come through governmental channels, and (although there were, in fact, budget deficits rising to 10 per cent. of the national income by the end of the war) the chief inflationary influence was German purchasing from the private sector of the Danish economy, which resulted in net exports rising by 1944 to an annual rate equivalent to a quarter of national income.

In the Middle East and India, on the other hand, it was Allied war expenditure that provided the main inflationary force. An excellent analysis of the inflationary experience of these and other primary producing countries is given in A. R. Prest's *War Economics of Primary Producing Countries*;[1] it is not necessary, therefore, to consider the subject at length here; it is interesting, however, to glance at certain aspects of it.

Palestine is an instructive case, because the national income has been estimated for 1939 and 1942–4, while rough estimates for 1940–1 can easily be interpolated with the help of price data. Direct estimates of private internal investment in the country are not available; it is possible, however, to obtain statistics of most of the remaining items of non-consumption expenditure—i.e. of the budget deficit, Allied military expenditure, and (a negative item) the foreign trade deficit on merchandise account. The total of these items, which may be roughly described as net public and foreign expenditure,[2] rose from a negative figure in 1939—the country having long been accustomed to consume more than it produced on account of the huge inflow of immigrants' capital and other foreign funds—to a positive figure equal to a fifth of the national income in 1943.

[1] Cambridge University Press, 1948.
[2] The only items which should be added to render this description exact are the net invisible current receipts in the foreign payments account, other than foreign military expenditure.

Allied military expenditure alone was equal in the latter year
to over 30 per cent. of the national income; if it had not
been partially offset by a substantial increase in the import
surplus, net public and foreign expenditure would have been
even greater than it was. If, however, one tries to relate the
share which this non-consumption expenditure claimed out of
the national income to the rate of increase of total money income, it is seen that, as happened in the United States and the
United Kingdom but in contrast to experience in Hungary at
this time, private spending habits probably changed in the
early years of the war very markedly. For the years 1941-4
inclusive, it was very roughly the case that the rate of change of
money income was proportional to net public and foreign
military expenditure in the country; each 1 per cent. of the
national income which these items of expenditure claimed being
associated with an annual increase of about 1·3 per cent. in
money income. Under these war conditions, a balanced budget,
a balanced merchandise account, and no foreign military expenditure would apparently have left the economy in equilibrium; under pre-war conditions these circumstances would
have entailed quite rapid inflation. The direct controls operated
during the war (price control, subsidies, and rationing), ineffective though they were by western standards, seem therefore
to have exerted a considerable effect upon private expenditure.

Much the same is seen in India. Net public and foreign expenditure[1] rose from about 3·5 per cent. of national income in
1939-40 to 15 per cent. of it in 1942-3; the proportion then fell
slightly (but only slightly) in the two following years. At the
beginning of the war, it would seem, the economy would have
been roughly in equilibrium with this expenditure at zero; by
1944 the increase of prices and money income had been stopped
with net public and foreign expenditure claiming some 13 or
14 per cent. of national output. The very limited rationing
system and price control (which began to have an appreciable
effect after 1943) were probably the main factors responsible
for the change in private spending habits which this implies.
Net public and foreign expenditure (of which foreign military
expenditure alone amounted to some 8 or 9 per cent. of national
income by 1942-3) seem to be adequate to explain the degree

[1] Including, in this case, non-military 'invisible' items.

of inflation which came about in the middle years of the war, before controls had achieved any considerable effect in limiting private expenditure.

Some countries which were not directly involved in the war felt the inflationary effects of the main belligerents' war expenditure mainly through the more normal commercial channels —that is to say, through positive balances of external payments on ordinary trade account. Argentina affords an example; by 1943 the positive balance of payments on current account amounted to 8·5 per cent. of the national income. Brazil had a positive balance equal to 7 per cent. of her national income in the previous year. Canada, until after 1941, sustained more inflationary pressure from her active balance of payments than from her budget deficit, and even when the latter rose to its maximum size (37 per cent. of national income) in 1942, the positive foreign balance, at 13 per cent. of national income, was still a major inflationary factor.

Inflation in those countries which were not involved in heavy war expenditure, however, clearly owes much to factors other than the foreign balance. The countries of Latin America are the chief ones in this group for which data are available, and these data have, fortunately, been admirably analysed by Keith Horsefield in the second issue of the International Monetary Fund's *Staff Papers*.[1] Despite the absence of heavy expenditure on military operations, there were some Latin American countries in which the greater part of the very substantial income inflation flowed from the government deficit. In Argentina this was the greatest source of inflationary pressure in every year of the period except 1947, when the increase of bank credit suggests that private investment was the main source. In Peru, where the inflation of the period under review was only a phase in a chronic process, the deficit was the main factor throughout. In Brazil it was the main factor in isolated years, notably 1938, 1943, and 1945.

The foreign balance seems to have been the predominant source of inflation in Latin America as a whole only in the three or four years beginning with 1941, and chiefly in the tropical or the oil-producing countries which were most affected by the wartime rise of United States' demand.

[1] 'Inflation in Latin America', vol. i, no. 2, Sept. 1950.

Internal private investment was also an important factor. In Chile and Mexico the increase of bank credit seems to have been a greater inflationary factor than either the government deficit or the foreign balance during all or most of the period; more generally, it became important about, or after, the end of the war, when the possibility of importing capital equipment removed what had hitherto been a restricting influence. War-time interruption of the supply of European, Japanese, and North American industrial products had, indeed, two opposing effects on the rest of the world; on the one hand, it gave industry in these other countries a greater measure of protection than it had enjoyed since the First World War, at a time when internal purchasing power was stimulated by inflation; on the other, it hindered the expansion and even the maintenance of industrial plant and equipment which could be supplied only or mainly by the great industrial countries. During the post-war boom the latter factor was diminished, while the former—protection —was only gradually weakened. Moreover, as elsewhere, there was a considerable tendency for purchases (perhaps largely purchases of capital equipment or consumers' durable goods, when these again became available), to be financed out of hoards of liquid assets, which had been accumulated in the middle and later war years. This fact tends to reduce the correlation between non-consumption expenditure and the rate of increase of income.

The spread of inflation from the great centres of war expenditure is thus by no means all to be accounted for by tracing that expenditure and its effects on balances of external payments. The generation of such balances in overseas countries was partly the effect of increased imports by the main belligerents, and of a diminution of their exports due to the inflation of their internal demands; but to a considerable extent, also, it was the result of shipping difficulties. The stimulation of overseas manufacturing industries in this period is a further inflationary factor, traceable only very indirectly, if at all, to expenditure in the main belligerents. Whether the budget deficits of Latin American countries are in any considerable degree connected with this expenditure is also far from clear; budgetary trouble has long been endemic in this region, though it was no doubt increased by loss of customs revenue during the war. Finally, inflation outside the main belligerents was in some degree attributable to rises in price of their imports and exports quite apart from any changes in balances of payments, which will be further discussed in Chapter 11.

Even in the main belligerent countries themselves the expenditure approach to the phenomena of inflation, so enlightening in most circumstances, turns out to be sadly inadequate during the period under review. Its efficacy depends primarily on the stability of the relation between the whole national income and some of its main components, notably private consumption; and the extraordinarily successful distortion of this relation by controls is perhaps the most outstanding feature of this time. Moreover, even when something like the 'normal' income–consumption relation was restored after the war, the main stimulus to income–inflation has often seemed to come, not from a traceable excess of non-consumption expenditure over the savings obtainable from income at its existing level, but from increases in factor prices leading mainly to augmentations of consumers' expenditure. It is to the mode of operation and the effectiveness of direct controls of expenditure, and to the mechanism of the price–wage spiral that one must therefore look for further light on the process of inflation.

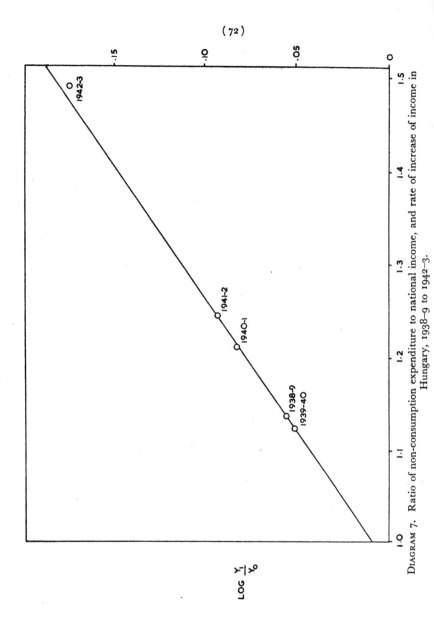

DIAGRAM 7. Ratio of non-consumption expenditure to national income, and rate of increase of income in Hungary, 1938–9 to 1942–3.

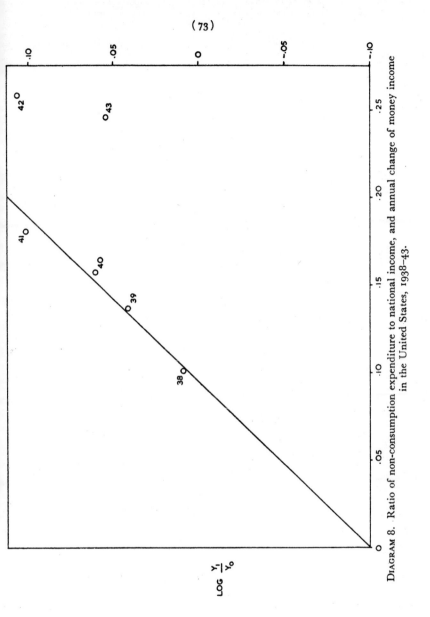

DIAGRAM 8. Ratio of non-consumption expenditure to national income, and annual change of money income in the United States, 1938–43.

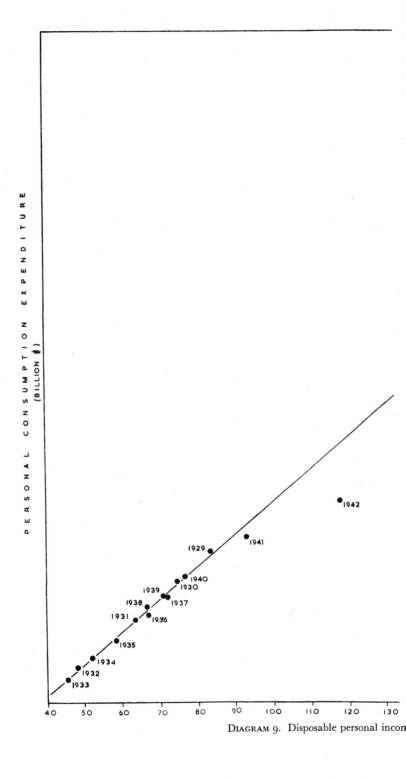

DIAGRAM 9. Disposable personal incom

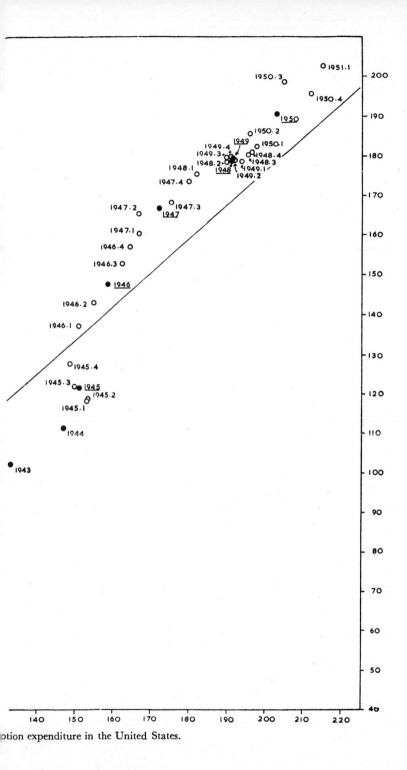

ption expenditure in the United States.

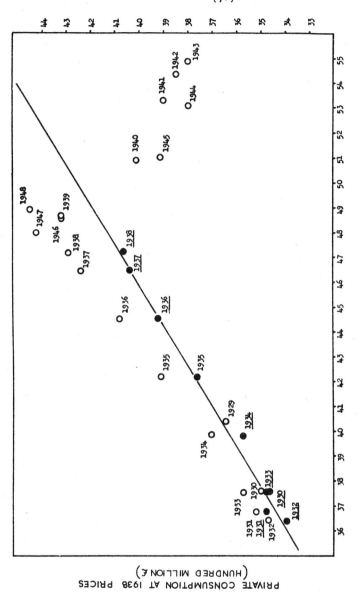

PRIVATE DISPOSABLE INCOME AT 1938 PRICES
(HUNDRED MILLION £)

PRIVATE CONSUMPTION AT 1938 PRICES
(HUNDRED MILLION £)

DIAGRAM 10. Private disposable income and consumption expenditure in the United Kingdom, 1929–38, at 1938 prices, allowing for a lag of consumption behind income. Black dots (to which the line is fitted) are plotted by eliminating, for the years up to 1938, an independent annual increase of expenditure of (25 million a year

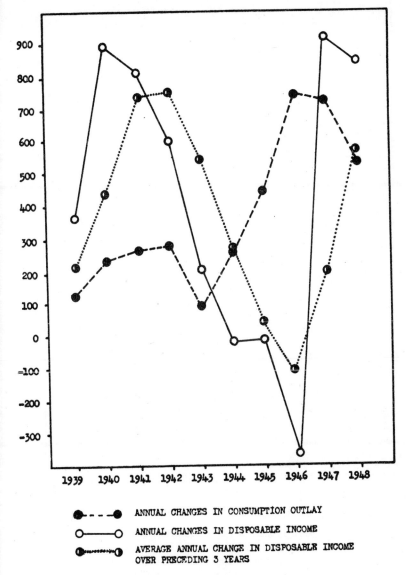

DIAGRAM 11. Annual changes in disposable income and consumption in the United Kingdom, 1938–9 to 1947–8.

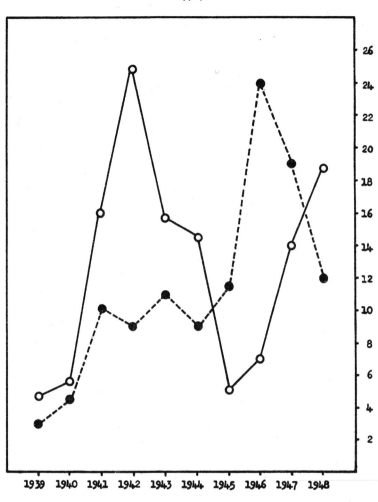

DIAGRAM 12. Annual changes in disposable income and consumption in the
United States, 1938–9 to 1947–8.

4

The Nature and Conditions of a Price–Wage Spiral

IT has been shown in Chapter 3 that the approach to the events of the war and the immediate post-war years through the theory of the 'multiplier' is of very limited usefulness. The theory of the 'multiplier' is based upon the assumption of a constant marginal propensity to consume—on the assumption that the proportion of any increment of aggregate income that will be spent on consumable goods and services can be taken as constant over the period under review. This may be a justifiable assumption in either of two circumstances; in the first place, if unemployed factors of production exist, so that additional expenditure will call forth additional supplies of consumable goods, or, secondly, if, in the absence of this condition, the prices of the goods in question are perfectly flexible, so that the ability of consumers to afford additional expenditure on an aggregate of goods whose supply is inflexible will be reflected in a rise in prices and thus in total expenditure. In so far as supplies are limited and prices are held down, by price control or otherwise, secondary increases in income will fail to be generated by primary increases in non-consumption expenditure.

Full employment of factors, their allocation to specified uses, and effective control of many prices produced this result during the war, and variation in the incidence of these conditions frustrates any attempt to trace a marginal relation between non-consumption expenditure and total income in most countries during the inflationary period, save for quite short stretches of time. The wartime conditions, however, differ only in degree from those which hold in a modern economy at other times of full employment so far, at any rate, as the very short run is concerned. Many prices of finished goods are governed by contracts of very considerable duration or are held constant as a matter of convenience; there is reason to suppose that many others are customarily held in some fairly constant relation to prime costs of production, which in turn depend largely on factor prices, such as wage rates, which are governed by contracts. If these circumstances applied generally, an increase in non-consumption expenditure would generate an immediate increase in consumption expenditure only so far as supplies were flexible. If supplies in general were inflexible, then an increase in consumers' expenditure could not occur until contractual or customarily stable prices of consumers' goods were revised, or until a rise in prime costs resulted in an increase in those prices which were cost-determined. In so far as these rigidities exist in the pricing system, therefore (and they certainly do exist over a wide portion of it in modern economies), the short-term operation of the 'multiplier' mechanism in times when the supply of goods in general is imperfectly elastic will tend to be jerky, the jerks corresponding to discontinuous adjustments of contractual or customarily fixed prices.

What, then, are the factors making for such price adjustments? Some prices which are fixed by contract for definite periods, or which are kept for convenience at fixed levels as long as possible, will no doubt be raised as soon as contracts fall to be renewed, simply because it has become abundantly clear that the market will bear an increase. Others will be raised as soon as the increase which the market seems able to bear is sufficient to outweigh the disadvantages of altering a fixed price. Others, however, will be raised because of increasing factor prices. These factor prices themselves may be raised by external influences (as will most commonly happen with imported raw materials), or through increased wage rates. These, in turn, may be due to a correct judgement that the market will bear the change, or, perhaps more commonly, they may result from demands based, in part at least, on a rise in the prices of consumers' goods.

The Relation of the Spiral to the 'Multiplier'

It is the tendency for prices to be fixed by producers in relation to costs of production (which depend on factor prices), and for wages to be fixed either automatically or by bargaining in relation to the prices of consumers' goods, that is principally responsible for giving the process of adjustment an inflationary power of its own. Any increase in wages unaccompanied by an increase in prices of finished goods naturally shifts real income to wage earners; the subsequent (and consequent) increase in the price of consumers' goods takes some of the increase away. Any increase in prices of consumers' goods unaccompanied by an increase in wages shifts real income away from wage earners, and is likely, therefore, to lead to a demand for an increase in their money earnings which will reverse the process. The distributional aspects of these changes will require further scrutiny later; the immediate question that arises is how a price–wage spiral is related to an inflationary process which (because all prices are perfectly flexible) can be analysed in terms of the 'multiplier' mechanism.

To ask this is, in fact, much the same as asking how a price–wage spiral is financed. In an open inflation, with flexible prices, the cycle of events may conveniently be thought of as starting with an increase in non-consumption expenditure financed either by a creation of new money (broadly defined) or by drawing on stocks of money previously held idle. Money is, at all events, injected into circulation, and will be spread between those who take part in transactions. If someone (say a wage earner) now receives more at the beginning of the week and spends all his earnings by the end of it (as he did before), then his average holding over the week as a whole will have been increased. Furthermore, he may now have some money left at the end of the week, or if he has been accustomed to having a balance left at the end of the week, this may very well be increased when his wage rises, if only because his spending habits may lag behind any sudden changes in his income. The balances which are active, in the sense that they change hands at regular intervals, are thus increased in each part of the economy in proportion to the increase in income in that part of the economy, while those balances which are idle, in the sense that they are not re-spent within the short period under consideration,[1] will probably also be increased. When

[1] This distinction between active and idle balances is, of course, arbitrary, in that it depends on the length of the 'short period under consideration'. In a sufficiently long run, all balances are presumably re-spent. To free the distinction from arbitrariness, it can perhaps best be thought of as a distinction between balances with rapid and slow rates of turnover, measured over a long period. This

equilibrium is reached at the higher level of income corresponding to the new level of non-consumption expenditure, the rate of leakage of the newly-created income into idle stocks will have become equal to the increase in the rate at which non-consumption expenditure is flowing. In the meantime, the injection of money into the active circulation will have exceeded the leakage back into idle deposits; thus, if the increase in non-consumption expenditure has been financed by drawing on formerly idle balances, without creation of new money, the whole process of income creation must be regarded as having been financed by a net transfer of existing money from idle to active balances. If, on the other hand, the increase in non-consumption expenditure was financed by creation of new money, this new money will have flowed into both active and idle deposits, equilibrium being reached when it has ceased to increase the former any more, the whole of the new credit being absorbed in additions to idle balances. At this point, the inflow of savings into idle balances will be sufficient to finance non-consumption expenditure at its new level, and, unless people have some reason for accumulating idle money rather than lending their savings through the capital market, the need for creation of new money will have ceased.

What, by way of comparison, is likely to be the monetary mechanism of a price–wage spiral? When wages are increased, the immediate finance may be provided either by drawing on firms' balances which would otherwise have been idle in the short period in question, or by increased borrowing from the banks. However it is financed, the increase in wages is likely to bring about an increased expenditure by wage earners— unless all consumers' goods and services are strictly rationed. The profit receivers, who obtain control of their incomes only after a considerable time-lag, may in some cases economize as soon as they know of the wage increase, but on the whole they are unlikely to be affected by it immediately, so far as their desire to spend is concerned. They will probably try to spend as much as before. In so far, therefore, as stocks of finished goods exist, the increase in total spending power due to the increase in wages not yet matched by a decrease in other dis-

distinction, in turn, can for many purposes be associated with a distinction between the different purposes for which the balances are held.

posable incomes may lead to an increase in consumers' total expenditure. Finally, however, profit receivers will feel the impact of increased labour cost, and the fall in their currently disposable incomes will begin to affect their expenditure, quite apart from the reduction that may already have been imposed upon it by the fact that wage earners are buying an increased amount for which the raiding of stocks can no longer compensate.

The net effect of an increase in wages with prices fixed and production inflexible, therefore, is to cause a temporary increase in consumers' total expenditure, to the extent to which stocks can be depleted, followed by a stabilization of expenditure at the old level. Since total money income is the same at the end of the process as at the beginning, active balances are unchanged in total quantity, except in so far as they bear different ratios to income in different parts of the community. Since there is a transfer of income (and of expenditure) from profit receivers to wage earners, and since the latter probably hold smaller active balances in relation to income than the former, total active balances may well be somewhat reduced. The temporary increase of expenditure while stocks of finished goods are being reduced is financed mainly by a transfer of money from the idle balances of profit receivers who in this period are paying increased wages without correspondingly reducing their own purchases. In part, they may ease the strain by increased borrowing from the banks at this time, and to this extent finance is provided by other peoples' idle deposits (transferred to the banks in exchange for, e.g. securities), or by a new creation of credit (through a reduction of the commercial banks' reserve ratios or an expansionary move by the central bank). In either case the idle balances, or new money concerned, pass into the hands partly (probably mainly) of traders or manufacturers in exchange for stocks of goods which they have sold but cannot replace; partly, perhaps, of wage earners who may be unable to spend all the increments in their incomes, especially if stocks of goods become inflexible before profit receivers have felt the impact of the reduction of their incomes. The whole process, therefore, is likely to result in some increase in idle balances and their redistribution in favour of those traders who have most drastically reduced stocks of goods, and of wage earners.

G

Consider now the mechanism and monetary effects of an increase in prices of finished goods, unaccompanied by any change in wages. The course of events will naturally depend to some extent on the policy followed by traders. If they sell their stocks at prices related to their historical cost, not the cost of replacement, the first impact of a rise of prices ordained by manufacturers will fall upon the wholesalers or retailers, who have to lay in stocks of goods at the new prices while selling off their earlier stocks at the old. This will involve a reduction of their reserves of idle money, unless they finance their stocks by bank credit or are financed by the manufacturers who supply them. In any of these cases, unless distributors foresee that higher prices will reduce the quantity sold, and cut their orders accordingly, or unless they are exceptionally short of credit or liquid assets, it is probable that the whole output will, in the first instance, be taken off the manufacturers' hands despite the price increase.

But will it be taken off the distributors' hands? Wage earners have no additional income to meet the increase in price, and no reason to expect it; how far they will increase their outlay in an effort to maintain the real level of their consumption will depend, therefore, mainly on the hitherto unspent margin of income on which they can draw, and on the extent of their liquid assets; though some increase in the extent to which they obtain credit may be possible (if, for instance, some of them now obtain on hire purchase goods which they would have bought outright before the price increase). The margin and the reserves in question are likely normally to be quite small, though there are times—when expenditure has been kept well below its normal level in relation to income by price control and inflexible supplies—when, even without any increase in their money income, wage earners may be expected to maintain their standards of consumption in the face of rising prices, especially if widespread rationing is in force.

Profit receivers have, of course, a prospect of increasing income when prices of finished goods are raised, and with some of them anticipation of this may be reflected in their expenditure as soon as the increase is announced, and before it affects the goods in the shops; certainly the unspent margins of their income and the extent of their liquid reserves are likely in many cases to be ample to permit some increase of expenditure in advance of a rise in income. Others, however, are likely to increase their expenditure only when retail prices rise; it is perhaps reasonable to expect that, at this point, they will increase it enough, or nearly enough, to maintain their previous level of real consumption. For most profit receivers, in any case, an increase in spendable money income will come only after the considerable time-lag involved in the distribution of profits (a lag which must vary from rather under a year to about eighteen months), and this will probably have to be awaited before profit receivers as a whole are likely to increase their real expenditure at all substantially, thus making up for any falling off in the volume of purchases by wage earners.

In so far as traders pass on at once rises in the prices charged by manufacturers—that is to say, fix prices in accordance with replacement costs—the burden of meeting such rises will be more immediately on the consumer and less on the trader. Profit receivers' spendable incomes will be increased in this case rather more quickly than under a régime of historical cost pricing, and a greater strain will be thrown on wage earners. The risk that the whole output will not be taken up by consumers at the increased price is, on balance, probably greater in this case.

A rise in prices of finished goods, unaccompanied by an increase in wages, is thus quite likely to be followed by a considerable hiatus during which the whole output of consumers' goods is not taken up by final purchasers. The economic effects of this will clearly depend on whether manufacturers and traders are willing to see stocks increase, and are able to finance the increase in question, either out of their own (or other peoples') idle balances or by an increase which the authorities are prepared to allow in the total supply of money. If stocks have been below the normal level in relation to sales, and liquid assets are plentiful (or new credit easy), a considerable price increase can be absorbed, especially if confidence in a further rise in prices makes increased stock holding attractive for speculative reasons. If stocks are already high in relation to sales, if there is fear of a fall in prices, or if the financing of additional stocks becomes impossible, then an increase in prices unaccompanied by a wage increase may lead to a cutting back of orders to manufacturers and so start a deflationary process. If this is not to happen, active deposits must ultimately increase; perhaps even more than in proportion to total money income (i.e. to the average increase in the prices of all goods and services), since the profit receivers who gain in money income, receiving their income in relatively large, infrequent instalments, probably require larger active balances in relation to their incomes than do wage earners.

This increase in active balances comes immediately from the idle balances, increased borrowings, or decreased savings of traders buying at the new prices while selling at the old (and perhaps, subsequently, buying more than they are selling at the new prices), of wage earners spending more in the absence of increases in their incomes, and of profit receivers spending more in advance of their income increases. The transfer from idle account (or from new money) into active balances goes on until the new level of transactions has established itself throughout the system. If this event is delayed—if, for instance, some receivers of increased incomes do not increase their consumption spending by the amount of the increase in their incomes when this increase has come into their hands—then there will be a new accumulation of idle balances which will have to be offset (if the level of income is to be maintained) by increased drafts on idle balances or increased borrowing by those who are willing to increase their stocks or to increase their consumption expenditure by more than the increase in their income. The mechanism of the money market may, of course, bring about a transfer of balances (by loan) from the points where they are accumulated to the points where expenditure is running ahead of current receipts.

Neither of the stages in a price–wage spiral, therefore, corresponds to either of the elementary stages in an open inflation with flexible prices—namely, the primary increase in non-consumption expenditure and the secondary increase in consumption expenditure. Wage increases unaccompanied by price increases (with real output constant) are likely to produce, apart from their more permanent distributional effects, merely a temporary increase in consumption at the expense of stocks and, probably, some fairly small increases in idle balances financed partly by slight withdrawals from active balances and partly by new creations of bank credit associated with increased wage bills. Price increases unaccompanied by wage increases are likely to produce a temporary decrease in real consumption (absorbed, unless a deflationary process ensues, by an increase in stocks), a permanent increase in money income, and a slightly more than corresponding increase in active balances, financed by drafts on idle balances and perhaps by new credit creation.

The injection of purchasing power which finances an ordinary open inflation is simply one aspect of the initiating increase in non-consumption expenditure (that is, the primary increase in factor incomes). In a price–wage spiral the increase in factor incomes—that is, the increase in prices which raises profits— is not already financed, but presents the economy with an invitation or challenge to finance it. If it is financed on a basis capable of being permanent—that is to say, if the whole output of consumers' goods is bought for consumption at the enhanced price—then there is no change in non-consumption expenditure, but simply an increase in the value of consumption. The increase in wages is not an increase in factor incomes as a whole at all, and can increase consumption expenditure only temporarily, apart from differences between wage earners and others in marginal propensities to consume. Essentially, therefore, the price–wage spiral is an alternation of simple increases in the value of consumption expenditure with purely distributional changes which set the stage for the next increase. In practice different parts of the economy will have different rapidities of response to the foregoing changes, so that it may not be easy to see this alternation as a series of discontinuous jumps; but that does not affect the nature of the process. Whether the spiral will have any tendency to converge will depend on two things, neither of them so definite as the leakages which determine the convergence of the income increase generated by an increment in non-consumption expenditure in an open economy— namely, the failure of entrepreneurs and wage earners to secure the price or wage increases they press for in their search for the maintenance or achievement of levels of real income which are incompatible, and the non-availability of money to finance increased transactions.

So far, the discussion has abstracted from the existence of fixed investment. If the price level of all output is raised, this will, of course, in any real case, affect non-consumption expenditure as well as consumption expenditure. If the demand for producers' goods is price inelastic, and credit is available to make it effective, the financing of the increase in expenditure demanded by the general price increase becomes to that extent less problematic than it would be if the whole of output consisted of consumers' goods. It is possible, however, that the price changes and wage changes of the spiral may affect the real volume of investment planned. A wage increase, since it diminishes prospective profits, is likely on the whole to lead to a reduction of investment plans, though in some instances it may lead to decisions to instal labour-saving machinery. An increase in prices of finished products, related to the foregoing increase in labour costs, is almost certain to increase prospective profits more, proportionately, than the prices of capital goods, and so to encourage expansion of investment plans. In all probability, however, the alternation of price increases and wage increases is too rapid in the ordinary course of the spiral to impose any detectable time pattern on the course of fixed investment, which follows behind the taking of decisions to invest by substantial intervals which vary widely from one type of project to another. In any case, an inflationary situation, with prices rigid and resources fully employed, is likely to mean a reserve of unfilled orders for producers' goods, so that variations in orders over a considerable range would fail to affect output.

The Conditions of Operation of the Spiral

In the foregoing analysis the fundamental conditions which enable the price–wage spiral to proceed have been stated only in the broadest terms and without any appeal to experience. It has been argued that it is essential to the working of the process that extra credit, or liquid reserves, should be available to finance each wage increase (and to finance increased expenditure on imports, if a rise of import price is the initiating factor); that credit, reserves, or some margin of unspent income should be available to take finished goods off producers' hands at increased prices, or to enable them to carry increased stocks of their products, in the interval between an increase in price and the distribution of the consequently increased profits; and that the state of expectations and of existing stocks should be such that those concerned are willing to undertake increased holdings without cutting down orders. It is clearly necessary, also, that sellers of goods should make the attempt to reimburse themselves for an increase in their costs by raising their prices, and that wage earners should not only attempt to preserve their real incomes in the face of a rise in prices by seeking higher wages, but that they should, for the time being, succeed. All these are, clearly, necessary conditions.

It has also been assumed, in discussing the working of the spiral, that full employment exists, in the sense that output is insensitive to increases in money income. This assumption makes for simplicity in exposition, since it assists in separating the mechanism of the spiral from that of the 'multiplier'. The 'multiplier' mechanism cannot work freely if output is fixed and prices are contractual or conventional; if output is expansible, on the other hand, changes in income and expenditure can come about through the 'multiplier' mechanism without changes in price, thus complicating the course of events associated with the spiral—if the spiral is working. There is, however, no obvious reason why the spiral should not work in a situation in which real output is expansible in response to increments in spending power; the existence of full employment is not an essential condition of the spiral's operation.

Nevertheless, it is clear that some of the essential conditions already mentioned are likely to be associated very closely with the level of employment of factors of production. Demands for increased wages, for instance, even though they are needed if the wage earners' standard of living is to be preserved, may not be made in deep depression, when there are few profits from which they could be financed, and when organized labour in each separate industry may fear that a rise in its own wage level would be bought only at the cost of increased unemployment. Certainly, there is relatively little chance that employers will accede to demands for higher wages in a depression, when their profits are low, price competition is keen, and when an abundance of labour in the market makes the maintenance of good relations with existing employees seem less important than at other times. Again, entrepreneurs are clearly much more likely to think that the market can stand a rise in prices—and much more likely to be right in thinking so—when output is limited mainly by the supply or distribution of one or more factors of production than when it is limited by a general deficiency of purchasing power.

This means that the rate at which wages and prices tend to be raised is likely to be related to the level of employment. The probability of a relationship of this kind has, of course, already played a considerable part in economic discussion; it is the basis of Professor A. C. Pigou's argument in his book *Lapses from Full Employment*,[1] and is a central theme also in Professor A. P. Lerner's more recent work *The Economics of Employment*.[2] It seems, however, that empirical investigation has not hitherto been directed towards verifying the existence of such a relation, or to finding the level of unemployment beneath which the price–wage spiral seems to come strongly into operation in any one economy.

One is tempted, therefore, to look at the year-to-year changes in wage rates that have occurred in the past along with the levels of unemployment prevailing at the time. In the United Kingdom, between 1880 and 1914, the index of wage rates was strongly influenced by certain industries—most notably coal-mining—in which (especially in the early part of the period) wages were related explicitly to the price of the product. This clearly reduces the probability that experience over these years will throw light on the present problem, but a glance at the data is, nevertheless, not entirely unwarranted.

The movements of both the variables (see Diagram 13, p. 99) were almost entirely of a cyclical nature, and the relation between them in their cyclical movement was fairly constant.

With the break of the boom—in 1890, 1900, 1907, and 1913—the rate of wage increase, which had been 4 or 5 per cent. per annum immediately before the crisis, was sharply reduced, sometimes becoming negative within a year, without, however, any considerable increase in unemployment. Thereafter, money wages usually continued to decline at a fairly steady rate of about 1 per cent. per annum until the onset of recovery, to the accompaniment of a steady increase of unemployment.

---

[1] London, Macmillan, 1945.
[2] New York, McGraw Hill, 1951.

During the upswing, the *rate* of increase of wages rose steadily as unemployment fell.

What would one expect to be the relation between the two variables during a fluctuation of effective demand? In the recovery and boom effective demand for labour is increasing, and, because it is expected to increase, it will be high relatively to the existing level of activity and employment. Labour is becoming scarcer, in the sense that the unemployed reserve is diminishing, so that its bargaining power is increasing, which will be likely to mean that the *rate* at which it can raise wages is increasing. When the boom breaks, not only does effective demand begin to fall (which by itself would presumably mean something like a *pari passu* fall in equilibrium wage levels), but it will, quite suddenly, become low relatively to the existing levels of activity and employment, because the expectation that these will increase is replaced by an expectation that they will decrease. Moreover, the increase in unemployment will *progressively* weaken labour's bargaining position and its power to secure wage increases or to resist wage cuts. Therefore, one would expect the break of the boom to be followed by a sudden fall in the rate of wage increase and then by a further fall *pari passu* with the growth of unemployment. When recovery sets in, expectations are again reversed, so that, in addition to a rise of the rate of wage increase correlated with the reduction of unemployment, one would expect a sudden, once-for-all, increase similar to the sudden decrease after the break of the boom.

This theoretical expectation is partly fulfilled. Recovery and boom are, indeed, marked by a rise of the rate of wage increase correlated with the reduction of unemployment, and the break of the boom is followed by a sudden fall. Thereafter, however, there was not generally, in the period just surveyed, a further fall correlated with the increase of unemployment; instead, the rate of reduction of money wages remained fairly steady despite the increase in the percentage of workers unemployed. In effect, the roughly parallelogram-shaped cycle which one would expect to find when rate of wage increase is plotted against unemployment in a scatter-diagram is cut off below by a horizontal line.

The explanation for this which comes most readily to mind

is that, once it is wage cuts and not wage increases that are in question, the belligerence of organized labour and the employers' fears of provoking disastrous conflicts are greatly strengthened. In a society in which labour is organized with any considerable degree of effectiveness, there is probably an absolute limit to the rate at which wage rates can be reduced —unless something very remarkable is happening at the same time to the cost of living.

It remains to inquire what light experience of cyclical fluctuations can cast upon the relation between unemployment and rate of wage increase which is relevant to the discussion of inflation. It is plain that, in the upswing of the trade cycle— an expansionary process starting and often even finishing well below the level of employment of resources which has been maintained throughout the inflationary period studied in this book—the rate of wage increase has at some point generally far outstripped the rate at which productivity per man-hour may be expected to rise over any considerable period, so that, beyond that point, money costs of labour per unit of output were rising. If the rate of increase of productivity per man-hour in industry generally is put, rather arbitrarily, at 1·5 per cent. per annum, it can be seen that the wage increase became inflationary (in the sense of raising labour cost of production) at somewhat different levels of unemployment in the various cyclical upswings examined. In that of 1886–90 the critical level was passed, perhaps in the early part of 1888, with trade union unemployment at 5 or 6 per cent.: in 1895–6 at 3 or 4 per cent.; in 1905–6 at 4 or 5 per cent.; in 1911–12 at 3 or 3·5 per cent. It is not possible to see in these figures any evidence of the increasing bargaining power of the trade unions, and taking account of the influence of the cost of living on wage demands will not help—1887–8 and 1895–6 were both periods when the cost of living was steady after a considerable decline, whereas 1905–6 and 1911–12 fell in a period of fairly steady increase which might have been expected to intensify wage demands.

It may be argued, however, that the rise of the rate of wage increase with increasing employment in the upswing of the trade cycle—when a further increase of employment is expected —is not relevant to the determination of the level of employment that could have been maintained indefinitely (*ceteris paribus*) without an increase in labour cost of production. In such a steady state, if it could be brought about, expectations would presumably be such that effective demand for labour, at any given level of employment and activity, would be somewhere between what it would be at that same level of activity in a downswing and in an upswing respectively. In this case the critical level of unemployment would be considerably less than that suggested by experience in the upswing—less by perhaps 1 or 2 per cent. of the occupied population.

How does experience in the United Kingdom after 1918 appear in the light of this analysis? Diagram 14 (p. 100) shows the changes in question. The violent movements of the years 1919–23 were quite unlike any experienced at other times. By 1919 the community had, with good reason, become acutely conscious of the rise of the cost of living, and, though only about a tenth of the recorded wage changes in 1919–20 were made in accordance with sliding scales, it was inevitable that the cost of living—which was 17 per cent. higher in 1920 than in 1919—should be the dominant factor in adjustment. By the time when the slump came, sliding scales had become so popular that more than half the recorded changes in wages in the years 1921–2 were made automatically in accordance with them. Thereafter, they again became of minor importance in effecting wage adjustments.

From 1924 until 1939 the relation between unemployment and rate of wage change was similar to that revealed in the cyclical movements of the generation before 1914; except that the level of unemployment throughout (so far as one can judge by comparing the post-war Unemployment Insurance statistics with the pre-war trade union records) was much higher. Another peculiarity of the inter-war cyclic changes was that there was no sudden reduction of the rate of wage increase at the break of the boom in 1929. Indeed, wage rates had already been falling since 1927, and with 11 per cent. of the insured population unemployed, and trade union strength at a low ebb after the great struggle of 1926, it is not surprising that what there was of industrial boom in the late nineteen-twenties did not raise wages. Nevertheless, when unemployment increased in the subsequent depression to over 20 per cent. of the insured population, the resistance to drastic wage reduction was as effective as it had been in the far less severe depressions before 1914, and the rate of decrease of wage rates never exceeded 1·6 per cent. in any year. Moreover, as in the recoveries from previous depressions, the rate of increase of wages rose as unemployment fell, even though unemployment was very high. By 1934, with unemployment still at 17 per cent., wages had ceased to fall; in 1937 and 1938, with unemployment still above 11 per cent., they were rising at 3 per cent. per annum.

From the upswing of the later nineteen-thirties it might be inferred that the critical level of unemployment, below which wages rose at such a pace as to raise unit labour cost of production, was as high as 14 or 15 per cent.—or, if allowance is made for the less buoyant condition of expectations in a steady state of employment, perhaps 10 or 12 per cent. Can this very large apparent rise in the critical unemployment rate since before 1914 be attributed simply to the increased bargaining power of organized labour? Some of it may well be attributed to this cause. The industrial strife of the nineteen-twenties, though it left the trade union movement for a time greatly weakened, induced in both parties to subsequent disputes a greater willingness to negotiate and to compromise, which probably, on the whole, tended to facilitate wage increase in a period of economic expansion.

There were, however, other points of difference between the periods before and after 1914 which may account for the apparently higher critical unemployment rate between the wars. The much higher average rate of unemployment after 1920 as compared with before 1914 was very largely due to a persistent mass of structural unemployment, which may well have affected the wage position in a very different way from the unemployment which was due to a general deficiency of effective demand. If there is unemployment confined largely to certain industries, and especially if these are highly localized, wages in those industries will probably be prevented from rising, and even made to fall—though, as was argued above, there is likely to be a fairly strict limit to the rate at which they will fall —but in so far as labour is immobile between those industries and others, wages in the others will not be prevented from rising as demand for labour in them expands, or as labour is able to assert its bargaining power. If, on the other hand, labour is distributed between industries in proportion to their requirements in full employment, a general deficiency of demand, though it may mean unequal unemployment in different industries, will be likely to mean a far less uneven distribution than is found when there is an underlying problem of structural unemployment. This more even distribution will mean that the critical level of unemployment below which there is a rise in average labour costs to industry as a whole will be lower than when a large part of the unemployment is of a structural character. In short, a considerable part of structural unemployment may be ineffective in depressing the bargaining power of labour as a whole. It seems likely that at least half the unemployment existing in 1937, for instance, was of a structural character, and, if that is so, one may say that, had there been no more structural unemployment than before 1914, the critical level of unemployment in the later nineteen-thirties would have been less than it actually was by something like 4 per cent. of the insured population. The greater part of the difference between the estimates of critical unemployment level for periods before and after the First World War may, therefore, be due to the heavy structural unemployment of the later period.

It is interesting to look at the comparable data for the United States between the two world wars. From Diagram 15 (p. 101) it will be seen that the points showing the relation of change of average hourly earnings in industry to rate of unemployment for these years fall into two well-defined groups; the first from 1921 to 1932, the second from 1935 to 1941. The point for 1934, quite understandably in view of the wage changes which accompanied the National Recovery Administration, lies well away from the rest, denoting a very large increase in earnings relatively to the unemployment ratio of the time.[1]

[1] It is also evident that the inter-war cycles in the United States did not follow the same course as any of those in the United Kingdom between 1880 and 1939. The correlation between unemployment and wage changes was higher and the relation more nearly linear. It may be a result of the less centralized nature and smaller scope of collective bargaining in the United States that wage changes vary more evenly with the state of the labour market. Certainly, one can deduce very similar 'critical' unemployment rates from the expanding and the contracting phases of these United States fluctuations.

The shift from one group of points to the other may, indeed, with some plausibility be attributed to the New Deal, which greatly strengthened the bargaining power of United States labour, both by promoting its organization and by the introduction of relief and unemployment insurance. Be that as it may, however, the shift was a drastic one; whereas the critical unemployment percentage before the New Deal seems to have been of the same order as that in the United Kingdom before 1914—perhaps 4 to 6 per cent.—it seems after 1935 to have been at least as high as it was at the same time in the United Kingdom—probably over 14 per cent.

The inflationary period, after unemployment had been reduced to a low level, displayed very little correlation between wage movements and the amount of remaining unemployment, either in the United Kingdom or in the United States. This, no doubt, is the clearest sign that the inflationary spiral was in full operation; wage changes ceased to be correlated with the rate of unemployment and began to be correlated quite closely with the movements of the cost of living. If one examines the record before 1939, for either of the two countries mentioned, one sees that the correlation between year-to-year changes of wage rates (or hourly earnings) and the simultaneous changes in cost of living was in general low (see, e.g. Diagrams 16 and 17, pp. 102, 103). This, at all events, is true of years when the change in the cost of living was small. In the years of high boom or sharp slump—1900, 1907, 1913, 1920 on the one hand, or 1885, 1894, 1922, 1931 on the other—sharp movements of both cost of living and wage rates tended to go together, the connexion being, no doubt, in some cases partly a direct causal one, and in others simply the common result of a drastic change in effective demand. In the inflationary period, however, with much greater variations in the rate of increase of the cost of living, the correlations become more impressive. In the United Kingdom, the percentage changes in wage rates in the years 1938–9, 1939–40, 1940–1, 1947–8, 1948–9, 1949–50, and 1950–1 were all equal to between half and the whole (averaging about two-thirds) of the corresponding changes in the cost of living index. In the intermediate years 1941–2 to 1946–7 the changes in wage rates were much greater than those in the cost of living index. In part, no doubt, this was due to the pressure to make wage rates up to the pre-war real level after money rates had failed to keep up with the cost of living increases of the early war years; in part, it is to be accounted for by the fact that the official cost of living index in these years—between the great wartime increases in indirect taxation and the introduction of the Interim Index in 1947—somewhat understated the rise in the working class cost of living. At all events, the correspondence between year-to-year movements of wage rates and the cost of living in the inflationary period—with some reservations about the later war and early reconstruction years—is a great deal closer than in times of substantial and varying unemployment.

These observations seem to point to a mechanism of operation of price changes which can be described as follows. The cost of living depends, in a simple way though with some time-lag, on two main factors; the internal wage level and the prices of primary commodities—which in the United Kingdom are mainly imported. The wage level again depends on two main factors, namely the level of employment and the cost of living, though in a more complicated way.

In slumps the connexion (in the United Kingdom at all events, though less so in the United States) becomes tenuous, but in periods of increasing activity the rate of change of wage rates increases in a fairly regular way with rising employment, and is also affected by the rate of change of the cost of living. The latter exercises a greater effect when unemployment is low than when it is high, and also, probably, increases its effect more than in proportion to itself—that is to say, large changes in the cost of living are more influential in proportion to their size than small changes. In ordinary times when employment fluctuates, therefore, wages rise at an accelerating rate in every recovery and boom, and cease to rise greatly, or actually fall, in every slump. This movement is imposed, with some time-lag and some reduction of its amplitude, on the cost of living, which, however, is as much or more affected by the much wider variations of primary commodity prices. In the United Kingdom the latter are sometimes correlated with home activity by virtue of the rough general parallelism between movements of activity and prices throughout the main trading economies of the world, but the correlation is very imperfect. In the United States primary commodity prices are more highly correlated with activity, since American demand is a high proportion of total demand for primary commodities, and since many of these are produced in the United States primarily for the home market. The direct influence of the cost of living on wage rates is probably confined largely to booms.

In a continuous period of low unemployment, on the other hand, the upward creep of wages due to general scarcity of labour and its consequent strong bargaining power will presumably proceed at a fairly constant rate, except in so far as it receives additional impetus from other forces. The influence of the cost of living, if that in turn were affected only by the increase of wages at some previous period, would also be constant. The whole inflationary movement would then proceed at a constant rate, or, perhaps (if wage demands over-compensated for increases in the cost of living, or price increases over-compensated for increases in wage costs) an exponentially increasing one. The further factor most likely to impinge upon such a process is a change in the cost of living arising from a change in primary commodity prices. If the economy in question is in a state of steady (because full) activity, such a change is most likely to arise either from a revision of expectations, from a change in supply of primary materials (such as a change in crop yields), or from a change in activity in some other part of the world. Any rise in the cost of living due to price increases of this kind is likely, because of the strong bargaining positions of both trade unions and entrepreneurs in relation to the ultimate purchaser, to be reflected very clearly, if not proportionately, by the consequential changes in wages and prices. Apart, therefore, from the more or less steady increase of costs and prices to which an economy may be subject if unemployment is stabilized below what has been referred to above as the 'critical point', the open economy at a high level of employment is probably more sensitive (so far as its price level is concerned) to changes in world commodity prices than it would be with a higher average level of unemployment. Of the closed—or almost closed—economy, this is likely to be less true. There, the fluctuations in commodity prices in ordinary times arise very largely from fluctuations in its own level of activity. If these are eliminated, or greatly reduced, commodity prices are less liable to fluctuate.

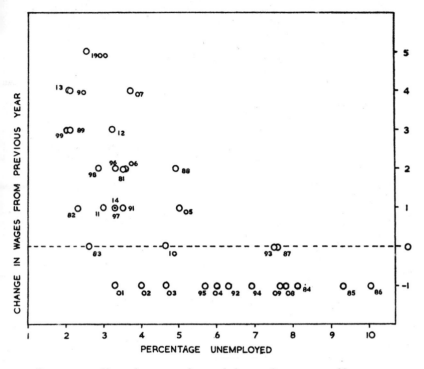

DIAGRAM 13. Unemployment and annual change of wage rates, 1881–1914: United Kingdom.

H

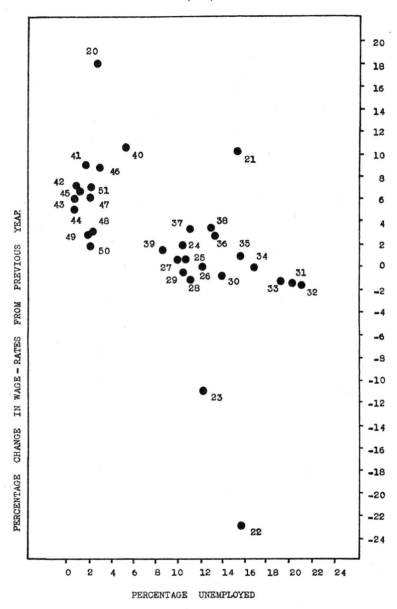

DIAGRAM 14. Unemployment and annual change of wage rates, 1920–51:
United Kingdom.

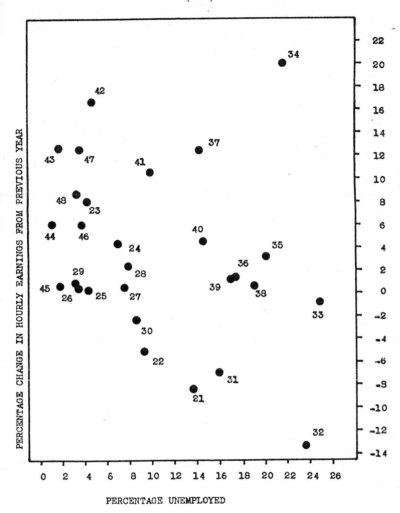

DIAGRAM 15. Unemployment and annual change of hourly earnings, 1921–48: United States.

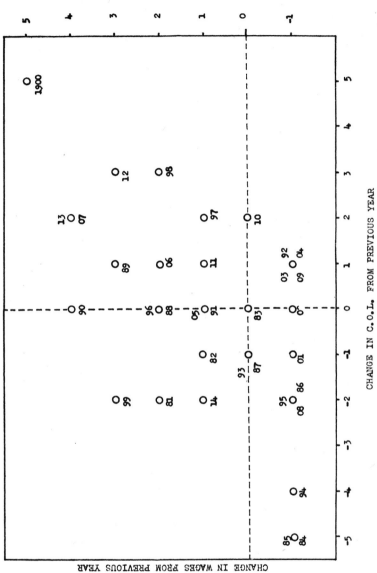

DIAGRAM 16. Annual changes in wage rates and cost of living, 1881–1914: United Kingdom.

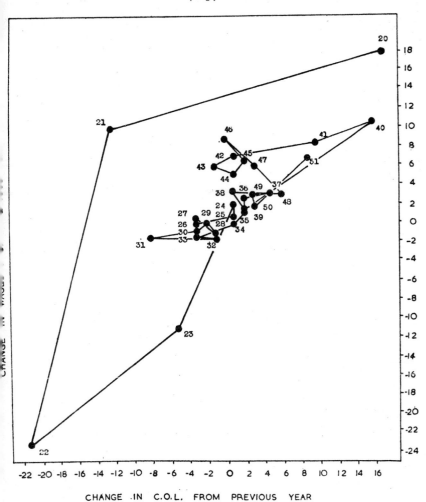

DIAGRAM 17. Annual changes in wage rates and cost of living, 1920–51 :
United Kingdom.

5

The Price–Wage Spiral and Income Distribution

The Role of Distributional Changes

IT has been pointed out that the motives which produce demands for wage increases and price increases are connected with distribution. It would hardly be surprising if, in a world where both prices and wages were contractual (or, at any rate, possessed some rigidity), entrepreneurs and wage earners respectively customarily sought all the time to raise them. The efforts of wage earners in this direction depend for their success, however, on various circumstances, two of which, at any rate, vary widely with the current pattern of distribution—namely, the size of profits and the level of real wages, both of which clearly influence public opinion in general in its attitude to the workers' claims. Moreover, the amount of pressure exerted by the wage earners is itself likely to vary with these two circumstances. Where wage rates are tied by agreement to a cost of living index (as is the case with Australian minimum wages, was the case with Canadian wages during the period of control, and is the case also with about one-seventh of British wage earners) the relation between wage increases and distribution assumes its most rigid form.

Similarly, entrepreneurial action in raising prices depends in practice very much on the distributional situation, since in some industries the maintenance of a fixed percentage profit margin over prime cost is conventional, and since many forms of price control and many contractual arrangements seek to keep producers' or distributors' profit margins fixed either absolutely or proportionately to costs. The result is that, apart from disturbances arising from outside the mechanism of the spiral, wages are most likely to move up when prices have moved up, and prices to rise when wages have risen.

Many kinds of price–wage spiral may be imagined, varying

with the assumptions that are made about the aims of the two parties who are competing for the real income of the country, or their success in achieving those aims. The modes of working of the simpler kinds can be easily represented and analysed either algebraically or geometrically. For the purpose of this chapter, it may perhaps be best to give a diagrammatic exposition of a few simple cases.

In Diagram 18 (p. 121) the wage bill is measured along the axis OW and total profits along the axis OP, it being assumed that these are the only two components of the cost of output; that is to say, the existence of rent, interest, and salaries (if these are distinguished from wages) and of imported raw materials is ignored. Since total real output is supposed to be fixed, the real income of either factor of production depends simply on its share of total money income, or on the ratio of its money income to that of the other factor. Suppose that wage earners seek to maintain that level of real income which is consistent with the ratio of wages to profits which rules for points on the line Ow, while entrepreneurs seek that which is consistent with the ratio of factor shares represented by points on Op. If factor shares initially are represented by the co-ordinates of the point A, entrepreneurs will be satisfied, but wage earners dissatisfied, and there will consequently be a demand for wage increases. If these are to satisfy the wage earners' demands, they must bring the point representing the new position on to the line Ow; since, however, there is no increase in total money income at this stage, wage earners' gains being at the expense of entrepreneurs' losses, the path by which the movement to Ow takes place must be the line AB, which slopes backwards at an angle of forty-five degrees. Entrepreneurs will now seek a price increase sufficient to bring the state of affairs back to something represented by a point on Op, and since they do this by increasing profits without changing money wages, the path traversed will be the horizontal line BC. Thus, the course of wages and profits in the spiral expansion due to this competition between wage earners and entrepreneurs will be represented on this diagram by a zigzag line $ABCDEFG$. . . . It is obvious from the diagram that the rate at which successive 'legs' of the zigzag (or 'turns of the spiral') involve increases in income will increase with the degree of divergence between the slopes of Ow and Op

which represent the factor distributions aimed at by the contending parties. It can also be shown that, for a given proportional degree of divergence between the factor ratios aimed at
by the two parties, the steps by which profits (and so total
money income) expand are greater if the ratio of wages to
profits is low than if it is high. It must be realized, however,
that this analysis tells one nothing of the actual rate, over time,
at which such a process will proceed, nor about the relative
speeds at which the horizontal and diagonal 'legs' of the zigzag
will be traversed.

A spiral of this kind may clearly arise if the two parties dis-
agree about their relative shares of the social product. It may
also be started from a situation in which both parties have been
content, if the real income available for distribution between
them is reduced, so that there is no longer enough to satisfy
them both. The significance of this can perhaps be brought out
by Diagram 19 (p. 121). A is again the initial position, corresponding to a distribution of money income which, with available real income at its original level, gives rise to no attempt to
raise wages or prices. Suppose now that the supply of consumers' goods is reduced, and that competition raises their
price. (Unit price is likely to be raised in at least the inverse
of the proportion in which supply is reduced, provided that
purchasing power is not removed, for instance, by additional
taxation; and the utilization of formerly active balances or of
new credit or the reduction of savings may enable price to be
raised by competition for the scarce supplies in considerably
more than this proportion.) Both wage earners and entrepreneurs will now require incomes to be raised in the proportion
in which prices have risen if they are to recover their old
standard of living—a thing which, clearly, they cannot both
do at the same time, in view of the reduction of total real
income. The price increase will mean that entrepreneurs maintain their share of total income better than wage earners at
first; if the price rise is sufficient, indeed, they might presumably increase their real income. Wage earners, however, if
they are determined to restore their real income, will press for
a wage increase which will bring them on to the line Ow, which
is such that its slope (RU/OU) bears to that of OA a proportion
equal to the ratio of the new prices to the old. Similarly, entre-

preneurs will try to achieve a position on the line Op, the slope of which measured from the vertical axis (that is to say, TV/OV) bears this same proportion to AV/OV. If the initial price increase, therefore, has shifted the position from that represented by A to that represented by T, subsequent events are likely to follow the course represented by $TBCD \ldots$, &c.

The processes so far considered have shown no tendency to converge. So long as both parties are determined to achieve standards of living which are incompatible with each other in view of the possibilities of supply, and are in a position to raise the prices of the goods and services they sell in pursuit of their ends, there is no end to the inflationary process. Shortage of liquidity or of new credit is, of course, likely to interfere with the process at some point, but that must be regarded as an interference from outside. If, however, there is some portion of the cost of output which is constant in money terms, the owners of the factors whose rewards are not constant can, clearly, all gain at the same time by inflating their money incomes. This fact has particularly important implications when the impulse which sets a price–wage spiral in motion is the raising of some element in cost which is constant thereafter —for instance, rents. Diagram 20 (p. 122) represents this case. What matters to wage earners now, with two other groups competing with them for the fixed national output, is not simply the ratio of their money income to profits, but its ratio to the sum of profits and rents. Thus, if the initial level of rents is represented by OR_1, a given level of real income for wage earners is represented by points on a line R_1w_1. Similarly, a given level of real income for entrepreneurs, so long as rents remain at OR_1 (or the equal length OS_1 measured off on the other axis), is represented by points on S_1p_1. If, before rents rise, both entrepreneurs and wage earners are contented with their real incomes (or, at least, are not taking steps to increase them), and the lines R_1w_1 and S_1p_1 are those which represent these 'satisfactory' situations, then they must have some point of intersection, A.

Suppose now that rents are raised to a level represented by OR_2 ($= OS_2$). The 'satisfactory' real income for wage earners will now be represented by points on a line R_2w_2, parallel to R_1w_1, while that for entrepreneurs will be represented by

$S_2 p_2$, parallel to $S_1 p_1$. Starting from A, therefore, the incomes of entrepreneurs and wage earners will follow some such course as $ABCDE \ldots$, &c., finally converging towards Z. When this point is reached (or virtually reached), the distribution of income between the three groups will be the same as before the increase in rents, and if that increase is not repeated, there will again be equilibrium. It can, however, hardly be a stable equilibrium, since both parties which are in a position to raise their money incomes can gain (in real terms) by raising them to values represented by points within the wedge of which $p_2 Z w_2$ is the tip. When there are only two parties competing for a fixed real income, they may, perhaps, agree, or learn by experience, to curb their inflationary competition, since general price inflation has disadvantages for both of them. If, however, there is a third party (rentiers or, in the shorter run, many classes of salary earner) whose money incomes are fixed, then price inflation may bring a real gain to all the parties in a position to raise their money incomes which for them may offset its disadvantages.

So far, only a closed economy has been discussed, and the introduction of foreign trade does, indeed, complicate the system very considerably, since importing entrepreneurs and exporting entrepreneurs have then to be distinguished as separate groups. It is possible, however, on the basis of the simpler cases so far discussed, to see in general how changes in the foreign trade situation may be expected to affect money income levels in the economy, on the assumption that entrepreneurs and wage earners can both raise their money incomes in an attempt to keep their real incomes constant.

Suppose (to take a practically important case) that prices in the outside world rise generally—that is to say, that the prices both of the country's imports and of its exports are raised. Entrepreneurial incomes as a whole (and, indeed, the national income as a whole) will not immediately be affected if trade balances, since the reduction of importers' profits will be matched by the increase of exporters' profits. Importers, however, will then raise their prices for resale on the home market so that their profits bear the same relation to the national income as formerly. In so far as they sell to exporters, the increase will probably be absorbed by reduction of the latters' abnormal profits; in so far as they sell to other entrepreneurs, who resell to or manufacture for the home market, the increase will probably be passed on, so that these entrepreneurs in turn keep their profits in the former relation to the national income. Prices of consumers' goods for the home market which contain imported materials will, in the end, rise by enough to cover the increased costs of those materials plus enough to raise the former profits of entrepreneurs who supply the home market in proportion to the increase in the national income which is involved. Wage earners' real incomes are thus reduced, and they in turn will seek increases to restore the original relation between the wage bill and the national income. The spiral which thus arises is, of course, convergent, provided that no section of the community insists on a real income larger than it originally had, and provided, also, that the outside world does not retaliate with a further price increase. The original distribution is clearly restored, and equilibrium re-established (on the assumption just stated) when home wages and prices have risen proportionately to those abroad. The attainment of this state of affairs is accelerated further in so far as the raising of prices of goods which are imported or exported leads entrepreneurs selling competing goods or similar goods on the home market to raise their prices, even in advance of any rise in their costs.

If the spiral is arrested before the point of complete adjustment to the foreign price level is reached, there must necessarily be some distortion of income distribution in relation to the initial position, the effect of which on the structure of the economy is clear. Importers will be discouraged, exporters encouraged, so that an export surplus will tend to arise, and home prices to be raised by the alternative mechanism of the foreign trade 'multiplier'. The increase of profits as a whole in relation to wages may, of course, do something towards offsetting this, in so far as it may increase home saving. A failure of the price level in a particular country to rise with that in the rest of the world is, therefore, likely to be retrieved through the foreign trade 'multiplier', or the price–wage spiral, or both, unless adjustment is made by raising the external value of the country's currency, or by reducing internal non-consumption expenditure.

The situation is, indeed, equally that which is brought about by a *fall* in the external value of the country's currency. In a state of full employment, an alteration of the balance of payments by this means depends on success in checking the operation of the price–wage spiral (which means maintaining some at least of the income distortion introduced by the depreciation), and, in so far as prices are flexible and market-determined, in preventing non-consumption expenditure as a whole from rising.

If the prices of a country's imports rise, but not those of its exports, the situation is rather more complicated. The initial effect will be to reduce total money income, since importers' profits will fall, those of exporters will not rise, and unless there is a substantial transfer of demand from imports, profits of non-importers supplying the home market will not at first be changed. It is possible that this may start a deflationary process; output might fail to be absorbed at the prices initially ruling, and unemployment or price reductions, or both, might result; this, of course, is the ordinary operation of an adverse change in the balance of payments, acting through the mechanism of the 'multiplier'. In so far as it led to a reduction of prices, it would still further worsen the position of importers, but would also strengthen the tendency for home-produced goods to be substituted for imports, and promote an expansion of exports by reducing exporters' costs and increasing their profits. An increase in unemployment might ultimately promote an increase of exports in much the same way. In an inflationary situation, however, with plenty of liquid reserves or plentiful supplies of new credit available, and with expectations sanguine, importers would be very likely to try to restore their profits by passing on the increase in import prices to the rest of the economy. In so far as they did this without impoverishing wage earners—that is to say, in so far as wages maintained their purchasing power, despite the rise in the prices of imported goods—the loss in purchasing power which initially fell upon importers would be transferred to exporters, whom we are assuming for the present purpose to be facing an elastic foreign market and unable to raise their prices.

It is clear that, as in the previous case, the full restoration or maintenance of the purchasing power of the incomes of both wage earners and those entrepreneurs who sell to the home market, using some imported materials, is possible only if wages and internal prices rise in the same proportion as import prices. When this has happened, however, exporters' profits will have been reduced; perhaps converted into losses. Both wage earners and non-exporting entrepreneurs in these circumstances are receiving higher proportions of the national income produced than before, though the purchasing power of their incomes is unchanged and the total amount of goods available for consumption in the country may be assumed to be unchanged— the deficit on external account being met by some form of borrowing abroad. Structural changes will necessarily follow; exporters will divert their energies to the home market, and if the consequently increased adverse balance can be financed, the total amount of goods available for use at home will be increased. In so far as all sections of the community are conservative in their spending habits and their ambitions with regard to real income—as we have assumed—this is clearly an anti-inflationary influence; the accumulation of stocks is likely to lead to an eventual reduction of orders which may remove the basic conditions as to expectations and credit supply which render the continuance of the spiral possible.

The assumption so far made, for simplicity, is that both entrepreneurs and wage earners aim at restoring their real incomes—that is to say, the purchasing power of their money incomes—to some conventional level. This is, of course, a highly artificial assumption, as, indeed, is any other that might be arbitrarily made about the *aims* of the competing parties. Institutional factors may, however, give definite and regular magnitudes to the steps by which wages and prices are raised. Thus, for instance, entrepreneurs may be accustomed to adjusting their prices so as to bring their percentage rates of profit over prime costs up to a conventional level; price controls, or government contract prices, may operate on the basis of fixed percentage profits over prime or perhaps total average costs. Similarly, wage rates may be adjusted automatically in relation to cost of living.

A constant ratio of profits to prime costs means, for the economy as a whole, a constant ratio between them and the aggregate of wages and costs of imported materials. This may be represented by a straight line such as S_1p_1 in Diagram 20, if Os_1 represents the cost of imported materials. If the policy is to keep profits at a constant ratio to total average costs, the appropriate line will have the same slope as before, but will be lower (like S_2p_2), since average fixed cost per unit of output may be assumed to be assessed on the historical cost, not the replacement cost, of fixed plant, and to be, therefore, independent in the short run of changes in wage and price levels. If wages are to be maintained in a constant relation to the prices of finished goods, then they must be kept in a fixed ratio to the aggregate of profits, costs of imported materials, and such other costs as are taken into account by entrepreneurs in fixing prices. The conditions of Diagram 20—namely, that $OS_1 = OR_1$ (or $OS_2 = OR_2$)—therefore adequately represent this particular case. The spiral will converge to a point (A or Z) where equilibrium is established. The equilibrium, moreover, will be stable, on the assumptions made, since from any point within the triangle p_1Aw_1 (or p_2Zw_2) the automatic adjustment of wages to cost of living and the reduction of prices into line with costs will bring profits and wages spiralling down to the point of equilibrium from a position where both are higher than the norm.

Here, therefore, it is the fixed costs—overheads and costs of imported materials—which anchor the whole price and wage structure. If they rise, the price and wage levels, which on the special assumptions here made are equilibrium levels, will rise proportionately. It is not improbable that in many countries the rise of import prices, in particular, has been more important in effecting adjustments of the internal price level in this way than have any changes in the pricing policy of entrepreneurs or in the aspirations and ability of wage earners to secure a particular share of the real national income. In terms of Diagram 20, the shift of the lines from (say) R_1w_1 and S_1p_1 to R_2w_2 and S_2p_2 may have been more important than any changes in their slopes.

The General Effect on Distribution

The price–wage spiral clearly involves alternate increases and decreases in real wages and real profits, with some trend increase in both at the expense of any elements in income which are constant, or relatively immovable, in money terms. The alternate increases and decreases cannot always be detected from the available statistics, though they sometimes show up clearly—the real wages of Thuringian miners, for instance, (according to Soecknick,[1] quoted by Bresciani-Turroni[2]) fell by half and recovered again in the course of each month from July to November 1923. The possibility of following the actual turns of the spiral will be examined later, with a view to determining the speed with which it has operated in some important cases. Meanwhile, can any generalizations be made about the effect of inflation on the average distribution of income over periods longer than those during which the spiral takes to 'turn'?

It seems that, apart from the obvious fact that factors whose money incomes are inflexible must lose in a period of price inflation, no such generalization is possible. Take first an open inflation due to an increase of non-consumption expenditure. While resources are still not fully utilized, it may well be that the elasticity of supply of products is less than that of the hired factors in general (especially labour), because of the necessity of bringing in previously uneconomic firms or plant in order to expand production. This will mean increasing the rent elements in the profits of firms or plant already employed, and so bringing about a 'shift to profits'. When, however, resources are fully employed, a further increase of expenditure will increase the competition for all factors of production, and there is no obvious a priori reason why the price of one will tend to rise more than that of another, except in so far as some are institutionally fixed and thus protected, for a time at least, from the effects of such competition. Often, wages are less immediately responsive than prices of finished goods (and so profits) to an increased pressure of monetary demand, and the lag of wage increases behind price increases reduces real wages and shifts the distribution of the national income in favour of entrepreneurs. In hyper-inflation this is normally the case; prices are then normally market-determined (which means that they are determined largely by the general expectation of continuing inflation) rather than cost-determined, whereas wages, though they tend to become more strongly linked to the cost of living than before, cannot keep pace with it.

[1] *Die Löhne in der Nachkriegszeit*, 1926.
[2] *Economics of Inflation*, trs. by M. E. Sayers (London, Allen & Unwin, 1937).

In the great German inflation of 1922–3 this can be seen relatively clearly, thanks to Bresciani-Turroni's analysis.[1] Until late in 1921 the share of labour in the German national income appears to have been much the same as in 1913. With the cost of living rising at some 20 per cent. per month in the spring of 1922, however, the share of labour fell, and by the end of the year was little more than half of what it had previously been. During 1923 the trade unions sought to remedy this by relating wages, first to the official cost of living index, then to the mark value of the dollar (which gave a more prompt indication of the progress of inflation) and finally (from August) to the price level *expected* to rule in the week in which the wages would be spent. The share of labour thus rose to something like its old level in March 1923, fell away to little more than half in July, and recovered again towards the end of the hyper-inflation. The variability from week to week was, however, very great, as is shown by the example of the Thuringian miners' wages which has already been referred to.

In the Hungarian inflation, also, the share of wages in the national income appears to have remained fairly high until hyper-inflation set in. Throughout 1945 and 1946 the real national income was probably less than half of what it had been before the war; real wages, however, seem to have been at about half the pre-war level in the early part of 1945, but, with the acceleration of price increases, fell to about 14 per cent. of that level by the end of the year. In February 1946 there was introduced a system of automatic adjustment under the title of 'calorie wages'. To the basic money wages a flat rate allowance was added consisting of food with a total calorific value of 14,000–16,000 per week, plus 5,000 for each dependent, or a sum of money supposed to be sufficient to buy this quantity of food, according to a price index which was brought up to date fairly frequently.

It is widely held that this system hastened inflation, partly because the calorie allowance was considerably higher than was, in fact, available from the food supply of the time. There seems, however, to be some misconception about this; the fact that the 'calorie wages' not distributed in kind were more than equivalent to the food supply (excluding that which was dis-

[1] *Economics of Inflation*, trs. by M. E. Sayers (London, Allen & Unwin, 1937).

tributed as 'calorie wages' in kind, or bought by non-wage earners) does not necessarily constitute an inflationary influence, since the excess money wages were not necessarily spent on food.

In fact, the introduction of 'calorie wages' is estimated to have pushed up total real wages from 14 per cent. of the 1939 level in December 1945 to 36·6 per cent. of it in February 1946. Thereafter, real wages fluctuated for a few months mostly between 20 and 30 per cent. of the pre-war level before sinking to 18 per cent. of it in June. The proportionate share of labour in the national income was thus probably much less during the 'calorie wage' period than before the hyper-inflation set in. With the share of profits in the national income so abnormally high, and prices determined, as they doubtless were at this period, by short-term demand based on expectations of further inflation, rather than on cost, it is unlikely that the raising of wages by this device appreciably hastened the course of inflation.

In other countries where there has been heavy inflation, stopping short of hyper-inflation, such evidence as exists does not always point to a decline in wages relative to the national income. In Greece, for instance, the ratio of the index of wages and salaries to the cost of living index (both based on 1939) did not fall below 71 per cent. during 1945 or 1946, despite the fact that even during the latter year the real national output was estimated to be no more than 55 per cent. of what it had been before the war. At this period, it is true, relief shipments were largely responsible for keeping the cost of living index down, and maintaining consumption, so that these figures probably somewhat misrepresent the situation. The weight of the evidence available, nevertheless, seems to be on the side of the view that the wage earners' share of the national income was well maintained, possibly because in a country little industrialized the effect of wage increases in raising prices is less than where wages form a higher initial proportion of national income. A similar appearance is presented by the Italian data for the years 1946–8. Real wages, according to the official indices (which in this case make some allowance for black market prices) were never in these years much less than 80 per cent. of what they had been in 1938, and, after the Einaudi reforms of late 1947, were actually above pre-war, although the real national income is estimated to have been in 1947 at only 70 per cent. of its pre-war level. In this case those in work doubtless benefited at the expense of the unemployed, as well as of some other classes. The adjustment of wages to the cost of living in Italy, by means of flat-rate bonuses, was fairly prompt, and it is likely that the share of wage earners in the national income was continuously maintained higher than before the war, so that prices of manufactures may well have been determined mainly by costs. The operation of this spiral ceased, however, when the Einaudi reforms suddenly cut off the supply of credit on which it depended, and at the same time caused a revision of the expectations that had induced anyone who could do so to buy goods for stock instead of holding money. The price of food in a country where it is mostly home-produced can hardly be regarded as cost-determined; it depends immediately on the momentary situation in the market; but here, too, the unloading of stocks, consequent upon the change of expectations just mentioned, seems to have served to bring inflation to an end.   ˙

In countries where inflation was only moderate there has generally been little change in the relative shares of the various factors in the national income. Wages in the United Kingdom, for instance, rose from 37·5 per cent. of the net national income at factor cost (excluding the income of the armed forces) in 1939 to some 42 per cent. in 1948. The increase was continuous, apart from a slight setback in 1945; it seems, therefore, to be associated with the existence (or rather the mode of operation under British conditions) of inflationary conditions themselves. Profits and professional earnings also increased during this period relatively to income as a whole—from 29 per cent. of it in 1938 to 33·5 per cent. in 1948, though in this case a maximum was reached in 1942–3, and there was a trough (not, however, as low as the 1938 level) in 1946. The common gain in the relative shares of wages and profits was, of course, at the expense of salaries and rents. Relatively to wages alone, profits rose until 1942 and then sank slowly until 1946.

Apart, therefore, from changes due to the relative fixity of rents and salaries, there has been no clear trend in the distribution of British income (before tax) between the main factors of production during the period of inflation as a whole. Such changes as have taken place in the relative shares of wage earners on the one hand and profit receivers and the non-salaried professions on the other may be traced to the relatively rapid rate of increase of prices and the relatively effective restraint on wage increase in the earlier years of the war, as compared with the subsequent period.

It is worth looking at these changes. G. E. Maxcy, in an unpublished thesis for the University of Leeds, has examined the behaviour of the ratio of profits to other factor shares (excluding the pay of the forces) in some detail. The index of this profits ratio rose from 100 in 1938 to 128 in 1942 and 1943, then fell to 103 in 1946, rose again to 109 in 1947, and fell to 100 again by 1949. Mr. Maxcy attempted to obtain an explanation of these movements in terms of two other variables —a price ratio designed to express the ratio of the price level of output to that of input, and an index of the total number of man-hours worked in industry. The attempt, as Mr. Maxcy shows, is only very partially successful, partly, no doubt, for lack of adequate data. The ratio of the price index for consumers' goods, with some highly conjectural allowance for producers' goods, to a cost index compounded of wage rates and the price of imported materials, fell fairly steadily throughout the whole period, though most sharply in 1938–9. This, therefore, gives little help in explaining the course of the profits ratio. The total number of man-hours worked in industry seems to have increased by about 16 per cent. between 1938 and 1940, which no doubt helps to explain the increase in the profits ratio in that period. Thereafter, however, it fell, owing to the transfer of manpower into the forces, until it was probably in 1944 below the 1938 level, and perhaps some 7 per cent. below it in the following year. Thereafter, of course, it rose. The high level of the profits ratio in the years 1941–5, when the number of man-hours worked was declining, and the ratio of non-war output prices to costs of input was also declining, must presumably be ascribed to the high and, until 1942–3, increasing proportion of the national income spent on defence equipment. Defence expenditure, other than the pay and receipts in kind of the armed forces, exceeded half the net national income at factor cost in 1942–3. The decline of the profits ratio after 1943 may have been assisted by the still diminishing scale of total manufactured production (as measured by the number of man-hours worked in industry), but it is most probably mainly due to the increasing efficiency of price control in the non-war industries (including the establishment of the utility schemes) and the more certain basis available for pricing war goods, especially where the cost-plus system was not followed. Nevertheless, the profits ratio until 1946 was much higher than before the war; it may be possible to connect this with the increasing efficiency of production in the war sector in cases where cost-plus did not rule, and the working of that principle itself where it did. The subsequent smaller rise of the profits ratio may be attributed, perhaps, to the increasing scale of production and efficiency of labour, and the slackening of price control. Its fall to the 1938 level by 1949 (as the White Paper on National Income and Expenditure points out in relation to total profits in that year) is partly illusory, being due to an increased legal allowance for depreciation and a smaller addition for revaluation of stocks than in the immediately preceding years. The profits ratio rose again in 1950.

When one looks at the United Kingdom indices of domestic prices, wages, and earnings in the inflationary period, it is impossible not to be struck by their general parallelism not only with one another, but with the index of import prices, which it is legitimate to regard as a largely independent variable. One is brought back to the conclusion, adumbrated at the end of the last chapter, that this has been the main determinant of British price and wage changes since 1939, though other factors must also be taken into account. The prices of imports rose in three great steps—by 79 per cent. between 1938 and 1942, by 47 per cent. between 1945 and 1948, and by 46 per cent. in 1950–1, with an increase of only 9 per cent. between 1942 and 1945, and a brief lull after mid-1948. The general price index of consumers' good embodied in the White Papers on National Income and Expenditure[1] reflects these steps on a smaller scale—a 43 per cent. rise to 1942, 8 per cent. 1942–5, 17 per cent. 1945–8, and 17 per cent. 1950–2. The rise in the early part of the war was partly due to purchase-tax;

[1] U.K. Treasury, *National Income and Expenditure of the United Kingdom 1938–1946* and *1946–1950*, annual Command Papers; see especially Cmds. 7099 and 8203 of April 1947 and 1951.

the cost of consumers' goods, excluding the effects of indirect taxes and subsidies, rose by only 35 per cent. between 1938 and 1942. Wage rates were at first slow to follow prices; between 1938 and 1942 they rose only by 30 per cent. This is probably to be attributed to two causes—in the first place, full employment was not attained until after the middle of this period; secondly, the lengthening of hours worked, including overtime, and the transfer of many workers to better-paid jobs were superimposed on the increase of rates, and raised average weekly earnings by some 60 per cent. The purchasing power of average earnings was thus actually increased, a circumstance likely to moderate demands for wage increases. In the later war years, 1942–5, with full employment, wage rates were pushed up by some 15 per cent.—considerably more than the prices of consumers' goods. The rate of increase, however, was only a little raised—to 18 per cent.—in the next three years, 1945–8, and closely matched the rise in prices of consumers' goods at that time. It may well be that the pressure for increased wage rates during this triennium of fairly rapid price increase was again reduced by the rapid increase in earnings, brought about largely by increased efficiency where piece rates ruled, despite some shortening of hours of work. It may also be the case that the pressure, which increased rates during the years 1943–6 very considerably faster than the prices of consumers' goods were rising, came in part from the fact that reduction of hours and the general dislocation attendant upon demobilization caused earnings to rise little—they rose only by less than 7 per cent. in these three years, which was slightly less than the percentage by which prices of consumers' goods rose. During 1948–50, when prices of consumers' goods were rising very little, and when the increase in efficiency was bringing a relatively rapid increase of earnings, the increase in rates of wages was less than in any two years since the beginning of the war. The price rises of 1950–2 stimulated a 17 per cent. rise in wage rates.

It has already been suggested that one may regard the price and wage movement in the United Kingdom as the products of two sets of forces—the pressure of import prices from without, and the pressure for wage increases from within. Import prices, throughout the period, have been much higher relatively to internal prices and wage rates than before the war—nearly 60 per cent. higher by 1949. The consequent pressure, mitigated by subsidies especially in the later years of the war and the first few years after it, was transmitted to prices of consumers' goods and to wage rates mainly in three great bursts between 1939 and 1942, between 1945 and 1948, and between 1950 and 1952 respectively. Independently of this, however, wage rates have tended to creep upwards during full employment—that is to say from 1940 or 1941 onwards. Their tendency to do this, in turn, has been modified by factors, other than wage rates, which affected earnings; when earnings were increasing owing to longer hours (involving more overtime) and increasing productivity, as in the early and middle war years and the years of post-war recovery, the pressure for increased rates seems to have been relaxed.

By 1949 the purchasing power of an hour's wages, at standard rates, over consumers' goods as a whole seems to have been almost exactly the same as before the war (its purchasing power over the goods normally bought by wage earners would be a little higher). The purchasing power of average weekly earnings over all consumers' goods, however, was some 30 per cent. higher than in 1938. Changes in employment and in the composition of the labour force (which are not allowed for in an index of earnings based on constant industrial weights) raised the increase in the total purchasing power (over all consumers' goods) of total wages paid to some 32 per cent., while the corresponding change for the total of all civilian factor incomes (before tax) was about 26 per cent. There was little further change in this respect during the two following years. The share of wages in the home-produced income was thus somewhat raised; their share in total personal incomes was, of course, increased considerably more, since the greater part of profits was not distributed in the post-war years.

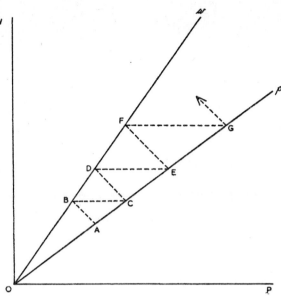

DIAGRAM 18.

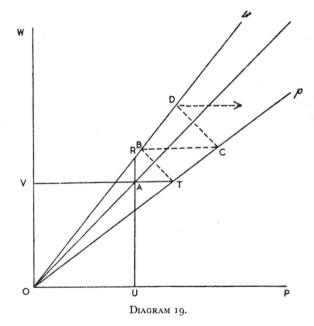

DIAGRAM 19.

The Price–Wage Spiral.

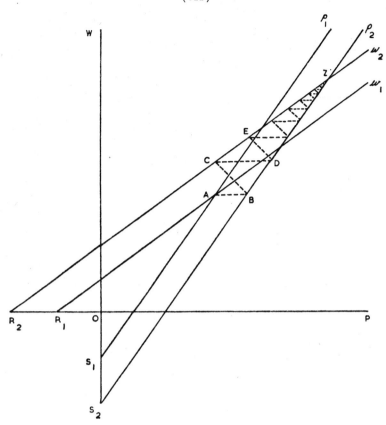

DIAGRAM 20.
The Price–Wage Spiral.

6

The Speed and Narrowing
of the Spiral

The Time-lags

THE foregoing discussion of the manner of operation of the
spiral throws little direct light on the speed at which it operates.
The speed of operation will clearly depend on two main factors
—how soon a rise in wages reaches the consumer in the form of
a rise in the retail prices of goods and services, and how soon a
rise in the cost of living is reflected in a successful effort to secure
increases in wages. It is clear from the outset that the effects of
either a general price increase or a general wage increase will
not be exerted at the same time on all parts of the economy,
but will be staggered as between different industries or departments of activity. A general wage increase, for instance, may
affect the prices at which some services are sold to the public
at once, but it will generally affect retail prices of manufactured
goods only after a time-lag which is likely to depend, among
other things, on the size of the stocks on hand of goods produced
before the increase in cost of production. Similarly, an increase
in the cost of living will be reflected in those wage rates which
are subject to an automatic adjustment for it after no more
delay than is involved in the publication of the index number
which shows the increase; but other rates will be affected, if at
all, only after the time required for the taking of a decision by
the trade unions concerned to press for an increase, and for the
negotiations by which they secure it.

The average time-lags for the economy as a whole will,
therefore, be nebulous, but their general order of magnitude is
clearly very important.

It may be useful, therefore, to examine the courses of events
in various countries, paying special attention to any sign of a
systematic lag of changes in wage rates behind changes in the
cost of living, and of changes in the prices of finished goods

behind changes in the rates of wages in the relevant industries. It is most convenient as a rule, in studying the wage–price time-lag, to confine one's attention to wages in manufacturing industry as a whole and the price index of manufactured goods. For the purpose in hand it is adequate to examine time series of the *monthly* changes in the variables concerned, looking for systematic gaps between the peaks and troughs of one series and the corresponding features of another. Naturally, it is only for relatively few countries that adequate data are available.

The data for the United Kingdom do not provide a very satisfactory basis for study, mainly because the advance in wage rates has at most times been too steady to be capable of being easily related to the other relevant variables. At the beginning of the war prices (both wholesale prices of manufactures and the cost of living) rose before wage rates, which gradually and partially caught up with the cost of living over a period of some six months. Later on, when isolated jumps occurred in the cost of living index (e.g. March and April 1941; October and November 1941), wages caught up in even more marked jumps within a month or two. In the later part of the war and the post-war years, however, the rise of the index becomes more regular. The biggest immediately post-war jumps in the manufacturing wage rates (December 1945 and June 1946) were not associated in any clear way with sudden advances in the cost of living. On the other hand, they were followed by sharp increases in the prices of manufactures with less than a month's lag in the former case and less than two months in the latter; but some of the outstanding rises in prices of manufactured goods (e.g. those of September 1947 and January 1948) could not be connected with any sharp rise in labour costs. The evidence does not suggest a systematic lag of cost of living changes behind those of wholesale prices of manufactures; at the beginning of the war and on a number of subsequent occasions (though by no means on all) the two seemed to have moved simultaneously.

It is important to remember that both wholesale and retail prices in the United Kingdom are subjected to powerful effects from overseas, in addition to those emanating from either the pressure of home demand or the price of domestic factors of production. The rise of the cost of living in 1939–40 was largely, in the first instance, due to the raising of import prices. The cost of living made considerable jumps almost simultaneously with the big jumps in wholesale (largely imported) commodity prices (August–November 1939), but then went on rising faster than import prices throughout the first six months of 1940. A rise of import prices, more than half of which was over in three months, was associated with a rise in retail prices which took five or six months to reach its half-way house. The devaluation of 1949 and the Korean War provide further examples of the effect of sudden, drastic increases in import prices. The big post-devaluation rise in import prices, which was spread out from October 1949 to May 1950, with the biggest jump at the beginning, was accompanied by only a slight and fairly regular rise in the index of retail prices. Import prices began to rise again in July 1950 and continued to do so fairly rapidly until May 1951, with the average rate of increase in the later part of this ten-month period rather greater than in the earlier part. Increases in the retail price index followed a not dissimilar pattern, except that they began two months later and made their first substantial pause in the autumn of 1951, some four or five months after import prices had ceased to rise. Retail prices, clearly, respond rather sluggishly to external shocks. Wage rate increases in the time of the Korean War bore much the same relation to retail prices as these bore to the prices of imports; they started a month later, and reached their first substantial pause in the spring of 1952, some five months after the first real halt in the ascent of the cost of living.

The data for the United States show very different regularities in the earlier and the later years under consideration. From 1939 to 1942 the lag between major movements of prices and the subsequent movements of wages is fairly clear. In 1939 it was about two months; when defence expenditure increased in the spring of 1941, prices and wages rose simultaneously; but when the price increase died away after March 1942, wage increases continued at a rapid rate for some six months. Movements of the wholesale prices of manufactures and of the cost of living in this period were practically simultaneous.

After the war the course of events was more complicated (see Diagram 21, pp. 134–5). The first major event was the wage increase of February 1946 (the 'first round'), which was brought about, not through an immediately preceding rise in the cost of living, but through a fall in earnings consequent upon demobilization, which provided an argument for taking steps to maintain 'total take-home pay' and purchasing power. This increase in pay was followed, within three months, by a comparable rise in the prices of manufactures, which, with the removal of price control from the end of June onwards, developed alarmingly. The cost of living rose a little later than the prices of manufactures, being influenced largely by the removal of price controls on foodstuffs.

It was doubtless the rise in the cost of living which was mainly responsible for the extensive 'second round' of wage increases, which occurred in three bursts, in February, June–July, and November 1947 respectively (the middle burst being the sharpest). These bursts were followed by advances in industrial prices after about one, three, and two months respectively. It appears, however, that the third of these bursts of wage increase in 1947 was stimulated to some extent by a further leap in the cost of living which occurred in September, contemporaneously with the rise in industrial prices for which the middle burst of wage increase may be held responsible. In the 'third round' of increases in the summer of 1948 industrial prices moved first, cost of living followed about a month behind, and wages rose a month or two later still. This increase appears to have originated with a revision of expectations following the authorization of the European Recovery Programme and the announcement, in the spring of 1948, of an enlarged defence programme. Actual or anticipated changes in effective demand had, by this time, become the initiating factors in such movements, whereas from 1946 to 1948 the cost and price revisions of the price–wage spiral proper serve best to explain the course of events. The recession in the last quarter of 1948 and early 1949 was, again, a matter of effective demand. Wholesale prices of manufactures and the cost of living fell virtually simultaneously from September onwards, though wages continued to increase, by virtue of earlier price increases and negotiations already started, until January 1949. Thereafter, with unemployment in excess of 5 per cent. of the labour force throughout the rest of the year, and with the cost of living first

falling, then nearly stationary, there were few wage increases—
even a few wage reductions. At the end of 1949, however,
recovery permitted further wage increases, which were reflected
in rises in prices of manufactured goods within a month or two,
and cost of living again rose some two months afterwards.

The sharp rise of industrial prices and cost of living in the
early months of the Korean War may be regarded as the main
cause of the rise in wages which began some three months later.
That increase, however, reached its highest peak in December,
simultaneously with the start of the second great expectation-
induced rise of living costs, which was prompted by the Chinese
intervention. The prolongation of the rise in both cost of living
and wholesale prices of manufactures into the first two months
of 1951 may be attributed largely to the heavy wage increases
in the last quarter of 1950.

It thus seems that, in the United States after the war, increases in wage rates have led to increases in wholesale prices
of the relevant goods within a period varying from zero to three
months (perhaps with some tendency to shorten); that rises in
the cost of living have, on the whole, followed changes in wholesale prices of manufactures at intervals of zero to two months,
and that major increases in the cost of living have been followed
by increases in wage rates after periods varying up to seven
months, but more usually about two or three. The total time
required for a 'turn of the spiral' in this period thus averages
about six months.

In Canada the very efficient price control and the gradual
nature of decontrol prevented any development of a systematic
spiral until very late in the inflationary period (see Diagram 22,
p. 136). Wages were frozen quite rigorously until 1946, and
only after the complete revocation of the control order in
November of that year were wage increases passed on into the
price of manufactured goods. The large burst of wage increases
during the last months of the year was followed, at an average
distance of three or four months, by increases in the wholesale
prices of manufactured goods, and, though a large part of this
price increase may be attributed to the decontrol measures of
January, February, and April 1947, it seems probable that some
of it is a lagged effect of the foregoing wage increases. The
large measure of price decontrol in August produced a spate of

increases which cannot be related with any precision to the fairly steady advance in wages which went on throughout the year; but the very sharp price rise of July–August 1948 seems to bear some relation to an almost equally sharp increase in wages two or three months earlier. There is, therefore, some slight evidence for a lag of two to four months between wage increases, and increases in the prices of manufactured goods in the period after decontrol.

Cost of living was kept stable by subsidies and direct control until after the war. There was considerable withdrawal of subsidies in 1945, but that could not affect wages until the relaxations of wage control, which began in January 1946. It is tempting to connect the very considerable increases in cost of living consequent upon the withdrawal of further subsidies in mid-1946 with the final decontrol and substantial increase of wage rates at the end of the year, but, since the precise timing of both was determined by administrative action, the lag between them cannot be regarded as typical. Indeed, after the beginning of 1947, the course of changes in the cost of living and of changes in wages does not suggest that there was any time-lag greater than a month. During this period, too, the lag between movements in wholesale prices of manufactures and those in the cost of living seems to have been no greater than a month or so. After decontrol, therefore, the total 'turn of the spiral' in Canada, as in the United States, probably took something like six months.

For other countries only considerably less frequent data are available, which limits the amount of information to be obtained concerning time-lags. From the Danish quarterly data from 1939 onwards, for instance, it is possible to deduce only that, at the beginning of the war and again in 1946–7, the cost of living and the price of manufactures have moved approximately together (between those two periods the movements of both variables were very small); while the substantial wage increases of 1945–6 seem to have resulted in corresponding movements in the prices of manufactured goods only after an interval of somewhat over a year.

Much more interesting, despite the shortness of the periods over which information is available, are the experiences of France and Italy, where the severity of inflation far surpassed that in the countries just discussed. For France only quarterly data are available, and those only from the beginning of 1946. The movements of the cost of living appear to have anticipated those of hourly earnings in industry by somewhat less than one quarter until the great increase of earnings in the first quarter of 1948: though that also may be regarded as in part the delayed consequence of cost of living increases which had gone on throughout 1947. Wage increases again followed the great retail price increases of 1949–51 with a lag of about a quarter. Industrial prices, on the other hand, followed earnings by about one-quarter (or perhaps a little less) again until the beginning of 1948, when they shot up in advance of earnings. The discrepancies of early 1948 are, no doubt, to be attributed largely to devaluation; but for that, prices of manufactures would perhaps have risen at a diminished rate in the first quarter of the year as earnings had done in the previous quarter. Again, therefore, there are very slight indications that the 'turn of the spiral' takes about six months, or rather less.

For Italy there are bi-monthly data from the beginning of 1947 only, with monthly data later. They show at first a considerable degree of simultaneity (if one allows for some differences of trend) in the movements of the cost of living, contract wages, and wholesale prices of finished goods. All three reached a maximum rate of increase in mid-1947; the two price series showed a maximum rate of decline at the end of that year, with wage rates, however, falling to a minimum (zero) rate of growth some four or six months later. In the price rises of 1950–1 there was a clear lag of wage changes behind those in the cost of living of anything from two to five months.

Partial relations, not sufficient to indicate the period of operation of the spiral as a whole, can be found in a few other countries. In Belgium, for instance, large jumps in the cost of living index in August 1947 and February 1948 seem to have been followed by gradual increases in earnings up to four months later. The conspicuous jumps in earnings in 1951 came as much as nine or ten months after those in the cost of living. The connexion between increases in earnings and increases in wholesale prices is, however, not at all clear (except in the metal industries, where they seem to move together) and the general index of wholesale prices seems to have been only loosely

connected with that of cost of living. Again in Hungary, during
1947 and the first half of 1948, the very large changes in cost
of living (due mainly to changes in food prices) seem to have
been followed at intervals of one to three months by corresponding changes in rates of earnings. The Government's
success in its policy of holding down the prices of finished manufactures seems, however, to have been sufficient to prevent a
very active operation of the spiral, and after mid-1946 both
wages and the cost of living were reduced. In Chile quarterly
data suggest that, between 1939 and 1946, increases in earnings
usually lagged anything up to one-quarter behind those in the
cost of living. The great rise in the latter at the end of 1946,
however, seems to have been connected with adjustments in
earnings which went on throughout the following year. Australian experience in 1950–2 suggests that, though some adjustment of earnings to the cost of living was almost immediate, a
substantial amount was delayed by one or two quarters.

In all these instances, therefore, the data, fragmentary though
they mostly are, suggest that some months must normally elapse
before a rise in prices can react to produce a further rise in
prices, or a rise in wages to produce a further rise in wages,
through the mechanism of the price–wage spiral. In hyper-
inflation, of course, the adjustments of wages and prices to
each other tend to become automatic and much more rapid
than in normal conditions; but in these circumstances the
inflationary process proceeds too rapidly and (so far as the
available data can show it) too smoothly for the propagation of
'jolts' through the economy to be traced from statistical records.

Light can, of course, be thrown upon the speed of propagation of these 'jolts' by other methods than that of examining
changes in prices and wages. Direct study of the delays which
take place in putting forward and in settling wage claims based
upon rises in the cost of living are of assistance here. A. T.
Peacock and W. J. I. Ryan[1] have found by studying a large
number of British wage claims in the years 1946–51 that 'the
time which has elapsed before an increase in the prices paid
for the major goods of everyday consumption was at least partially reflected in an increase in the wages being paid to workers
varied between about three months and twelve months'. Even

---

[1] *Manchester Guardian*, 15 May 1952, and *Economic Journal*, June 1953.

where a sliding scale agreement is in operation, the time between a price increase and the consequential wage increase has been shown by these writers to vary between one and thirteen months, according to the terms of the agreement and the timing of the initial price increase. They show that the average time taken to settle claims, after they had been put forward, was about four months.

To this lag we must add that between the rise in wage costs and the rise in the wholesale prices of manufactured goods. No precise direct evidence seems to be available here; clearly, the lag may be very short, or, if wholesale prices are bound by contract, it may be very long. We still have to add the delay which arises between increases of manufacturers' prices, or transport costs, and the raising of retail prices. This will depend on the rate of turnover of retailers' and middlemen's stocks, since it is most usual for distributors to sell goods at prices related to their historic costs, or, occasionally, at prices related to the average of these and replacement costs. There will not, of course, for any broad class of goods, be a clear-cut lag corresponding to the traders' period of turnover, since that period will be an average of probably quite widely different periods for the different types of goods within the broad class. The average period, moreover, varies enormously from one broad class to another. Nevertheless, the information available about rates of turnover can, clearly, give one a very useful indication of the range and the average length of the lags likely to exist at this stage.

According to evidence from the United States and the United Kingdom, the total period of turnover in distribution before 1939 varied from over a year in some extreme cases, such as jewellery, through a range of from two to six months in the footwear and clothing trades, and two to three or four months in groceries, down to a matter of days for perishable goods. Turnover generally in normal times seems to be rather more rapid in the United States than in the United Kingdom; in the latter, however, it has clearly been much more rapid during the greater part of the inflationary period than usual; during the war, indeed, monthly quotas of some goods (such as footwear) were largely sold within a few days of arrival in the shops. It is clear, however, that for most manufactured goods in any but these very exceptional conditions of shortage, the lag between a rise in labour costs and the main part of the consequential rise in retail price will seldom be less than two months, and in many cases will be four or more.

Adding these lags to those which arise between increases in the cost of living and the granting of wage increases, even without allowing for a considerable gap between rising wage costs and rising list prices of manufactured goods, one arrives at a range of total times extending all the way from perhaps two months to two years, with the greatest probability apparently attached to something considerably longer than the six months which has emerged from a scrutiny of price and wage series as a common apparent time for a complete 'turn of the spiral'. All the evidence is of a highly indefinite nature, and it is, perhaps, hardly necessary to seek a reconciliation of two such vague indications. All that need be said, perhaps, is that a sharp rise in the cost of living may be expected to result in a further rise through the mechanism of the spiral, the greater part of which is likely to be completed by a time six months or a year after the initial rise.

The Narrowing or Widening of the Spiral

It is clear, however, that the course of an inflationary process for which the price–wage spiral provides the chief mechanism is dependent not only upon the time-lags which separate the increases in wages, wholesale prices, and cost of living, but also upon the ratio of each of these increases to the one which had preceded and motivated it. If, for instance, a 1 per cent. increase in wholesale prices normally provokes $\frac{1}{2}$ per cent. increase in the cost of living, a 1 per cent. increase in cost of living provokes a $\frac{3}{4}$ per cent. increase in wage rates, and a 1 per cent. increase in wage rates a $\frac{3}{4}$ per cent. increase in wholesale prices, then a 1 per cent. increase in wholesale prices now will lead to an increase of $\frac{1}{2} \times \frac{3}{4} \times \frac{3}{4}$ per cent. or $\frac{9}{32}$ per cent. six months hence. In these circumstances it is plain that any inflationary movement will soon be damped out, unless constantly renewed by some factor outside the mechanism of the price–wage spiral. If, on the other hand, a 1 per cent. increase in prices now leads to a 1·5 per cent. increase in six months' time, then any inflationary movement will be explosive, the rate of the development of the explosion being governed by the size of the factor of increase (1·5 per cent. in this example) and the period of six months in which it acts.

The data available do not seem to justify any elaborate attempt to analyse the price–wage spiral in terms of these factors of increase; by simple inspection, however, it is possible to form some rough idea of these magnitudes in certain cases. For instance, in the United States the fluctuations in rate of increase of cost of living were probably less than half as great in amplitude as the corresponding movements of wholesale prices; those in wage rates distinctly less than the corresponding (preceding) variations in cost of living; those in wholesale prices of finished goods perhaps twice as great as the preceding changes in wage rates. The factor of increase was thus apparently less than unity; the operation of the price–wage spiral, by itself, would in this case not be explosive. Moreover, since each 'turn' took something like six months, the speed of the inflationary process set in motion by some 'jolt', such as the removal of price control, was likely to be fairly slow.

Indeed, if one examines a chart of prices of finished goods in the United States (either the index of wholesale prices of processed goods or that of consumers' prices) for the period 1946–8, it does not seem too fanciful to regard it as showing an exponential or asymptotic adjustment towards an hypothetical equilibrium level, following upon the shock of decontrol. The hypothetical ceiling towards which prices were tending seems to stand at a distance above the level of June 1946, equal to some three or four times the immediate price adjustment of the month or two succeeding decontrol, and the rise towards it proceeded at a rate which diminished fairly steadily. In each 'turn of the spiral' (roughly, on the evidence above, each six months), the rate of change of prices diminished by something like a quarter.[1] In hyper-inflation, on the other hand, expectations of further price increase would have caused the contending parties to raise their prices to such an extent as to overcompensate at each stage for the recent increases imposed against them, and the price increase would have steepened instead of slackening off.

[1] A detailed 'model' of the United States inflation in this period is described in F. D. Holzmann, 'Income Determination in Open Inflation', *Review of Economics and Statistics*, May 1950. See also J. Duesenberry, 'The Mechanics of Inflation', ibid.

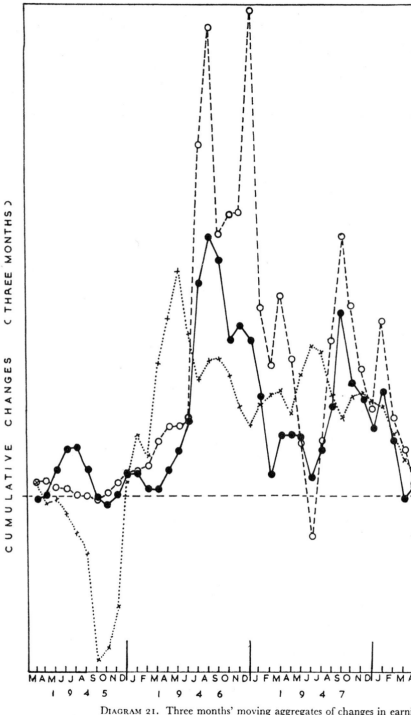

DIAGRAM 21. Three months' moving aggregates of changes in earnir

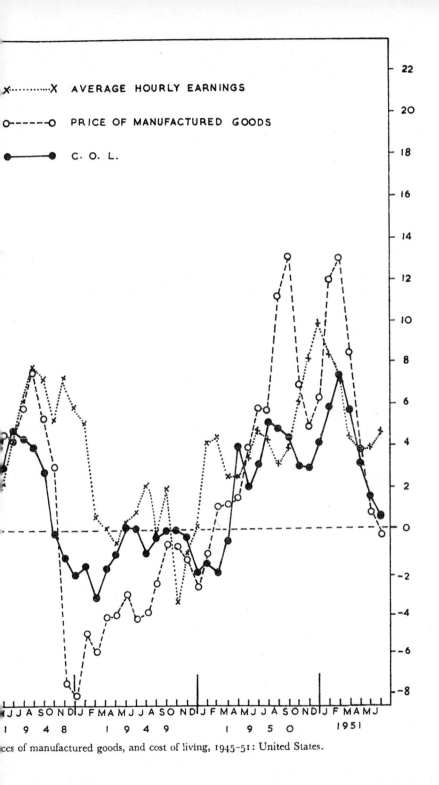

...ces of manufactured goods, and cost of living, 1945–51: United States.

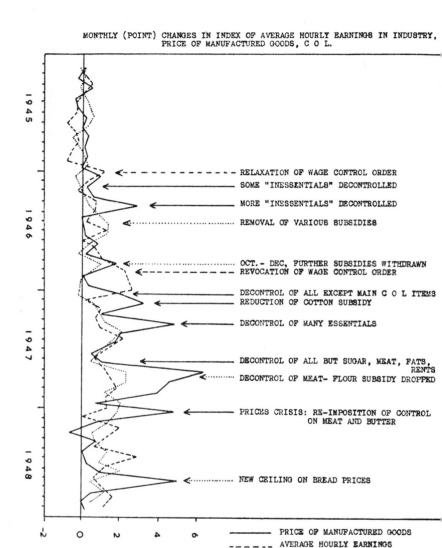

MONTHLY (POINT) CHANGES IN INDEX OF AVERAGE HOURLY EARNINGS IN INDUSTRY, PRICE OF MANUFACTURED GOODS, C O L.

1945

1946

← — — — — — — — — — — — — RELAXATION OF WAGE CONTROL ORDER
← — — — — — — — — SOME "INESSENTIALS" DECONTROLLED
← — — — — — — MORE "INESSENTIALS" DECONTROLLED
← .... REMOVAL OF VARIOUS SUBSIDIES

← .... OCT. - DEC, FURTHER SUBSIDIES WITHDRAWN
← — — — — — — — REVOCATION OF WAGE CONTROL ORDER
← — — — — DECONTROL OF ALL EXCEPT MAIN C O L ITEMS
← — — — REDUCTION OF COTTON SUBSIDY

← — — — — DECONTROL OF MANY ESSENTIALS

1947

← — — — DECONTROL OF ALL BUT SUGAR, MEAT, FATS, RENTS
← .... DECONTROL OF MEAT- FLOUR SUBSIDY DROPPED

← — — PRICES CRISIS: RE-IMPOSITION OF CONTROL ON MEAT AND BUTTER

1948

← .... NEW CEILING ON BREAD PRICES

-2   O   2   4   6

——————— PRICE OF MANUFACTURED GOODS
— — — — — AVERAGE HOURLY EARNINGS
.... C O L

DIAGRAM 22. Monthly changes in prices of manufactured goods, cost of living, and hourly earnings in Canada, 1945–8.

7
Price Control

The Reasons for Price Control

SINCE inflation—in the sense in which it causes alarm—is essentially the inordinate rise of prices, it is natural that the attempt should be made to combat it by direct administrative prohibitions of price increase. Action of this kind has, indeed, been taken from ancient times. In a more sophisticated age, however, under the influence of classical political economy, such policy tended to fall into disrepute, as being a necessarily futile attempt to suppress symptoms without attacking the roots of the disease. The great controversy about the inflation of the Napoleonic Wars centred on the nature of these roots—whether excess of money or shortage of goods was to blame, and whether, for this purpose, bank credit counted as money. The financial controversies on the First World War, likewise, were mainly concerned with the unwisdom, or the unfortunate necessity, of financing war expenditure partly in a manner that increased the volume of bank credit. The mechanism by which money income is generated by increased expenditure was, however, not understood, and that by which money incomes and prices can be indefinitely expanded through the unwillingness of any section of the community to bear a reduction in real income which is, in fact, inevitable was little discussed. After his brilliant exposition of these two matters in his pamphlet *How to pay for the War*,[1] John Maynard Keynes commented: 'During the last war I was at the Treasury. But I never at that time heard our financial problem discussed along these lines.'

The price control of the First World War was directed not at a suppression of the price–wage spiral so much as at particular social injustices and hardships—profiteering and prices for necessities which would have put them beyond the reach of the poor. These, indeed, are clearly among the most cogent reasons for ever introducing price control, together with its concomitant

[1] London, Macmillan, Feb. 1940.

(for important commodities) of rationing. The free market system would, in the first place, bring about the optimum distribution of a given supply of goods and services if the purchasers had roughly equal purchasing power—or, to be precise, equal marginal satisfactions from income. The qualification here means that, with incomes as unequal as they are, the free market system brings about a distribution which is always open to attack on grounds of welfare, even though it may be argued that much inequality is inevitable; but when there are barely enough of certain necessities for general health and efficiency, even assuming distribution according to physiological need, the fact that free markets do not produce this distribution will reduce national efficiency, and so lay them open to stronger attack. This may happen in peacetime; it is more likely to happen in war, partly because shortages (in relation to physiological need) are then more probable, partly because wartime inflation often produces abnormally great inequalities of income.

Similarly (with approximate equality of purchasing power) the free market would, in the long run, cause the available resources to be used to produce the kinds of goods and services in the relative quantities most conducive to the satisfaction of the community's wants. The qualification about income distribution, however, is again an important one, especially in war when inequalities may become abnormally great. The qualification 'in the long run' is also of fairly widespread importance; the inelasticity of supply of many commodities in the short run notoriously causes prices to be raised by a sudden, permanent increase in demand, or a sudden, permanent worsening of supply conditions to heights well above those that are necessary to call forth an appropriate supply in the longer run, often with the consequence that an excessive supply is stimulated, and fluctuations of price and supply are set up. In war the danger of this is again unusually strong because the changes both in demand and in supply are abnormally violent and sudden, and the time-lags involved in adjusting the structure of production to them are often long. House-room becomes scarce because building is stopped, or because of enemy action; but the correspondingly high equilibrium price can have very little effect in calling forth an increased supply until after the war, and then it may stimulate an over-supply because the high price will continue until the appropriate number of houses is finished, and further houses will have been started meanwhile. Food becomes scarce because of blockades or shipping difficulties, and high prices, though they may stimulate home agriculture, cannot bring increased supplies into existence for a season at least, and will, in the meantime, probably have drawn too many resources onto the land. Moreover, while high prices due to scarcity will bring about some immediate relief by causing those holding stocks to reduce them *if* they think the shortage temporary, it often happens that many people increase their stocks in anticipation of worse shortage, so raising price temporarily still further above its longer-term equilibrium level, with still further distorting effects on the allocation of producers' resources.

These considerations—the intensification in wartime of the injustices and inefficiencies which spring from the inequality of incomes, and the imperfection of short-term equilibrium price as a regulator of supply—are likely to create a strong case for piecemeal and sporadic price control in wartime even if there were no general price inflation. In practice, however, war always involves some tendency in this direction, partly, or perhaps mainly through the price–wage spiral, and this creates a further and sometimes a stronger case for price control of a more general nature.

The Adoption of Price and Wage Controls

It is clearly possible, in principle, to check the operation of the price–wage spiral completely by administrative control of prices and/or wages, and it is very difficult in wartime (or, indeed, in other times of continuous full employment) to check it by other means. Whether wages or prices or both are chosen, depends on many circumstances, doctrinal and political.

So far as doctrine is concerned, it seems to have been the case that the necessity of wage control was sooner and more clearly perceived than that for control of prices of goods. Thus the British Treasury Memorandum of 1929 on *The Course of Prices in a Great War*[1] concludes:

The real conclusion is that the problem of banking and general financial policy in time of war and the problem of controlling profits

---

[1] Quoted by W. K. Hancock and M. Gowing, *British War Economy*, H.M.S.O., 1949.

and the price of labour (including remuneration for personal services of all kinds) must be dealt with together. The limitation of wages is probably more important than the limitation of profits, since, all other methods failing, taxation can be applied more easily to correct inflated profits than to correct inflated wage payments. . . . The programme must include fixation of wages and prices so as to reduce to the smallest possible dimensions the demand for additional credit. . . .

This is essentially a 'purchasing power' approach to the problem; it is perceived that, since taxation cannot mop up all the excess of income over that which is required to buy the available goods at the existing price, the generation of new income by the spending of this excess must be directly controlled. The perception of the price–wage spiral as a simple competitive bidding-up of sectional prices does not, however, seem to have been clear; if it had been, the case for control would have been strengthened, and it would have been seen that, from this point of view, the control of prices is as important as that of wages. Indeed, in a country with strongly organized labour, and at a time when large-scale elimination of the higher-cost producers and distributors cannot be faced, any major divergence between prices and wages spells trouble, and failure to prevent an upward movement in either will make it very hard to hold the other down.

The political difficulty—in most countries—of wage control, however, and the demand for price control as an anti-profiteering (rather than an anti-inflationary) measure caused the latter type of control to be attempted first; or to be the only one of the two that was seriously attempted in most places.

Germany had both kinds of control before the war. The story of German price control is a long one, dating back to the Emergency Decrees of 1931, by which a Price Commissioner was appointed; but really effective control (as distinct from supervision of cartel agreements) began with the appointment of Joseph Wagner as Commissioner for Price Formation in October 1936 and his famous 'price-stop decree' of the following month, which attempted to freeze at the October 1936 level all prices except those of labour. Modifications of the price structure were gradually made, partly to allow for changes in cost of imports or the employment of substitute materials, partly by way of reduction of cartel prices which were thought excessive. This German price control sprang mainly from two roots

—first, the National Socialist mistrust of the free market, and secondly, the high degree and long tradition of cartellization. It was thus, in its origins, very unlike the measures of control introduced in other countries during the war, though in some degree it is, no doubt, to be regarded as a precaution taken on reaching full employment by a community disposed to be highly nervous of price-inflation. German wage control, in the full sense of a wage-stop decree, came into force only on the eve of the war. From 1934 the powers of the 'Trustees of Labour' had included the fixing of minimum wages; in 1938 maxima were laid down, in every case 10 per cent. above the minimum for the trade and type of labour concerned, and in the following year the scheduled rates were frozen. Both controls remained extremely effective through war and occupation.

In France and Italy wage control was effective and price control was not. Freezing of prices and wages was attempted from the outbreak of war in France. The ineffectiveness of price control under inflationary pressure, before, during, and after the German occupation, frustrated the intention of providing stability; nevertheless, it is probable that the existence of wage and price control considerably slowed down the working of the price–wage spiral, mainly at the expense of the wage earners. Italian wages were frozen in 1940, but inability to control prices necessitated the granting of bonuses, and (after the Allied landing) increases in rates. In November 1944 the whole institutional framework of state wage control was abolished, and collective bargaining resumed.

Elsewhere, price control has generally been found—for political reasons—easier and more effective than wage control. A beginning was made on both at about the same time—the spring of 1942—in the United States, and the attempt made to prevent all further wage and salary increases (with minor exceptions) from the following October. Wages, however, were freed from control almost immediately on the close of hostilities, on condition that the relaxation was not used as a basis for a claim to raise a controlled price, while price control itself was abolished only in the summer of 1946. Price control was generally successful, in that the consumers' price index rose less than 10 per cent. during its currency; hourly wage rates rose somewhat, but not much more.

In the other principal countries operating effective direct controls—Canada, Australia, New Zealand, and the United Kingdom—price control came first, and direct wage control (if it was introduced at all) was not rigid even in intention, but mitigated by cost of living provisions. Canada set the pattern for the type of control in which wages were rigidly linked to prices, which were controlled. The Wartime Prices and Trade Board, established at the outbreak of war with extensive powers over the prices, supply, and distribution of necessities took little drastic action in regard to prices in the first two years—in which the movement of North American prices generally was moderate—though wool, sugar, and butter were brought under control. The rapid rise of prices due to United States rearmament in the autumn of 1941, however, called forth a freezing of the prices of all goods and many services at the level of September–October, followed by the gradual introduction of specific price ceilings. Wages and salaries were frozen at this time also; but it was provided that, when the cost of living index rose by a specified amount, bonuses should be given to compensate the lower earners fully and the middle earners partially for the rise. This Canadian control was exceedingly effective.

Australia and New Zealand took strong action to control prices at earlier dates than did Canada, but otherwise largely followed the Canadian model. New Zealand froze prices on the outbreak of war, allowing increases only to the extent of increases in cost of production or importation, and from September 1941 fixed rigidly prices of certain principal commodities (subsequently increased in number), irrespectively of cost changes. In December 1942 wages and salaries were frozen, a 5 per cent. increase being permitted after the first 2·5 per cent. rise in the cost of living index, and a further similar increase after each subsequent 5 per cent. rise. In Australia specific prices were fixed by the Price Commissioner for some 200 commodities during the first two years of war, account being taken of cost increases. From February 1942 wages also were pegged —the existing mechanism of minimum wage fixation by the Commonwealth Arbitration court being simply strengthened by the specification of maxima as well. This, however, meant merely that basic rates were pegged, automatic cost of living adjustments continuing according to established Australian

practice. Finally, in April 1943 the structure of control was
completed by the stabilization of the cost of living index, as in
the United Kingdom.

In the United Kingdom, apart from rent control which was
introduced promptly at the outbreak of war, price control did
not arrive until the beginning of 1940. In the autumn of 1939,
when import prices were rising fast, government trading departments were instructed to cover replacement costs. The
Prices of Goods Act came into force in January 1940 with the
object of limiting profits to the pre-war absolute level per unit
of commodity sold. Prices of foodstuffs were, in effect, largely
stabilized from the end of 1939, and from April 1941 were
lowered or raised as was necessary to offset the less controllable
movements of other prices entering into the cost of living index.
Specific price fixing for selected commodities, other than food,
was undertaken from July 1941 under the powers granted by
the Goods and Services (Price Control) Act. No compulsory
wage freeze or maximum wage fixing was ever attempted; the
principle that wages are determined by collective bargaining
was retained—though strikes were made illegal and additional
compulsory wage-arbitration machinery was established. The
political atmosphere at the beginning of the war—with prices
rising and a Conservative government in office—was particularly unfavourable to any attempt to infringe this general
principle (which would in any case have been difficult). A
co-operative policy on the part of trade unions had to be relied
upon; it was achieved with the help of cost of living stabilization to the extent that the rate of increase of hourly wage rates
was steadily reduced until 1944, after which it remained until
1951 at less than 6 per cent. per annum except for the post-war
jump in 1944–6, as follows:

*Percentage Annual Increases of Index
of Weekly Money Wage-Rates; United Kingdom*

1938–9	1·5	1945–6	8·8
1939–40	10·5	1946–7	6·0
1940–1	8·5	1947–8	3·0
1941–2	7·0	1948–9	3·0
1942–3	6·0	1949–50	1·8
1943–4	5·0	1950–1	8·7
1944–5	6·5	1951–2	8·0

In view of the fact that output per man-hour was probably increasing, on the average, in the latter part of the war, and was certainly increasing quite rapidly again from 1946 onwards, the rate of increase of labour costs cannot have been more than, perhaps, 2 or 3 per cent. per annum in the period of stabilization, apart from the demobilization year, 1945-6.

The Contribution of Other Controls

The practical lessons which have emerged from the attempts to apply the controls in question, are mainly straightforward ones, consistent with the simple theory of market equilibrium. A free market does not produce. optimum results under war conditions, and the need for direct control for checking the price–wage spiral (when circumstances favour its operation) is inescapable; but this does not mean that the teachings of price theory can be ignored. Prices influence both consumption and production; keeping a price down where it would otherwise rise will tend to increase consumption of the commodity concerned up to the limit of the supplies available, and (perhaps in the longer run) to reduce production of it. This is most markedly and obviously true if prices of some other commodities are less efficiently held down; in this case consumers will tend to substitute the cheaper, price-controlled commodity for dearer, less efficiently controlled ones, while producers will tend to switch to the commodities which have risen most in price. If *all* prices, including those of the hired factors of production, are successfully frozen, this substitution effect will not occur; moreover profits, also, and so total incomes, will be roughly stabilized (apart from the effects of changes in productivity and employment). Any subsequent change in the structure of production, however (which can only be brought about consistently with this general freeze by some process of priorities, allocation of resources, or orders to produce), will leave prices, incomes, and supplies out of equilibrium. A shift of resources from civilian supply to war production, for instance, will leave demand unsatisfied at existing prices and income levels in the civilian sector, unless the extra expenditure on war material is balanced by extra taxation of civilian incomes. Even if this is achieved, particular commodities will generally be scarce in relation to the civilian demand for them, since a reduction of civilian disposable incomes will not necessarily reduce demand for particular goods to the same extent to which the government's demands for them have increased.

It is possible, in principle, that a general, perfectly efficient freeze of prices (including those of the hired factors of production) might succeed for a time without these ancillary controls in peacetime, when the economy was not undergoing rapid structural change. Such change is, however, the main feature of the period here under discussion. Moreover, price fixing never can be perfectly efficient and comprehensive, so that direct controls of production and consumption are all the more necessary to deal with attempts at substitution. Where (as is the case in any truly inflationary situation) private consumers have an excess of disposable income over the value of the available goods and services at the controlled prices, rationing is all the more necessary to secure equitable distribution.

Nevertheless, though ancillary controls cannot be dispensed with, the extent to which they are necessary depends very markedly on the efficiency with which price regulation can be employed, as opposed to mere price freezing. With completely comprehensive and efficient administration it might in principle be possible to control a war (or other) economy by price manipulation and fiscal policy alone, without ancillary controls, in such a way that the average level of prices was kept fairly steady. Wages and profit margins could be raised in industries required to expand, reduced in those required to contract; selling prices (including tax) could be fixed so as to clear the market at the level of disposable income so produced. It is doubtful, however, whether the drastic and rapid changes required in war could be thus brought about by this market mechanism without engendering great inequalities of income, leading to an inefficient distribution of scarce necessities.

Price control thus, generally, demands both some system of direct allocation of resources and some rationing of finished products, and the less comprehensive and flexible the price control is, and/or the greater are the changes to be brought about in the structure of production, the more necessary those direct controls of production and consumption will be.

Does it follow that, with comprehensive allocation of factors and comprehensive rationing, price control would become

unnecessary? Clearly it does if the monetary system is altogether superseded, and each consumer's ration of essential
goods is delivered to him without payment—a situation which
has been approached in certain economies (i.e. Poland immediately after the war) where money wages became almost
valueless on account of price inflation, and wages were mainly
paid in the form of essential goods. Given fixed factor prices,
the *status quo* can equally well be preserved if rationed goods
are sold through ordinary channels, provided that rations are
correctly calculated. If the price of a good is initially so high
that some consumers are unable to afford their rations, the
market will not be cleared, since the wealthier consumers cannot
exceed their allotted share; and price will fall until the market
is cleared, which can happen only when all rations are fully
taken up.

Rationing alone, however, cannot suppress the price–wage
spiral. It may reduce the incentive for any group in the community to seek a higher money income (since extra money
income cannot bring an immediate increase in consumption),
but it is unlikely to eliminate it. Wage earners, therefore, may
be expected to continue to press for increases of wages, and in so
far as the importance of marginal income to employers is reduced
by rationing, they will be the more willing to risk the loss
of some profits by granting wage increases. If the wage increase
raises the income of the poorest consumers (as it probably will),
there is nothing to prevent sellers of goods from raising their
prices to the point where these poorest consumers can, once
more, only just afford their rations. The price increase which
the raising of wages may be expected to motivate, therefore, is
likely to prove possible, in part or in whole.

This, however, is a digression or, at least, an appendix to the
argument by which it has been sought to show that price
control (especially an imperfectly comprehensive price control)
requires some direct controls of production and consumption
if it is not to lead to distortion of production and gross inequity
in distribution. The success of price control has clearly depended to a large extent on this support. Rationing was very
widely adopted to ensure an equitable distribution of necessities.
It covered the main foodstuffs in all European countries and
Japan during, and for various lengths of time after, the war

(except that the United Kingdom and certain other countries found it necessary to ration bread and potatoes only during the post-war food shortage, if at all), while clothing was rationed in most European countries, Japan, and also in Australia and New Zealand. Soap, also, was very generally rationed in Europe and coal in some European countries, while the acute shortages of motor spirit and rubber were met by rationing in many parts of the world. Rationing, or some form of licensing, covered most of the principal consumers' goods in Europe generally, including the United Kingdom; the price mechanism was substantially in abeyance as a distributing mechanism except where (as in France or Italy, for instance) a significant proportion of rationed goods found their way into a black market. In legal markets price control had, and needed, the support of very widespread and vigorous quantitative limitation.

Outside Europe (and Japan) rationing of consumers' goods naturally played a smaller part. Food shortages being far less pressing than in Europe, the level of civilian consumption was less a matter for concern. Nevertheless, considerable recourse was had to rationing in the later part of the war; Australia, for instance, ultimately rationed clothing, meat, butter, tea, and sugar, and operated priorities systems for milk and eggs; the United States from 1943 rationed meat, canned fruit and vegetables, sugar, fats and butter, petrol (locally) and tyres while many of the consumers' durable goods in these and other overseas countries were available only to restricted groups of consumers. That further recourse was not had to it must be attributed mainly to the fact that supplies of necessities were expansible. In all the main countries which employed price control food became cheaper than before the war in relation to hourly earnings—in the United Kingdom some 25 per cent. cheaper, in the United States about 15 per cent., in Canada and Australia about 12 per cent., in Germany about 4 per cent. (These figures refer to 1943, which was, in general, the year of fullest mobilization of resources.) Consumption of food per capita fell at the same time by some 16 per cent. in the United Kingdom, while it rose about 9 per cent. in the United States and Canada—comparable data are not available for other countries. The need for drastic rationing in the United Kingdom, and the reason why only isolated items had to be rationed (and those not drastically) in North America are, therefore, clear.

With clothing experience was somewhat different, since prices generally rose more than those of food—notably in Australia and the United Kingdom, where clothing became about 30 per cent. dearer and about 10 per cent. dearer respectively than before the war in relation to hourly earnings. These price increases may have helped to choke off demand; the 10 per cent. cent. increase in the United Kingdom can have made only a relatively small contribution to the 44 per cent. reduction in per capita consumption which was brought about under the rationing scheme, but the greater Australian price increase must have helped considerably towards bringing about the reduction of per capita consumption to a level some 30 or 40 per cent. below pre-war.

In Canada and the United States clothing prices rose less than hourly earnings, and it is not surprising that per capita consumption increased very markedly—by about 25 per cent. in both countries. This increase, however, was within the capacity of the economy without hampering the war effort. In fact, if one asks how the United States and Canada were able to achieve such a high degree of conversion to war economy, and such a high degree of success in wartime price control with only slight recourse to formal rationing of the consumer, the answer seems to lie, not in the smaller degree (as compared with, say, the United Kingdom) in which it was necessary to compress *total* civilian consumption below the equilibrium level to achieve these results, but in the plentiful supply of the main necessities— food and clothing—which meant that civilian consumption as a whole could be cut far below the level which would normally have gone with the wartime income and price position by such simple expedients as the total cessation of production of passenger cars, refrigerators, and other durable goods which normally enter largely into marginal purchases when North American incomes rise. The European economies, on the other hand, suffered from shortages of food and clothing (and certain overseas economies from clothing shortages) which had to be met by rationing if price control was to be applied, whatever might be the supply position and policy with regard to other consumers' goods.

So much for the effects of price control on consumption; on the supply side, also, the main economies were well equipped with direct controls. In the United Kingdom allocation of manpower came to be the chief instrument for determining the structure of production, but allocation of raw materials was also available for ensuring that, the inducements offered by the price structure notwithstanding, resources should not be drawn into inessential uses. Equally stringent direct controls were available in Germany, where official penetration into the government of industry was peculiarly complete. In the United States allocation of labour did not become the powerful instrument for control of production that it was in the United Kingdom. There was no direction of labour, though by 1944 men could be hired only by arrangement with the United States Employment Service, which observed an industrial priority system in referring men for employment. Local ceilings on employment in non-essential industries and the selective use of deferment of military service also gave some control over the distribution of manpower to the authorities; but materials rather than men were the instruments by which production was directly influenced—a reflection, no doubt, of the fact that in the initially under-employed United States economy, it was in regard to materials that shortage arose long before there was any general shortage of manpower. The United States, like the United Kingdom and all other economies whose approaches to the problems of wartime production were empirical, 'planned on the bottleneck'. The American approach to full planning—i.e. allocation—in this field was, however, gradual, and various systems of priorities preceded the adoption of the Controlled Materials Plan in April 1943.

The direct control of labour is, of course, as much a supporting measure to wage control as to price control. It is impossible to freeze wages, and difficult to control them at all, if they are at the same time being left to control the distribution of manpower between industries, especially at a time when the economic structure is being transformed, and no large pool of unemployed exists. Where (as in most countries) the freezing of wages was imperfect, however, relative wage rates in different occupations tended to change during the war and post-war period, though not always in such a direction as to assist the structural changes of the time.

An unpublished investigation by Mr. Garas of the University of Leeds throws light on the operation, or supersession, of wage incentives in relation to the wartime and post-war changes in the occupational structure of the United Kingdom. His method is to study the relation between changes in the average weekly earnings in an industry (expressed in terms of the average for all industries) and total employment in it (expressed in terms of total employment in all industries). Both of these variables are measured in such a way that their value for the year 1938 is 100.

If relative employment in an industry expands because demand shifts in the direction of its product, rendering it capable of bidding more strongly for labour in the open market, then the correlation between relative employment and relative earnings in it will be positive. The same will be true if relative employment in it falls because demand has shifted away from its products, and it has, therefore, been able to keep the reduced amount of labour it requires without bidding vigorously against other industries. On the other hand, if labour is directed into an industry, or is removed from it for military service less rapidly than from other industries, its share of total employment may rise while earnings in it are falling relatively to earnings elsewhere; if labour is being removed from it very rapidly by direct controls, its share of employment may fall while earnings in it are raised relatively to the average. A negative correlation between relative employment and relative earnings is thus a very clear indication that the price mechanism is superseded by direct control; a positive correlation suggests that the redistribution of labour is taking place mainly through the price mechanism.

In the two industrial groups most essentially connected with the production of armaments—chemicals and the metal, engineering, and shipbuilding group—it is quite clear that the correlation between relative employment and relative earnings is negative. Moreover, for the latter of these two groups there is some evidence that movements in earnings lag behind those in employment, suggesting that the latter are the independent causal factor. The elasticity of the curve (the change in relative employment that goes with a unit change in relative earnings) is high—ten or more—which suggests, not so much that the demand for labour in these industries was elastic, as that both the demand curve and the supply curve (and consequently their point of intersection) were moving rapidly to the right during the war years.

In some industries from which labour was moved in the course of the war, the correlation between relative employment and relative earnings was, on the other hand, mainly positive; both variables fell (and subsequently recovered) together. This was true of textiles, the food, drink, and tobacco group, and the paper and printing group. In the two former cases, however, the middle period of the war (1940–3) brought falls in relative employment with little change in relative earnings, which suggests that the removal of labour from the industries concerned was virtually keeping up at that time with the shift of demand away from their products. In the clothing and woodworking industries the pattern was similar, except that, in this middle period, the correlation became negative, showing that the removal of labour in the former case and the relative increase of the labour force in the latter had outpaced the decrease and increase respectively in the pressure of market (including governmental) demand for the product. Coalmining shows a negative correlation in the years up to 1943, when first, the relatively slow calling-up of miners and the fall in the total demand for coal, then the relative shrinkage of the labour force caused a fall and a rise respectively in relative earnings. Subsequently, direct controls failed to keep the labour force up to the desired level, and the correlation between relative employment and relative earnings became positive, changes in the former variable being about three-quarters of those in the latter. Building and contracting shows a negative correlation until 1941, as the removal of labour outpaced the fall in the demand for its product; then, till the end of the war, the correlation became positive. The over-manning of the building industry at the end of the war, in relation to the rate of building which the supply of materials and the investment programme rendered possible, is reflected in the re-emergence of a negative correlation.

Thus, at the time of most active mobilization (say 1941) the operation of the market mechanism, as reflected in a positive correlation between wage inducement and the movement of labour into or out of an industry, was superseded for almost every important British industrial group, and it was only in a minority of instances (notably coalmining in the later part of the war) that a substantial relative change in wages took place in such a way as to assist the movement of labour that the economy required. The direct control over British labour, therefore, seems to have been quite sufficient to have rendered a wage freeze compatible with the necessary changes in the distribution of manpower. No doubt it was this which made it possible to secure such moderation of wage increases, even despite the absence of any compulsory stabilization of rates.

The Technique of Price Control

Granted that adequate control can be exercised over the use of resources, so that price control is possible without distortion of the economic structure, or gross inequity in distribution, the three techniques of control which may be employed are, a freezing of the existing structure of prices, a limitation of profit margins which leaves the prices of commodities to change in some way with costs, and the fixing of specific prices. Each of these has its peculiar difficulties. A freeze has to reckon with the fact that, for any open economy, some prices are determined externally, and the only way of maintaining the frozen price structure in the face of a rise in the prices of imports is to make use of subsidies. Further recourse must be had to subsidies if a complete stabilization of wages is not accomplished, or if, in spite of such a stabilization, costs of production rise (as they well may under war conditions) because of decreased efficiency. For these reasons a more elastic form of control, which makes some allowance for increases in certain costs, is often preferred to a rigid freezing of prices, and a system emerges which goes part way, at least, towards being a mere fixing of profit margins at various stages of production and distribution. Any such system suffers from two disadvantages—it is difficult to enforce, since it demands very full accounting control, and it fails to provide incentives to keep costs down. The third form of control—the separate fixing of specific prices for each commodity—certainly provides incentives to cost reduction, but it, in turn, presents difficulties; the determination of the prices to be enforced entails much labour (especially in view of the multiplicity of grades and models which must generally be covered), enforcement is impossible unless each grade is very accurately specified to prevent evasion through lowering of quality, and trouble arises through excess profits where there are great cost differences between the best and the marginal firms, a uniform selling price being stipulated for all.

In the period under discussion, so far as civilian supplies are concerned, the tendency has been to start with one of the first two of the systems just distinguished (or some compromise between them) and to work towards the third. The initial approach was different in different countries, as has already been explained; Germany wanted a system of rational prices; the United Kingdom and Australia at first wanted merely to prevent profiteering and gradually came to regard price-stabilization for the sake of preventing a spiral as the main end of price policy; New Zealand and Canada had this latter object in mind from an earlier stage in the history of their drastic action in the field of price control.

The United Kingdom, the United States, and Australia all began, in effect, with measures for controlling profit margins. In the two former countries cash profits per unit of commodity sold were to be limited to the level of some pre-war base period. Great difficulty was encountered in the United Kingdom because traders' records and accounting methods were often inadequate for the distribution of the selling price of each particular line of goods between cost and profit, and there was not adequate machinery for enforcement. The American practice was to look at the profits of the industry as a whole—not the firm, still less the particular line of goods—in judging whether a price was excessive. There, also, enforcement was at first very inadequate. In Australia the scope of this kind of control grew only slowly, commodity by commodity, cost being mostly calculated outside the retail field as an average of historical and replacement cost. In the earlier stages, however, the Prices Commissioner was empowered to use a variety of methods, including the fixing of specific maximum prices. New Zealand, like Germany, began with a general freeze, and gradually was obliged to permit increases of price to cover increases of cost: these increases, however, applied only to specific firms and specific consignments of goods; no general increases of prices with costs according to a formula were allowed. Historical, not replacement costs, were generally taken as the basis of calculation, and the maintenance of the pre-war cash profit per unit of sales (unless the pre-war profit in the business as a whole was judged excessive) was the utmost that was allowed. The New Zealand economy, however, more than almost any other, was dependent upon import costs over which it could exercise no control.

The United States, in March 1942, moved from an attempt to control profit margins to an attempt to hold the general price level steady by a freeze. Adjustments were still allowed on the ground that a fair profit could not be earned by the industry, but the determination to prevent further increase gradually grew. The strong attempt to stabilize wages and salaries after October 1942 helped considerably; and increasing use came to be made of subsidies. In other countries there was no attempt at a general freeze so late in the development of control, but rather a gradual evolution from the widespread use of 'formula' prices, or the adjustment of frozen prices for increases in cost, towards the specific determination of prices by the controlling authority, and then towards the use of subsidies, if necessary, to prevent further adjustment in the face of still rising costs.

The possibility of successful specific price control is limited, as has already been pointed out, by the degree in which quality can be controlled. In the United Kingdom food prices (since the main foodstuffs were distributed to the retailer by the Ministry of Food) were easily fixed in this way. Specific control was extended to other goods and services under the Act of July 1941 only gradually, and, in the main, as adequate control of quality was achieved. Control of the prices of clothing, for instance, awaited the Utility Cloth scheme, under which the quality of the cloth, if not that of the workmanship in the garment, could be adequately specified. Similar quality control was achieved for furniture. In the United States, also, food quality was maintained with considerable success, despite the absence of government trading—the difficulty there arose mainly from interregional differences in cost, which had to be met by a complex and decentralized system of price fixing—but great difficulty was encountered with clothing, and there was strong evidence of evasion through deterioration of quality.

Australia, like the United Kingdom, introduced standard cloths.

In all those countries, indeed, which became fully converted to a war economy there was some standardization of products in various fields, and this certainly assisted the effectiveness of specific price controls—even though standardization or simplification generally involved a deterioration of quality (in the sense of the *amount* of workmanship involved), whereas the price controller's problem was to see that reduction in either amount or quality of workmanship did not take place unless accompanied by a reduction of price. This standardization and simplification probably went furthest in Germany, so far, at least, as civilian supplies were concerned—armaments were notoriously under-standardized until the last two years of the war. Quality-changes seem, nevertheless, to have given rise to trouble under the very rigid and comprehensive German system of price freezing modified by specific adjustments on account of general economic policy or change of costs. It may have been for this reason that limitation of profits—or rather, an obligation on the firm to reduce price if profits exceeded a standard level—was introduced in 1941.

The second main difficulty in specific price fixing arises from cost differences between firms. The hard fact was soon perceived that a uniform price based on the high-cost producer's costs will mean abnormally high total profits, while one based on the low-cost producer's costs will before long mean cessation of production by the high-cost producers. In normal times, under a competitive system, prices are not uniform in most markets, and the constellation of prices is, moreover, such that the high-cost producers are making losses—there are either firms passing through temporary difficulties, or firms on their (sometimes very slow) way out of business, to be replaced, partly at least, by new entrants. In war, in essential industries, the high-cost producer cannot be dispensed with; in industries which are to shrink he can be removed, as he was under the British Concentration Scheme, but increased social need for a product will make it desirable to push its margin of production to new, higher, levels of cost.

There are various ways of facing this difficulty. Where the buyer is the government, acting as a monopsonist, there is no reason why buying prices should be uniform, and the problem does not arise. Where prices are being fixed for sale to the public, uniformity sometimes matters, and sometimes does not. New Zealand refrained throughout from any uniform price fixing, allowing considerable variations of market price to persist. In some places (especially in the United States), large inter-regional price differences could be—indeed, had to be—allowed. The administration of a system in which a constant cost of living is important, however, becomes much more difficult in the face of large differences of this kind, while non-uniform prices for basic materials introduce complications into the whole process of costing and price fixing, and may lead to considerable inequity. If, for these reasons, a uniform market price is desired in the face of substantial cost differences, profits can be kept down and high output secured at the same time only by subsidizing the high-cost producer at the expense either of the exchequer or of the low-cost producer. The United States did the former in a very large number of instances, particularly non-ferrous metals; the United Kingdom did the latter in the notable cases of steel and coal, for each of which there was operated a pooling system, under which the various plants or mines paid a levy on output, or received a subsidy, so as to bring selling prices to a uniform, average level.

There is clearly great advantage for the government in acting as a monopsonist in cases where costs vary widely; where the problem is to control prices charged to private buyers, there is much to be said for preventing marginal cost in the least efficient firm from governing the price level in a situation where the public is sensitive to profiteering (even if the excessive profits are all removed by taxation) and where any rise of price is liable to set a price–wage spiral in motion. Nevertheless, there are objections to most systems of price differentiation, the main one being that they may not promote the optimum use of re-sources as powerfully as a system of prices which are uniform, apart from the geographical variations arising from transport costs. The British pooling system for coal, for instance, may possibly have prevented as intensive a utilization of the resources in the low-cost mines as was desirable; by taxing their output to subsidize the high-cost mines, it may have meant that part of the nation's coal requirements was being produced under adverse conditions when the same amount could have been produced under physically and economically easier conditions. Similarly, if the government pays a lower price to a low-cost firm than to a high-cost firm, it may cause some goods to be produced in the latter with a high average expenditure of labour and materials which could have been produced at lower real cost if the low-cost firm had worked its plant more intensively, up to the point where marginal costs became the same as in the (now less intensively utilized) high-cost plant.

To avoid all possibility of inefficient use of resources through differential pricing, while holding down profits, it would be necessary to carry the discrimination further, and not merely to pay each producer for all units of his output according to the cost of the marginal unit, but to pay for each unit separately at its marginal direct cost, adding some lump sum to cover the firm's essential overheads. This, of course, is quite impracticable.

How much waste of resources is brought about by the impossibility of carrying discrimination to this theoretically desirable length will depend on two factors—how far the intensity of utilization of plants or mines in wartime is governed by strictly economic calculations on the part of their managers, and how marginal costs vary with output. It is likely that, under war conditions, most manufacturing plants on war production are in fact worked to some technically-determined point of full capacity without any fine balancing of marginal costs against marginal revenue, and that a change in the pricing system for their output would not affect its volume appreciably. Moreover, it is probable that, in manufacturing plants, marginal cost rises very steeply with output after some point of practical full capacity is reached, so that even under a system of fine economic calculation output would not be greatly affected by price beyond a certain level. In mining marginal cost doubtless varies with intensity of working very much more gradually and over a wider range of intensity, so that output is probably normally quite sensitive to price. Even there, however, it is doubtful whether, under war conditions of direct control, economic calculations of this kind influence the output of a mine very much. Even in agriculture, where output is still more sensitive to price offered (in industrial countries, even if not in peasant economies), direct control of output, such as was exercised by the

War Agricultural Committees in the United Kingdom, might be adequate to prevent under-utilization of the more productive farms under a system of differential pricing. None of the industrial countries, however, were troubled by large profits to farmers as much as they were troubled about large profits to manufacturers, and price discrimination between high-cost and low-cost agricultural producers was not used to a significant extent, while subsidies (with the exception of ploughing-up subsidies) were mainly such as to encourage the advancing of both the extensive and the intensive margins.

The field in which the issues of price fixing and profit limitation arose most acutely during the war was, of course, munition production. The State's concern with price control here is somewhat different from what it is elsewhere; being connected less with price levels as such (since the cost of munitions does not enter into the cost of living, and the price–wage spiral is, therefore, not affected), and more with incentives. The simplest of all forms of munitions contract is the cost plus (a contract specifying an agreed percentage profit). Though generally condemned as encouraging inefficiency, it was still used widely by the British Ministry of Supply and the War Office, doubtless because of its convenience when costs are difficult to ascertain in advance and are liable to rapid change with the expansion of the scale of production. The British Admiralty and Air Ministry tried, on the other hand, to negotiate fixed-price contracts, which should give an incentive to minimize cost; but, since the contract price had generally to be based on the costing of the goods already produced by the same firm, the incentive was not as clear as might at first sight appear. The United States policy was to aim at fixed-price contracts, subject (because of rapidly changing conditions) to frequent re-negotiation; but there, too, especially in the early stages of mobilization, and in production of an experimental kind, reliance had often to be placed on contracts which specified cost plus a fixed fee (cost plus a fixed percentage appears to have been avoided). German practice seems to have been based on separate cost-plus contracts with each supplying firm up till 1942, when, in the interests of promoting efficiency, the government decided to forgo, in part at least, the monopsonistic advantages of differential pricing, and to base the price of each item on its cost of production 'by a well-run firm'. Compromises between the two systems—such as the division of firms into groups according to size or location, and the fixing of a standard price for each group—were also used. Australia, also, started with mainly cost-plus contracts, and moved on to a system of prices fixed in advance in 1943, when industry was fairly fully converted to war production.

This would appear, indeed, to be an almost inevitable pattern of development. During the process of conversion to war production, efficiency is too unpredictable and too rapidly changing for any fixed or ceiling price system to be workable over much of the field (United States real costs in munition production generally are estimated to have fallen by some 40 per cent. between 1939 and 1943); while cost differences between firms are so great as to make the government's gains from price differentiation very large. During the mobilization period the advantage of speed in building up war production is greater, in relation to the advantage of securing efficiency in the use of the national resources, than it is once a full war economy has been achieved; so that forms of contract for war material tend to provide incentives to bring the greatest number of firms into war production during the earlier period, while during the later one the emphasis is on reduction of real costs.

Subsidies for Price Stabilization

In a closed economy, where all prices (including those of the hired factors) were under control, it would in principle be possible to freeze all prices permanently (so long as direct controls were available for bringing about changes in the structure of output and for distributing products), or to manipulate relative prices so as to bring about some, at least, of the desired structural changes, without any great increase in the general level of prices. All actual economies, however, are in some degree dependent on imports, the prices of which rise during a period of general inflation. Moreover, both these increases in import prices and the rises in price which are necessary to call forth the required increase in supplies of certain essential home-produced goods (such as foodstuffs) may be such that, in the absence of complete control over the pricing system, they would set the price–wage spiral in motion if passed on to the consumer. It was in the light of the realization that the price–wage spiral might lead to a really immoderate increase in the general price level, and that certain cost increases, such as the increase in import prices, could not be prevented, that most of the advanced economies fully converted to a war economy found it necessary to interpose a cushion of subsidy between the unavoidably rising costs and the general cost of living.

The United Kingdom was the pioneer in this respect. In the first autumn of the war the Ministry of Food and the raw materials departments had plans to freeze the prices of the commodities they handled at the pre-war level; the Treasury, however, considered this policy inflationary, and gave instructions that the prices at which these commodities were sold should cover their replacement costs. A change of mind concerning the relative inflationary powers of subsidies and the price–wage spiral came about before the end of 1939, when the trade unions, with an eye on the rapidly rising cost of living, were responding unsympathetically to exhortations to refrain from asking for wage increases, and when important increases had, in fact, been asked for and granted, with immediate effect on prices. The first 'temporary' trading losses of the Ministry of Food were sustained in November 1939; food prices were stabilized (again 'temporarily') from the following January; the policy of stabilizing the cost of living as a whole was announced in April 1941, from which date food prices were manipulated so as to offset (in the Ministry of Labour index number) any changes in the prices of essential items less thoroughly under control.

Power to give subsidies to keep down prices of essential goods was vested in the Canadian Wartime Prices and Trade Board from December 1941. Between then and April 1943 the use of this power had been largely instrumental in rendering a 30 per cent. increase in wholesale farm prices compatible with a 5 per cent. increase in retail food prices. The New Zealand Government gave subsidies (as elsewhere, as a last resort, when other means of absorbing cost increases were exhausted) in connexion with its stabilization policy, inaugurated in August 1941; the United States gave subsidies (most notably on meat, feeding-stuffs for dairy cattle, bread-grain, and oilseeds) which reached considerable magnitudes by 1944; Australia began to give isolated subsidies as early as July 1941, but began to give them wherever necessary to hold down all prices (except those

of 'perishable primary products') from April 1943. Norway
and the Netherlands also had recourse to subsidies on a large
scale. Thus, of the countries which were highly successful in
price control, Germany was the only one which achieved this
success without any large recourse to subsidies—a fact due, no
doubt, largely to her trading, not with the free world market in
which commodity prices rose rapidly in the earlier part of the
war, but with occupied and satellite countries whose supply
prices and Reichsmark exchange rates she could in some degree
manipulate. Moreover, a number of countries where price
control has not succeeded so well in preventing price-inflation
—France, Belgium, and Poland—have nevertheless used subsidies extensively.

The amount of subsidy varied greatly from country to
country, not only with the thoroughness with which it was
sought to stabilize prices, but also with the extent to which costs
outside the control of the government rose, thus calling for
subsidies to prevent corresponding increases in the prices to
which stabilization policy applied. The countries most dependent on imports naturally had to subsidize to the greatest
extent; in Norway and the Netherlands subsidies reached some
7 per cent., or more, of gross national product, the United
Kingdom in 1948 was spending on subsidies some £570 million,
or about 5·7 per cent. of the gross national product, for Belgium
the corresponding figure for 1947 was not much under 5 per
cent., while New Zealand in this year had paid subsidies amounting to some 3·5 per cent. of gross national product. In Australia
where the degree of dependence on imports in regard to the goods
whose prices were most firmly held down was lower, subsidies
closely related to the stabilization programme reached about
1·7 per cent. of gross national product; in the United States,
where the degree of dependence on imports was very small, and
where most of the expansion in home production of the foodstuffs to which subsidies were applied had already taken place
(with most of the increase in real marginal cost) before stabilization policy was firmly applied, subsidies never reached 1 per
cent. of gross national product.

These figures may be misleading in that indirect taxation was
in some cases kept down in the interest of price stabilization,
so that actual subsidies paid do not reveal the whole direct

budgetary cost of this policy. In all countries total indirect taxes were, of course, far greater than total subsidies throughout, so that the effect of fiscal policy as a whole was to raise the general price level, as measured by a correctly weighted index of all goods and services. In some countries, indeed, the excess of indirect tax revenue over subsidy payments continued to rise throughout the inflationary period; this was the case in the United States. But in others the rise in subsidies at some point surpassed that in indirect tax revenue; thus, in the United Kingdom and Canada the net figure fell from 1943 until 1945, in New Zealand from 1943 until 1944, in Australia from 1942 until 1944. The rate of *net* indirect taxation on the national output as a whole fell in Australia from 12·1 to 10·3 per cent. over the period just mentioned; in the other countries the reduction was smaller.

That the net reduction in the rate of taxation on output (minus subsidies) was everywhere small and, in some countries which employed subsidies, non-existent, is, however, not very relevant to the efficacy of the subsidy policy. The effects of that policy can be appreciated only when one remembers the nature of the economies in which it was operated. They were economies in which the price–wage spiral constituted by far the most important inflationary danger, and in which the political pressure and the case in economics and in equity for general wage increases depended on the prices of a *restricted* group of goods and services, which were generally agreed to be necessary to the maintenance of health, efficiency, and the minimum standard of comfort as conceived of by the community as a whole. To keep down the prices of those goods was, in these circumstances, anti-inflationary, even though it released purchasing power for expenditure on other goods, and even though it might involve levying taxation which would raise the prices of 'other goods', because increases in the prices of these 'other goods' would (during the war, at least) have relatively little effect in provoking or justifying wage demands. The policy might still be anti-inflationary even though it involved an increase in the government deficit. The economies which operated it were ones in which the prices even of 'other goods' were controlled in some degree, and in which the ancillary controls over use of resources were adequate to prevent a drawing-off of factors of production to the manufacture of these 'other goods', even if their prices rose relatively to those of subsidized necessities. Income released or created by the cheapening of necessities or the enlargement of the public deficit could, therefore, find little outlet; it flowed mostly back to the exchequer either directly through purchases of savings certificates and government bonds, or indirectly through the banks. Even where the prices of 'other goods' were not very efficiently held down, their increase, though it might put a strain on the ancillary controls by which resources were directed to the production of war material and necessities, might well be less mischievous .than the increase in the price of necessities together with the cumulative spiral movement to which it would lead.

An economy of this kind is to be distinguished very clearly from one in which there is no effective control of prices or of the allocation of resources, except the forces of the market, and in which market forces, rather than bilateral bargaining, are mainly responsible for fixing wage levels. In such an economy the increase of wages with the pressure of entrepreneurs' competitive bidding (and the concurrent rise in selling prices) will not be checked by holding down the prices of wage earners' necessities; moreover, expenditure on non-subsidized and non-rationed goods will be unchecked, so that the process of inflation will be explicable very largely in terms of the 'multiplier' mechanism. Subsidies in such an economy will increase the rate of income inflation in so far as they involve increase in the public deficit. They may well result in a distribution of necessities more conducive to health and efficiency than that which would occur in their absence, but in so far as this involves a net transfer of income from the rich to the poor it may bring about some further addition to the rate of inflation by diminishing the marginal propensity to save. It is, emphatically, in the economy where wages are fixed by collective bargaining, or official arbitration, in some kind of implicit or explicit relation to a restricted range of prices, particularly if there is a fairly effective control of prices in general, that subsidies can play an important anti-inflationary role. It was in economies of this type that they were used in the period under review, in general with great success. In so far as these conditions fail to be realized

—through a tendency for wages to be governed mainly by competition between employers, through their being based on the prices of the whole range of consumers' goods and services, or through a failure to limit expenditure on unsubsidized commodities—subsidies become ineffective against inflation.

Post-War Control and Decontrol

In the economies where price control had been effective during the war there had come, by 1945, to be a situation such that it could not be removed without a large immediate rise in prices. The essence of this situation was the existence of arrears of demand for goods together with large stocks of money, and, in addition, of serious physical shortages of many commodities, especially foodstuffs, the demand for which in a free market is inelastic with respect to price. In some countries—most notably Belgium and Czechoslovakia—the stocks of purchasing power were reduced from abnormal to normal size, in relation to the current level of money income, by currency reforms carried out before or shortly after the end of the war. Even in these countries, however, important measures of price control and rationing were continued or instituted, primarily in order to guard against rises in the prices of the necessities which were abnormally scarce in relation to the supply of goods and services as a whole.

The circumstances of subsequent decontrol in various countries, and the consequences which followed it, may be divided, broadly, into three groups. First, there were those countries which decontrolled prices and abolished rationing while there were still considerable arrears of unsatisfied demand for goods, backed by purchasing power sufficient to make them effective. Of these, the United States and Canada are the chief examples. Secondly, there was the decontrol in Germany which coincided with a drastic currency reform. Thirdly, there were those countries which waited until the expansion of supply, together with price increases which the controls had permitted, brought about a rough correspondence between the ruling, controlled, prices, and the equilibrium levels which would rule in an uncontrolled market. In addition, there were some countries, particularly the United Kingdom, New Zealand, and Norway, which retained comprehensive price controls throughout the period.

So far as the market for goods is concerned, there was clearly still disequilibrium in the United States when price controls (though not rent controls) were completely removed in the middle of 1946, as there was in Canada when the main price controls on necessities were removed early in 1947. In the United States, it is true, expenditure on consumption in the first quarter of 1946 conformed to the same linear relation as had held good, in general, between it and disposable personal income from 1929 to 1940; but it is also clear that the distribution of spendable income was considerably changed, in a way likely to promote consumption, and in every subsequent quarter up to the time of writing consumption expenditure has been higher than this relation would require. Meat, fats, and sugar were still rationed (the rations being, apparently, fully taken up), and in all the more durable goods, including clothing, there were large arrears of demand waiting to be satisfied. Moreover, stocks of notes and demand deposits were some 30 per cent. higher than pre-war in relation to the money value of the national income, and, indeed, holdings of all liquid assets, however defined, were higher in relation to income than before the war, so that there was plenty of purchasing power to make demand effective once the barriers were down.

When price control and rationing were removed, the consumers' price index rose by 9 per cent. in two months, and its food component by twice that amount. The price–wage spiral thus touched off has been described in Chapter 6; it is relevant to remark here, however, that, with the lifting of controls, profits increased markedly as a proportion of total factor incomes —gross corporate profits from 11·6 per cent. of gross private income in the first half of 1946 to 14 per cent. a year later—and that wages and salaries did not recover their pre-decontrol ratio to total incomes in the succeeding two years. That the changes after decontrol were primarily the result of a breaking loose of hitherto constrained expenditure on consumption is further confirmed by the fact that non-consumption expenditure as a whole was quite sharply reduced in relation to total national income during 1946—the impulse to price rise clearly did not arise from an increase of government deficits, external surpluses, or private investment.

The general course of events was very similar (except that

decontrol came later and somewhat more gradually) in Canada. Another country which removed controls at a time when they had been maintaining the system out of equilibrium was Belgium. There price controls on unrationed goods were removed during 1946 and early 1947 without giving rise to price increases, but the abolition of food rationing and subsidies after mid-1947 led to very considerable immediate rises in price, in excess of those for which the removal of the subsidies alone would account. Belgium, like most of the food-importing countries of Europe, was still at this time suffering from shortages of many foodstuffs in relation to other goods. It is noteworthy that the rises in question in food prices, and in the cost of living as a whole, took place despite the fact that the supply of money was no greater in relation to national income than before the war, and that a very considerable shortage of effective demand for the products of Belgian labour as a whole became apparent in 1948. The situation was like that in the United States and Canada in that foodstuffs were the commodities which had most notably been kept low in price by the controls, but unlike in that Belgian consumers had not, at the time of decontrol, large arrears of demand for durable and semi-durable goods, backed by ample reserves of purchasing power. Monetary reform had removed to some extent one of the essential conditions of a general expansion of consumers' spending, but with a scarcity of food or other necessities, consumers will concentrate their purchasing power on the scarce items, at the expense of saving and of expenditure on other goods. Other prices may fall, but the scarce items may well be of overwhelming importance, not only in the weighting of cost of living indices, but in the actual budgets of most of the population.

The effect of specific shortages of essential items of consumption in rendering decontrol dangerous was particularly evident in India, where at the end of 1947 sugar and textiles were decontrolled and the rationing of grain was limited to the large towns, despite the fact that total food and clothing consumption was well below the pre-war level, and the 1947 wheat harvest had been particularly poor. Severe price increases followed (about 15 per cent. in a year), and controls were reinstated in the later part of 1948. The course of events there is to be contrasted with that in Czechoslovakia, where price control and

substantial measures of rationing were instituted at the same
time as the monetary reform of 1945, apparently on the ground
that no monetary reform which was not so drastic as to produce
a deflationary slump could keep food and textile prices from
rising in a free market in the existing conditions of scarcity. So
severe, indeed, was the strain placed upon the Czechoslovak
price control by food and textile shortage that there developed
a widespread black market, systematized in the autumn of 1948
as a legal system of double prices—low prices for rations, and
high but also controlled prices for quantities bought in excess
of the ration. These experiences in general emphasize the fact
that the early post-war situation was marked by a much greater
distortion of the composition of supplies available to consumers
than was either the war period, when scarcities were general, or
the period after (say) 1948, when the worst of the post-war
specific shortages has passed. The extremely high equilibrium
price of some of the main necessities, the supplies of which were
improving, but were generally inelastic in regard to price in the
short run, very greatly increased the dangers, and diminished
the advantages to be expected from decontrol of prices at this
time.

The German currency reform and decontrol of prices came
in mid-1948, when the supply situation in the world as a whole
was considerably eased. Moreover, more than in the other
countries which have been discussed, the effect of lifting price
control was to bring greatly increased supplies of food and some
other necessities to market. The official prices of food, before
reform, had been lower relatively to those of industrial goods
than before the war; but there was an extensive black market
with very high prices, especially for foodstuffs, and it is impossible to say with any precision what the effective pre-reform
prices had been. Prices in general rose by some 11 per cent. in
the six months after decontrol and reform, for the supply of
money had not been reduced to a very low level, by pre-war
standards, in relation to the level of income, and consumers'
stocks of practically every kind of goods were exceedingly low.
As in the United States two years earlier, the share of profits
in the national income rose. Unlike the countries which had
removed controls in earlier years, however, Germany did not
experience a rise in food prices much greater than that in prices

of other consumers' goods. The general price increase was of short duration. In the face of rapidly rising supplies and a restrictive monetary policy, prices began to fall again from the early months of 1949, to the accompaniment of a considerable increase in unemployment, and a slowing down of recovery.

The German policy of reform and decontrol must be judged to have been, on the whole, remarkably successful, but in comparing it with the policies of other countries where there was virtually full employment and where black markets were of minor importance, it must be remembered that the move towards market equilibrium in Germany was made from both sides at once. Not only was the supply of money reduced by the reform, but real income (and, still more, the portion of it flowing through the market) rose to meet monetary demand once money became valuable again. Later, when money began to be scarce in the crucial quarters, the rate of growth of real income slowed down. Such a flexible real income level did not exist in any other country, and where the level of real income was rigid, excesses of demand in relation to the fixed supply were fully reflected, after decontrol, in rises of price.

In many countries conditions arose during 1948 or 1949 which permitted large measures of decontrol without any special accompanying monetary restrictions, and without serious immediate consequential price increases. The rise of real incomes, the mitigation of particular shortages of key commodities (such as foodstuffs), the gradual creeping up of controlled prices, largely because of the rise in world primary commodity prices not offset by increased subsidies, and, finally, the satisfaction of many of the abnormal needs to replenish stocks, all helped to bring supplies and effective demands together at something not far different from existing controlled prices. Rationing tended to be abandoned before price control—it is normally the most unpopular and administratively expensive part of a system of controls. Australia, Austria, France, Denmark, Sweden, and the Netherlands were most conspicuous in the partial abolition of rationing between June, 1948, and the beginning of 1950, while the United Kingdom, Norway, New Zealand, and some other countries made smaller but notable relaxations. Price controls, however, remained in most of the countries in question (though often diminished in scope) and in no case is it possible to trace a rise in prices immediately attributable to decontrol. The devaluations of September 1949 complicate the issue, and it is probably more reasonable to attribute some of the changes in distribution of income in this period to them rather than to measures of decontrol. In short, the decontrol measures of these years were easy and painless, but partial.

That price control could be so widely maintained in the absence of rationing as it was from 1948 onwards, in many countries, is perhaps at first sight surprising. It should not, however, occasion more surprise than the fact that many modern 'uncontrolled' economies have worked reasonably well in spite of the existence of very many rigid prices. If demand for a good is high, it disappears from the shops for part of each month; if it is low, orders to the manufacturers are reduced and their production curtailed, probably in favour of a better-selling line. Systems of price control usually take account of changes in factor costs sufficiently to ensure that few established commodities will disappear from production through unprofitability. The inconvenience caused by price rigidity without rationing is not great except where necessities are concerned, or where the rigid prices are allowed to move very far from equilibrium.

These considerations help to explain the workability of many economies particularly in the period after 1948, though, since the scope of price control in these countries had always greatly exceeded that of rationing, their applicability is fairly general. The difficulties of price control should not, however, be overlooked; in time of war it proved to be workable and to a large extent harmless; but in peace, especially after it had continued in operation for many years, its disadvantages and difficulties were multiplied. The United Kingdom provides many examples of this. In March 1948, for instance, when the pressure of rising import prices had for some time been troublesome, an attempt was made to strengthen the existing price controls. It was then found, not only that these controls had been weakened in the course of time by the multiplication of goods which were in some sense 'new' since 1939, and, therefore, not covered by the Price of Goods Act, but that some sellers whose goods were covered by the Act had apparently remained unaware of the fact. It was not difficult to impose a new freezing policy, but for the necessary alternative basis of control which had, of course, to be laid down to deal with the eventuality of rising costs (especially of imports), no acceptable basis could be found better than the notoriously objectionable cost-plus system. This system was again applied in certain cases when controls were tightened once again against the inflationary pressure of the Korean War. In between—in 1949—a considerable amount of decontrol had taken place, but even after it the Board of Trade estimated that between a half and three-quarters of all consumers' goods and services were subject, directly or indirectly, to maximum-price regulations.

The Korean War boom brought about a fairly widespread tightening or reimposition of controls. Both price and wage freezes were instituted in the United States at the beginning of 1951 (their importance was small since the inflationary pressure, generated mainly by abnormal buying for stock, subsided soon afterwards). The United Kingdom reimposed some controls shortly after this time; New Zealand had ceased its gradual decontrol at the end of 1950; Finland had restored price control in July of that year. Some generally minor tightening or restoration of rationing took place at about the same time in many countries, including Hungary, Yugoslavia, Ireland, Austria, and Czechoslovakia.

In Western countries these measures were not of great or long-lived importance. Without subsidies, which were nowhere reintroduced or increased to any great extent, price control is essentially a limitation of profits, which, in turn, threaten to become excessive only when there is rising demand. Budgetary and monetary policy in this period were such as to keep total demand fairly well in check, apart from the short-lived spell of panic buying in late 1950 and the first two or three months of 1951. For most of the economies in question, the pressure came largely from outside in the shape of high import prices—which collapsed quickly, though not before they had sown a crop of wage demands. The technique of dealing with this factor—the liability of every externally-caused rise in prices to set in motion the price–wage spiral—has not generally been mastered. Price control, without subsidies, is clearly useless against it. Indeed, hindsight shows that the primary commodity-importing countries of Europe might have done well to use subsidies to insulate themselves from the temporary high import prices of 1950–1. Subsidies would have been more in place there than against the great, still unreversed, rise of prices from 1939 to 1948. But in addition to price control and subsidies as measures of insulation against temporary excesses of demand, internal or in the world markets, a wage policy is needed; and this, though achieved by some Western countries in the war, and by some east European countries since, has not been securely established by any Western country in time of peace.

8

Hyper-inflation and the 'Flight from Cash'

Hyper-inflation and Expectations

HYPER-INFLATION is generally recognized to be closely connected with a highly abnormal condition of expectations concerning the future of prices. In normal circumstances prices reflect the general state of expectations concerning their future. If people generally, at a given moment, come to believe that prices in future will be higher than they are at that moment, because, for instance, a war has broken out, prices will be changed at once to take account of this fact. In a free and active market prices at each moment reflect a supply and demand situation which is governed partly by expectations, which, in turn, are governed largely by the present price. If all the operators in the market had the same expectations, prices could not normally differ from what they were expected to be at any future point of time by more than the costs of holding stocks until that future time—that is to say by the costs of interest and storage. With perishable commodities, of course, the cost of storage may be high—indeed, it may be impossible to store the commodity in good condition for any long period, in which case one may reconcile the situation with what has just been said by regarding the cost of storage as infinite. One effect of a general expectation of a price increase will, therefore, be to induce people to produce durable rather than perishable goods, and to the extent to which this shift is technically possible the prices of the latter will be dragged up by reduction of supply in some sort of relation to the expectation-induced rise in the price of the former. This, no doubt, is a long run effect; the more immediate point is that any general expectation of price increase is bound to be self-verifying.

It is possible, of course, for expectations of price increase and their automatic realization through the working of a free market to be mutually self-reinforcing. Some concrete cause, such as a war, having caused the market generally to expect some increase in price over a finite future period, the generally expected increase (apart from allowances for storage costs, &c.) will be realized at once. This increase may be quicker than many people in the market had expected, in which case there may be a further upward revision of expectations, and so on indefinitely. The process may be divergent, and constitute hyper-inflation.

Other forces, however, will be at work, either opposing the development of a hyper-inflation or pushing it on. Opposing it there will generally be certain important prices in the economy which, being contractual, are not affected, or not quickly affected, by changes in expectations. Wages may be among these. In so far as they are stable, upward revisions of the expected (and subsequently realized) prices of finished goods will tend to be undermined by convictions in at least some quarters that, in the somewhat longer run, prices must return to something like their customary relation to costs of production. Any stable item in cost will tend to damp down the cumulative raising of price expectations in this way, and to an extent related to its importance in the whole cost structure. Only if the prices of all factors are very quickly adjusted to the price level of finished output will this drag be entirely eliminated.

Another important factor which might be expected to oppose hyper-inflation is the difficulty which may be experienced in financing the increases in price which are expected. Every buyer may expect prices at some future date to be substantially higher than at present, but may be unable to afford his customary purchases at the expected future price out of his present income, and unable to obtain credit to finance the difference. The sellers, if they share the buyers' price expectations, will be unwilling to part with their goods at less than the expected price, *minus* the cost of holding until the time when it is expected. The fact that they may not be able to sell their whole output at the expected price (less this allowance) would not, in itself, disturb them, since they would be happy to accumulate stocks to sell later. The difficulty of financing such stocks, however, may prevent their doing this. The same shortage of credit, *plus* imperfections in their personal knowledge and trust of their customers, would also prevent them from selling to the latter on credit.

The Financing of Hyper-inflation

What are the prospects of a shortage of credit, or of money, in the widest sense? If the expectations of price increase are general, it follows that every holder of idle money, expecting his holding to depreciate in purchasing power, will wish to hold goods instead. The whole idle money of the community will, therefore, be mobilized to finance the price increase. In any real situation, of course, there will be differences of expectation, and only those who expect a price increase will liquidate their idle money holdings in this way; but, if the inflationary process proceeds in such a way as to make expectations of further increase more general, more and more idle balances will be drawn into the active circulation, so that eventually no idle balances—in the sense of balances not regularly turned over—will be left.

If expectations of price increase become very strong and general, however, they will not only cause people to reduce their idle balances—the minimum balances they have left just before each pay-day. They will lead to changes of financial habits affecting the relation between active balances, which are turned over regularly, and the amount of transactions which they finance. It is necessary to pause for a moment to consider how this comes about.

Imagine a simplified economy in which all the factors of production (or, more precisely, their owners), are paid n times a year, their total annual income (national income at factor cost) being Y. Suppose that they spend the whole of this income, paying it out at a constant rate throughout the year. Then, their income each pay-day is Y/n, and their average holding of active money between pay-days (and consequently over the year as a whole) is $\frac{1}{2}Y/n$. Suppose, however, that they also keep a reserve of idle money, I_f, which is the sum they have in hand just before each pay-day when their balances are lowest. Their average money holding throughout the year is then $\frac{1}{2}Y/n + I_f$.

On the other hand, there are the enterprises. They receive an annual income Y from the owners of factors of production, who make up the community, and we have already implied that they receive it at a constant rate throughout the year—that is to say, Y/n comes in at an even rate between any two successive pay-days. Since this sum Y/n is paid out at each pay-day, the average sum in hand over the whole year is $\frac{1}{2}Y/n+I_e$, where I_e denotes the idle balances kept by enterprises. Adding up, therefore, one finds that the total money held by the whole community—consumers (factor owners) and enterprises together is $Y/n+I$ (where I denotes total idle money, I_f+I_e). It is to be noted this last result does not depend upon the assumption that money is spent at an even rate between pay-days. If consumers, through apprehension of a price increase, or for any other reason, chose to spend their incomes immediately after pay-day, then the average holdings of enterprises would be raised just as much as those of consumers were lowered. In this simple model the amount of money required depends only upon the level of income, the amounts of idle money demanded, and the frequency of pay-day.

This, however, is due to the assumption that all enterprises pay for their factors on the same day. If pay-days are spread evenly over the year, then enterprises will receive their revenue at a continuous rate even if consumers spend all their money on pay-day; since every day will be pay-day for someone. With pay-days thus staggered, a reduction of consumers' average balances through rapid expenditure of each instalment of their income will not affect the average active balances required by enterprises, which would remain at half the income of a period between consecutive pay-days ($\frac{1}{2}Y/n$).

Of course, many features of any existing economy have been left out of account. In the first place, different factors of production (or rather, their owners) are paid with different frequencies—wages weekly, salaries monthly, rent, interest, and dividends anything between monthly and annually, and so forth. Some of these payments—notably those of dividends—are staggered; different firms pay at different dates throughout the year; with the result that considerable amounts of wealth, which would have to be held in the form of money if all such payments were made at the same time, can in fact be held in other forms. Nevertheless, it is possible to conceive of some average frequency of factor payments, modified by an allowance for the degree of staggering, which could stand in place of the uniform frequency assumed above.

Secondly, consumers' incomes are not all spent in the week in which they are received, and that fact affects the argument. Suppose (to take an absurd example) that consumers spent all their income in buying goods in such large batches that they had to save up three weeks' wages to buy each batch. Their average money holdings (assuming no idle money—nothing left in their purses after they had made their three-weekly purchase) would then be half of three weeks' income—not half of one week's, as it is if they spend their income at an even rate in the week in which they receive it. At the same time, since the purchases of consumers as a whole might be supposed to be evenly spread over time, the three-weekly purchases of separate families being staggered, the enterprises would receive payments at an even rate, and, if they paid for their factors of production weekly, would still need to keep average balances equal only to half a week's income.

Thus, consumers' average active balances are related not only to the frequency of their receipts but to how quickly they spend each instalment of income (if they do so continuously), or how many instalments they accumulate between expenditures where their expenditure is discontinuous—as it normally is where clothing or durable goods are concerned.

In order to be realistic, one must allow further for the existence of very large payments between enterprises; some frequent, some less so; against which active balances have to be held. E. H. Phelps Brown and G. L. S. Shackle[1] estimated that in the year 1930 these inter-firm payments in the United Kingdom were approximately equal to the factor payments and expenditures by consumers which have already been discussed. In any given state of industrial and financial organization, however, these payments may be expected to vary in proportion to the national income, and the balances held in consequence of them to vary in much the same way as other balances connected with production and consumption. Again there is the financial circulation to be considered. So far as the United Kingdom is concerned, financial transactions within the City of London greatly exceed all other payments in the whole country. It

[1] Royal Economic Society, Memorandum 74, Sept, 1938.

seems, however, that the balances held in connexion with them are fairly small, and that they do not greatly modify any conclusions that may be reached about the demand for money in a modern economy without taking them into account.

It appears, therefore, that the amount of money required in a given economy for the purpose of carrying on transactions bears to the national income a ratio which depends upon the average frequency of periodical payments made by firms for factors of production or intermediate products, the average frequency of the discontinuous payments (for durable goods, &c.) made by consumers, and the extent to which either consumers or firms arrange their more continuous payments so that they follow quickly on their receipts.[1] It is in the light of this that the ratio of money holding to national income, generally called 'Cambridge K', or its inverse, generally called the income velocity of circulation, are to be interpreted.

Thus, in the simple model discussed on pages 174–5, in which there are only factor payments and corresponding expenditures on consumption, all factor incomes being spent at a constant rate in the period before the next instalment, the income velocity, V, (which is Y/M where M is the quantity of money), is clearly equal to $n(1-I/M)$. If there were no idle money, I, V would coincide with n, the frequency of payments to factors of production. The fact that money is needed to finance inter-firm payments will mean that, even if consumers still spend their money in the way assumed, the income velocity of active money will in fact be less than this. It will be still less in so far as either consumers or enterprises save up to buy durable goods or other assets. It is, perhaps, worth noting that, whereas the average annual frequency of factor payments in the United Kingdom and the United States must be about 25, Dr. Khusro has estimated the income velocity of circulation of active money in both countries to be about 6 (see page 208).

It must be made clear that the income velocity of circulation is simply an inverse measure of the money holding in relation to the national income, and that, though it is related in the ways which have been discussed to the average frequency of payments in the economy, it must not be confused with another

[1] See Howard Ellis, 'Some Fundamentals of the Theory of Velocity', *Quarterly Journal of Economics*, May 1938.

velocity which is important in the study of inflation—the rate at which changes in income are propagated through the economy, and at which, therefore, an increase in expenditure raises income through the mechanism of the 'multiplier'. This, as has been shown by several writers,[1] depends not merely on the interval between factor payments, but on (i) the interval between an increase in expenditure by consumers and either an increase in output or an increase in price resulting from it; a lag which depends on the extent to which stocks can be drawn down, and on other things; (ii) the interval between an increase in output, or in the price of output, and the distribution of the correspondingly increased earnings of enterprise to factors of production; and (iii) the interval between an increase in consumers' incomes and the consequential increase in their expenditure. Clearly, also, the income velocity of circulation is unrelated to the rate at which changes of prices are propagated through the system by the mechanism of the price–wage spiral. Its relevance is entirely monetary; it measures the extent to which a unit quantity of money is made, by the institutional arrangements in force, to facilitate transactions.

It has already been pointed out that expectations of rising prices will cause people to seek to reduce their holdings of idle money, thus bringing about (and automatically financing) the price increases which are expected; and the foregoing paragraphs have sought to explain how active money can be economized so that further expectation-induced increases of price can be financed without any increase in the supply of money. Consumers can spend their incomes as soon as they get them; firms can spend their revenue on stocks of materials, &c., as soon as they come in; owners of factors of production are likely to insist on being paid at more frequent intervals; nobody will save up to buy durable goods if it can be avoided—spare cash already in hand will be invested in such goods as far as possible, but the use of money as a store of value against future purchases is unattractive.

There is thus a good deal of scope for the financing of an

[1] Erik Lundberg, *Economic Expansion*, Stockholm Economic Studies, No. 6 (London, P. S. King, 1937); Lloyd A. Metzler, 'Three Lags in the Circular Flow of Income', *Essays in Honour of Alvin Hansen* (New York, 1948); W. T. Newlyn, 'The Phillips/Newlyn Hydraulic Model', *Yorkshire Bulletin of Economic and Social Research*, vol. ii, no. 2, July 1950.

inflation due to cumulative upward revision of price expectations by means of drafts on idle money and economies in the use of active money—these means will, indeed, be brought into action by the changes in expectations which provide the mainspring for the whole process. Nevertheless, there must be some limit to the use which can be made of any finite monetary stock. In the great German inflation of 1923 the income velocity of circulation of money as a whole rose perhaps forty-fold; in the Hungarian inflation of 1945–6 it rose several hundred-fold. The values of transactions in these instances, however, rose respectively several hundred thousand million-fold, and several million million million-fold. The amount of money in existence rose proportionately very much more than the average rate of turnover of a unit of money. Clearly, if there were no expansion of the supply of money, a hyper-inflation could not proceed very far.

In practice, however, the process is never simply a matter of revised expectations; it is always aided by an injection of new purchasing power to finance non-consumption expenditure, or perhaps to finance increases in working capital. Indeed, the process of hyper-inflation itself helps to bring about such injections of new purchasing power. Governments are unable to collect revenue quickly enough to keep pace with advancing prices, income, and public expenditure; they are unable to borrow from the general public (who have ceased to be attracted by obligations of fixed money value) and have to borrow from the banks.

This tendency for hyper-inflation to go with large creations of credit is the first of the main circumstances which help it on. The second—not by any means always present—is a mode of operation of the price–wage spiral which tends, not merely to mitigate or eliminate any tendency for sticky factor prices to impose a drag on the inflationary process, but actually to accelerate it. This happens when one of the hired factors, usually labour, has come for some reason to claim a higher proportion of the available national product than is consistent with either internal or external equilibrium. Internal equilibrium may be made impossible in this way if, for instance, the real national product has been reduced at the time of the inflation by some material disaster, so that the customary real

N

wage, which labour is still able to seek by bargaining successfully for increased money wages, is no longer compatible with the customary profit margins in pursuit of which entrepreneurs are still able to raise their prices. External equilibrium may equally well be made impossible if money wages are tied to the external value of the currency (or, more precisely, the domestic-currency value of foreign currency in a free foreign exchange market) at a level which keeps domestic costs inconsistent with equilibrium in the balance of payments. In either of these cases expectations of higher prices are continuously fed by the evidence of rising wage costs, aided in the second case by the direct (as well as the indirect) effects of collapsing foreign exchanges.

Hyper-inflation is thus characterized by a continuing general expectation of rising prices which, because it is continuously reinforced, largely by the events for which it is itself responsible, continues to exist for considerable lengths of time, whereas without this continuous reinforcement, general expectations of any price level considerably different from that ruling at the moment are self-extinguishing. It follows that one should be able to detect it by the symptoms of a widespread attempt to avoid holding money, or assets of fixed money value: that is to say, by an increase in the velocity of circulation of money (or a decrease in its inverse, 'Cambridge K'), and by a rise in interest rates. The latter will be discussed in Chapter 9; the remainder of the present chapter is concerned with the symptoms of a 'flight from cash'.

The 'Flight from Cash'

In so far as people behave rationally, one would expect them to adjust their holdings of money in all circumstances in accordance with (among other things) their expectations as to changes in its value. Matters are not, however, quite as simple as that. In the first place, as was pointed out at the beginning of this chapter, expectations of a change in the value of money are normally quite quickly discounted by changes of market price, so that it is only during processes which involve their continual renewal that there can be said to be persistent expectations of further price change. Secondly, the quantity of money in existence may well be inelastic, so that the whole community, as opposed to any particular group within the community, cannot easily reduce its money holdings; all it can do is alter the relation of these holdings to income by altering the latter. Thirdly, changes in the relation of money holdings to income—that is to say, in the income velocity of circulation—may come about for all kinds of reason; moreover, in order to understand them thoroughly, one would have to take into account at the same time changes in interest rates, which may be either symptoms of the community's adjustment to increasing or decreasing shortage of money in relation to the amount of work money has to do, or changes imposed by some external force (such as a change in profits) which will, nevertheless, influence velocity.

Thus, in some non-inflationary periods (such as the inter-war years in the United Kingdom)[1] income velocity can be shown to be quite highly correlated with both interest rates and the rate of increase of the prices of goods. It seems most reasonable to suppose that this is due to the ordinary cyclical changes in the economy, which are associated with changes in expectations—though not always with persistent expectations of change. In an expansion, for instance, expectations of price or demand improve; prices and, perhaps, output are raised accordingly; the consequent increase in money income (in face of an imperfectly elastic supply of money) entails an increase in velocity, or an increased scarcity of money, which causes a rise in interest rates.

Something like this no doubt happens in any 'open' inflation once upward revision of prices, as opposed to injection of purchasing power, has become the leading feature. Thus, it will happen not only when, as just described, price expectations with regard to finished goods are pushed upward by the development of stronger and stronger evidence of increasing demand, but also when factor prices are pushed upwards by any means, such as rising import prices, or the price–wage spiral. In any of these circumstances, money income is likely to outrun the supply of money, so that velocity and interest rates rise. There is likely, in any given country, to be some positive correlation between the rate of increase of prices (or money income) in such a process

---

[1] See A. J. Brown, 'Interest, Prices, and the Demand Schedule for Idle Money', *Oxford Economic Papers* (Oxford, Clarendon Press), No. 2, May 1939; reprinted in *Oxford Studies in the Price Mechanism*, 1951.

and the velocity of circulation, not because of any enduring expectation of further price increase, causing the population to seek to reduce its money holdings, but because the faster prices (and money incomes) rise, the further they are likely to run ahead of the supply of money in any given state of the institutional arrangements determining the latter.

As inflation becomes more rapid, however, true hyper-inflation will set in; the rate at which price expectations are revised will become so rapid that the expectations are constantly ahead of the actuality by a finite margin. From then onwards, there will be, not merely an upward push on velocity of circulation, as more work is imposed on the monetary stock by price increases, but also an upward pull, as holders of money seek to unload their idle stocks and to cut down their active stocks also by more frequent payments and the other changes in monetary habits which have been discussed earlier in this chapter. The relation between rate of price increase and the velocity of circulation then becomes more interesting, being closely connected with an important part of the hyper-inflationary mechanism.

This relation between the change in velocity and the recent change in prices which may be regarded as causing it (in hyper-inflation, at least) is obviously quite an important parameter, closely related to the elasticity of expectations of the principal money holders with regard to prices. It will be necessary to refer to it frequently in the discussion that follows and for lack of a better name it may perhaps be called the 'coefficient of sensitivity'.[1] It will be interesting to see what happens to this

---

[1] The coefficient is most conveniently defined as

$$\frac{dV}{V} \bigg/ \frac{d(P_t/P_{t-1})}{P_t/P_{t-1}} \quad \text{or} \quad \frac{d \log V}{d \log (P_t/P_{t-1})},$$

where V is income velocity of circulation and P_t/P_{t-1} is the annual ratio of increase of the price index calculated from the period (either a year or a shorter time) ending at the moment for which velocity is measured. This measure is not a true elasticity, since its magnitude is dependent on the arbitrary decision to measure the rate of change of prices as an *annual* rate. A true elasticity could be obtained if the rate of price change were measured by the rate of compound interest (*continuously* compounded) at which prices were increasing. If prices rose, exponentially, from P_{t-1} to P_t in a year, this rate would be $\log_e (P_t/P_{t-1})$. A 'coefficient of sensitivity' defined as $\dfrac{dV}{V} \bigg/ \dfrac{d \log (P_t/P_{t-1})}{\log (P_t/P_{t-1})}$ or $\dfrac{d \log V}{d \log \{\log (P_t/P_{t-1})\}}$ would be quite independent of the time units employed. It would, however, be unsuitable for the coefficient. Does it remain roughly the same at high rates of price increase as at more normal rates? Does it increase as the fact of the unreliability of money comes home to more and more people, or is all systematic relation between the velocity of circulation and the rate of increase of prices lost in a disorderly 'flight from cash'? Again it may be worth looking first at experience in some inflations which have not reached the hyper-inflation stage.

One would not expect any signs even of a submerged adjustment of money holdings (or velocity) to the rate of price increase to be evident during the inflationary period in economies like the United States or the United Kingdom which operated under fairly general price control. Where total expenditure on current output is under control, savings are, perforce, very large. Even if the owners of these savings are apprehensive of a fall in the value of money, they have little chance to hedge against it. They can acquire equities or existing real property only so far as the present owners are willing to part with them for money which they would then have for the most part to hold idle, so that, though the prices of such assets may rise, they are not substituted for money by the economy as a whole. Government fixed-interest securities are plentiful, and provide an escape from the holding of money; but they furnish no hedge against inflation. Moreover, with taxation at high levels their net yield, like that of other investments, is low. There is thus a very strong tendency in the presence of the controls on expenditure for monetary liquidity to become high, whatever expectations about the future of prices may be.

In the years before controls on expenditure became effective there are some signs of a positive correlation between income velocity and rate of increase of prices in the United Kingdom and the United States. In the former they rose together from 1938 to 1939, but the large increase in prices from 1939 to 1940 was associated with only a small increase in velocity (price control began to be important from the beginning of 1940), and thereafter velocity fell fairly uniformly, at about 10 per

present purpose since (P_t/P_{t-1}) is quite liable to be unity or less, and $\log(P_t/P_{t-1})$ to be, therefore, zero or negative. It, therefore, seems better to keep to the simpler form of the coefficient which is not independent of the time-unit chosen to measure the rate of price increase; stipulating merely that the unit chosen shall be one year.

cent. per annum, until 1946, despite the fact that the rate of price increase, though falling from 1940 to 1943, was virtually constant at a low level for the next three years. After 1946 there was again a positive correlation, though it is hard to believe that, in the circumstances of the time, this meant very much. Liquidity was again being reduced, and this happened to coincide with an advance in the rate of price increase, but the latter is not likely to have been responsible for the former.

In the United States the period of positive correlation between price increase and income velocity runs from 1939 to 1943. It is only after the latter date that there begins to be a great fall in velocity, uncorrelated with rate of price change, and due, presumably, to controls of expenditure. As in the United Kingdom, velocity began to rise again after 1946 (when price controls were abandoned), but this is not correlated with the rate of price increase. It was greater in 1947–8, when prices were rising slowly, than in 1946–7 when they were rising fast. Like the concurrent changes in the United Kingdom, therefore, it is to be regarded as a movement back from the abnormal liquidity imposed on the community in the later war years.

One might reasonably expect to see a much closer connexion between velocity and the immediately previous rate of price increase in France, where controls were much less successful than in the United Kingdom or the United States, and where the rate of price increase has at times exceeded 60 per cent. per annum. Any such expectation, however, is only very imperfectly fulfilled. Controls in France were, at all events, capable of bringing about a great decrease in velocity between 1938 and 1943. With the great fall in real income in 1944–5, the velocity of circulation appears to have fallen to only a quarter or a third of its 1938 value, though the existence of black market transactions at high prices must have raised true velocity considerably above this low figure. From 1944, however, it rose continuously until 1948, when it was 89 per cent. above pre-war, according to the official national income estimate. Up to 1946 this increase in velocity went with an increase in the rate at which prices were rising; it continued from then onwards, however, despite a slight moderation of the rate of price increase. When the price increase slowed down, and actually ceased for a considerable time in 1949, income velocity

did not fall appreciably, but remained at about the same level
as the previous year. The French economy was, of course,
subject to some measure of price control throughout this period
—though it was not possible (up to late 1948) to hold even
official prices, and there were large black markets. It is, therefore, not possible to regard the income velocity of circulation of
money in France, even after the end of the war, as the product of
a free choice by the community of the degree of monetary
liquidity it would maintain. The measures to restrict bank
credit from 1947 onwards probably, in these circumstances, had
a considerable effect in raising velocity. That there was considerable monetary stringency is suggested by the rise of interest
rates—the yield of Government bonds increasing from under
3 per cent. in 1945 to a maximum monthly average value of
4·84 per cent. in June 1948. Nevertheless, it seems likely that
the greater part of the more than 80 per cent. increase in income
velocity between 1938 and 1948–9 reflects a decreased liquidity
preference, consequent upon the experience of wartime and
(still more) post-war price inflation.

A sharp contrast with the experience so far discussed is
afforded by two countries at a much lower level of economic
development, which have both undergone price inflations of
somewhat similar magnitude followed, however, by virtual
stabilization of their price levels. In those less developed countries, income statistics are lacking, and it is, therefore, necessary
to use a price index in place of an income index. Instead of the
income velocity V (which is Y/M), therefore, one uses P/M,
which is identical (by Irving Fisher's exchange identity) with
V/T, the ratio of income velocity to real income. In both Syria
and Iran the correlation between the rate of price increase and
P/M has been extraordinarily close, ever since 1939. In Syria
(see Diagram 23, p. 196) there may be discerned also some
rising of P/M in 1939–41, over and above that which is correlated with price increases, and a subsequent fall in 1946–7
which is not correlated with a price decrease. The sensitiveness
with which velocity appears to have responded to alterations
in the rate of price change is, however, remarkable; there
appears to have been a fixed 'coefficient of sensitivity' with a
value in the neighbourhood of three-quarters. In Iran the
correspondence is equally close. There is, indeed, little sign

here of any large systematic forces operating upon velocity except recent experience of the rate at which prices were changing, though the foregoing period of price change which seems to have been taken into account in adjusting velocity appears to have been longer here than in the other countries studied. (Velocity is most closely related to the average price change of the preceding *two* years in Iran.) The 'coefficient of sensitivity' was very slightly under one-half.

It seems hard at first sight to account for this apparently close adjustment of cash holdings to current price change in countries which are relatively undeveloped. It may be, however, that a large part of the note circulation (the only kind of money taken into account in these instances) in Syria and Iran is in the hands of the mercantile community which might be expected to be more sensitive to current economic events than the population at large.

In other Middle Eastern countries and in India only a much less regular relation is observable between price increase and P/M. It is probable that the official price indices in these countries substantially understate the wartime increase in prices, because, during periods of price control, official prices are used and no allowance made for black market transactions, which were generally of considerable importance. Variations in the volume of goods entering into transactions are also a disturbing factor, difficult to allow for because of lack of data. The most substantial evidence of a systematic connexion between velocity and price increase relates to Turkey where the latter variable increased fairly steadily from 1939 to early 1943, and then declined rapidly, prices actually falling for a time in the second half of the year and in 1944. From early 1941, when the rise became rapid, P/M began to increase, showing some correlation with price movements over the previous year, but also rising independently, at some 20-25 per cent. a year, until early 1944 (a year after price increase had ceased). In later 1944 and 1945 velocity seems to have fallen again. There is thus something to suggest that the six-fold price increase between 1939 and 1943 caused a general reduction of liquidity, which was not reversed for a year after the increase had ceased, and that there was also some more detailed adjustment of real balances to the year-to-year changes in experience of price change. The latter was, in fact, quite a sensitive adjustment with the 'coefficient of sensitivity' in the region of three-quarters.

Iraq affords some evidence of a fairly sensitive adjustment of velocity to price change (coefficient about one-half, or slightly higher) if the weight of the four principal crops is taken as an index of the volume of income transactions (T), and if a uniform decrease of velocity after 1940. at a rate of some 20 per cent. per annum is allowed for. The downward trend in velocity eases off after 1945; it seems to have been due largely to difficulty in spending, coupled with anticipation of greater ease later on, since price control (introduced in 1942) is said to have been very ineffective. It is, however, hard to account for the difference of monetary behaviour between Iraq, where the tendency was towards greater liquidity, and Turkey and Syria, where it was the opposite.

Egypt and India also show apparent trends towards increased liquidity during the period of rapid price inflation. In the former, P/M seems to have fallen more rapidly in the years of rapid price increase, 1940–3, than after 1944, when the price inflation moderated and was reversed. There was a fairly general attempt at price control in Egypt from 1939 onwards, which, so far as it was successful in limiting payments, would produce the increase in liquidity which the data suggest, and in so far as it was ineffective (that is to say to a large extent) would distort the data. In spite of the apparent fall of P/M by 59 per cent. between 1939 and 1946–7, it is not certain that velocity fell at all, though it seems probable that it did. Price control and restriction of supplies covered a considerable number of products in Egypt; and though the control was clearly not very effective, it may well have been sufficient to keep consumers' expenditure lagging well behind the increase in the means of payment which the great military disbursements of the Allies created.

Much of this is true of India also. The events of 1938–40 seem to show P/M responding to the rise and fall of the rate of price increase with a sensitivity measured by a coefficient of about one-third. From then until 1943, however, P/M appears to have fallen by some 40 per cent., a high rate of price increase (about 30 per cent. per annum) notwithstanding. Again, the imperfection of the price data may give a misleading impression, but it seems probable that there was some fall in true velocity. After 1943, when price control became considerably more effective, however, velocity fell but little. The Indian and Egyptian data are thus hard to interpret, but they show, at all events, that there was no sign of a 'flight from cash' in either of these countries.

Price control appears to have had some effect in most Latin American countries in bringing about an increase in liquidity, despite considerable price inflation. In three of them, however, Brazil, Chile, and Costa Rica, this is not so, and some correlation is observable between rate of price increase and velocity of circulation. The latter is readily calculated from its reciprocal, the 'index of liquidity', provided by J. K. Horsefield in his article 'Inflation in Latin America'.[1] For Brazil the correlation is fairly close throughout the period 1938-47, the 'coefficient of sensitivity' being about 1·5. For Chile it is less impressive, being marred by low velocities of circulation (in relation to the foregoing rates of price increase) in the years 1940-2; though a 'coefficient of sensitivity' of about one-half is quite strongly suggested. In Costa Rica the very rapid price increases of 1942-3 failed to bring about any appreciable immediate increases in velocity, presumably because of direct checks on expenditure; after the war, however (as, indeed, had been the case in 1938-41) a connexion between price increases and succeeding velocity became apparent, the 'coefficient of sensitivity' being between 1 and 1·5, though there was some further tendency for velocity to increase independently of immediately preceding price changes.

Of the inflations so far discussed in this chapter, the most severe was the French, in which prices rose about twenty-fold. It is possible for a much greater increase than this to take place in a similar time without the situation exploding into anything that deserves the name of hyper-inflation—Italy, where prices rose sixty-fold, and Japan, where they rose more than twice as much, afford examples. For Japan there are fairly reliable statistics of national income, so that income velocity of circulation can be calculated and plotted against the rate of change of prices (in this case wholesale prices), as in the cases already discussed (see Diagram 24, p. 197). Between 1938-42 this

[1] I.M.F., *Staff Papers*, vol. i, no. 2, Sept. 1950.

velocity seems to have fallen by about 30 per cent. Thereafter, it rose, but by 1944 had not regained more than half of the foregoing decline. This may be taken as *prima facie* evidence of the effectiveness of controls on expenditure—the price increase, certainly, had averaged less than 10 per cent. per annum up to this time. With defeat controls were loosened and supply of goods reduced simultaneously. Prices almost quintupled during 1946 and roughly trebled in each of the following two years. Velocity shot up to nearly three times the value ruling in 1937-9. There was, however, a time-lag; the maximum velocity was reached in 1948, two years after the maximum rate of price increase. Indeed, a reasonably close relation is observable between income velocity in a given year during this violently inflationary phase and the average rate of price increase during that and the preceding two years; the 'coefficient of sensitivity' in this relation is about unity.

For Italy the data are less satisfactory, in that there are no estimates of the money value of the national income, so that P/M has to serve instead of true income velocity as an index of the 'flight from cash' during most of the period. This variable, like velocity in Japan, fell drastically during the earlier part of the war; by 1943 it was less than half of what it had been in 1938. To some extent this may be accounted for by the under-statements of the official index of wholesale prices and perhaps, also, some expansion of the real volume of production. In 1944, even on the evidence of the price index, P/M (or V/T) rose again to the 1938 level, but since real income has been estimated to have been only 71 per cent. of what it had been in 1938, it is unlikely that velocity had risen above pre-war levels—although prices were nearly four times as great as a year before. Thereafter, the rate of price increase moderated; it rose again sharply in 1946-7, but settled down to a normal level after the credit restrictions at the end of the latter year. Taking the available estimates of income at pre-war prices for 1944, 1945, and 1947, and revaluing them with the help of the available price indices, one arrives at the conclusions that true income velocity, though it rose by perhaps 40 or 50 per cent. between 1944 and 1947, did not appreciably exceed its pre-war value. The process of price inflation in Italy seems barely to have reached the magnitude at which a 'flight from cash' begins to be induced.

We come now to hyper-inflation proper. It seems appropriate here to distinguish between the short run and the longer run relations that might exist between rate of price inflation and the income velocity of circulation. One might well expect some sections of the community to change their monetary habits rapidly with month-to-month changes in the rate of price inflation; others to change them (perhaps after a time-lag) only in response to inflationary experience extending over longer periods. Of this there is some evidence in the hyper-inflations on which adequate data exist—and here it may be useful to draw on evidence from the First World War, as well as the Second. The short-term relation will be considered first. The great German inflation of 1922–3 affords on the whole a good instance of a close relation even in the short run between velocity and the rate of price increase. Up to the beginning of 1922 velocity in Germany was lower than before 1914, despite the fact that the cost of living had risen to twenty times the pre-war level. Beginning in February 1922, however, there were three consecutive months in which the cost of living rose by about 20 per cent. and it was this experience which appears to have begun the 'flight from cash'. The flight was an orderly one, and, while there was a fairly close relation between the increasing pace of price increase and the increasing velocity, the 'coefficient of sensitivity' was surprisingly low—one-tenth or one-twelfth. Indeed, in the last violent phase of the inflation after June 1923, there is some departure from the relation—not, as might be expected, in the direction of greater velocity but in the opposite direction. The Austro-Hungarian 'flight from cash' in the same period was also relatively orderly, velocity showing little increase except that which was closely correlated with rapid price increase, and returning to normal level promptly when each burst of price increase ceased. The 'coefficient of sensitivity' here appears to have varied between about one-fifth and one-twelfth.

What appears to be an orderly pattern of behaviour is to be seen also in China since 1937, although for the more recent of the years concerned information is exceptionally unreliable, particularly with regard to the volume of money in existence (see Diagram 25, p. 198). By 1939 prices were doubling each year, but velocity had risen by only some 20 per cent., so that the 'coefficient of sensitivity' was less than one-third. After that, however, the rate of price increase made a steady advance until 1943 when prices were rising 3·6-fold each year, and velocity had risen nearly five-fold. One would hesitate to suggest that any close causal relation existed between this acceleration of price rise and the concurrent rise in velocity of circulation, if it were not that, after 1944 when price increase was greatly slowed down, velocity appears from the statistics available to have declined *pari passu*. For the whole period 1940-6, therefore, there is a close relation between price increase and velocity, the 'coefficient of sensitivity' apparently showing the remarkably high value of three.

At the other extreme stand the hyper-inflations in which the 'flight from cash' has not been wholly correlated with current price movements. One remarkably clear case of this is the Russian inflation after the October Revolution of 1917. On the eve of that revolution the velocity of circulation of notes appears to have been less than pre-war, despite the fact that prices had trebled in the preceding year. Immediately after the revolution prices trebled in three months, and this (together, no doubt, with the political changes which accompanied it) appears to have begun the decay of confidence in money. In the backward and conservative Russian economy, however, confidence decayed slowly. During the following two and a half years P/M rose, trebling each year, until it gradually came to rest at a level some fifty times as high as before the revolution. Behind this steady advance in velocity, however, there may be discovered an adjustment of velocity to changes in rates of price increase, the 'coefficient of sensitivity' being about one-fifth.

Greece, in the Second World War, presents a somewhat similar picture. In the months of hyper-inflation, September 1943 to October 1944, velocity rose three hundred-fold. This increase can be analysed into a steady rise of 10 per cent. per month—again, a trebling each year—plus a less regular increase which is closely related to variations in the rate of price increase by a 'coefficient of sensitivity' of about one-twentieth.

In the great Hungarian inflation—the greatest of all—the course of events was more complicated, Velocity was, apparently, still not supernormal on the eve of the government's flight from Budapest in December 1944, despite the fact that prices had more than doubled in the previous twelve months. After the flight price data are lacking until September 1945, by which time V/T had risen to six times its pre-war value. This rise (equivalent to about 20 per cent. per month) was associated with only a relatively small increase in the rate of change of prices but it must be remembered that the real national income was, perhaps, halved in the interval, so that true income velocity rose probably no more than three-fold. After that, although the rate of price increase fell somewhat, velocity rose rapidly. If a steady rise by 10 per cent. per month is allowed for from the end of September to the end of December 1945, the remaining changes in velocity during those months are reasonably well correlated with the immediately preceding rates of price increase. By the last mentioned date P/M was about thirty times pre-war. From January 1946 until the end of June 1946 (the last point for which simultaneous price and note-circulation data are available) the independent increase in velocity appears to have ceased, and the velocity changes are closely correlated with variations in the immediately preceding rate of price increase. The 'coefficient of sensitivity' connecting velocity with rate of price increase is, therefore, less than one-twentieth, and the major part of the 'flight from cash' in the great Hungarian inflation thus seems to have been uncorrelated with immediately preceding rises in price. The collapse of confidence during 1945 was not a process closely geared to month-to-month economic developments, but a substratum of fine adjustments of cash holdings to current price changes is nevertheless traceable for as much of the year as is covered by adequate data, while, in the following hectic six months, the sixteen-fold rise of velocity has all the appearance of a systematic and reversible adjustment to the diminishing purchasing power of the pengo.

In Rumania cash holdings during the early years of the war were, again, abnormally high, though to a much smaller extent than in Hungary. It was not, surprisingly, after the invasion of 1944 that prices and the velocity of circulation began to rise alarmingly. Data are lacking for the early part of 1945, but by the third quarter prices were rising 2·4-fold per annum, and P/M had risen to three times its pre-war level. Production, however, had fallen to little more than half the level of early

1944; the true income velocity of circulation, therefore, had probably risen by little more than 50 per cent. during a period of rather over a year. There are, nevertheless, indications that between the autumn of 1945 and mid-1946 it showed a steady increase equivalent to an annual doubling. Thereafter (ignoring changes which appear to be closely correlated with variations in the rate of price increase), P/M fell somewhat, but this may be due to some recovery of real income in late 1946. After the beginning of 1947 there seems again to have been an 'autonomous' increase in P/M, at something like 25 per cent. per month; but a fall (at a somewhat slower rate) followed in the second quarter. Allowing for these 'autonomous' movements of P/M, velocity appears to have been connected with price change by a low, but fairly well-defined, relation, characterized by a 'coefficient of sensitivity' of not more than one-tenth.

The longer-term relation between velocity and price change can be investigated by considering the total changes in these two variables in the whole period from the beginning to the end of hyper-inflation (see Diagram 26, p. 199). This relation is, of course, characterized by a higher 'coefficient of sensitivity' than that which relates to the shorter-term adjustments, since it is raised by the gradual 'flight from cash' of the great mass of the community, which in most countries probably responds in this way only to a long-continued and severe increase of prices. In post-revolutionary Russia, taking the average price rise and the total increase in velocity over the whole period 1917–21, and in Greece during 1943–4, it was above unity; in Rumania during 1944–7 and Japan during 1945–8, about unity. In the most explosive of the hyper-inflations, however,—the German of 1922–3 and the Hungarian of 1944–6—this longer-term sensitivity over the whole hyper-inflationary period was low, being about a quarter in Germany and perhaps a sixth in Hungary. It is clear that a country which normally uses money extensively has great difficulty in dispensing with its services altogether, and the degree in which this can be done can hardly be expected to increase indefinitely in direct proportion to the rate at which the value of money is depreciating. Provided, for instance, that wages and salaries are paid in money at all, there is bound to be an upper limit to the velocity of circulation, set by the rate at which employers can fetch cash from the banks and hand it out, employees can run to the shops after being paid, and so on. A more primitive economy can retreat further and further in the direction of barter; an advanced one has great difficulty in doing without money as a means of payment, even after it has ceased almost entirely to use it as a unit of account—not to speak of a store of value.

The still longer-term effects of a hyper-inflation (or something approaching it) on liquidity are yet another matter. The Economic Commission for Europe in its *Economic Survey of Europe in 1949* (p. 55) suggests that velocities of circulation had been permanently altered as a result of experience in the inflationary years. The decrease in velocity in most countries is a matter which can more conveniently be discussed in Chapter 10; here it is more important to note that in Greece and Hungary velocity was, in 1947–9, twice as high as pre-war, in Japan more than 2·5 times as high as pre-war, in France and Poland more than 50 per cent. above the pre-war level (see Diagram 26, p. 199). Whether the change is to be considered permanent is, however, dubious. The Greek and Hungarian velocities show a marked fall between the end of 1946 and 1949, and Polish velocity between 1947 and 1948. Previous experience suggests, however, that the effect of inflation in this direction may be long-lasting even after price increases have moderated or ceased. The income velocity of the note circulation in Germany at the height of inflation in November 1923 was perhaps forty times as high as pre-war, but fell to five times the pre-war level within a fortnight of the introduction of the Rentenmark, and was down to twice that level by March 1924. After that, the rate of decline of velocity was slow; in 1928–9 velocity seemed to have settled down at a level about 50 per cent. higher than in 1914, though the depression, of course, subsequently changed this state of affairs.

What conclusions can be drawn from these diverse experiences? The first impression they leave is that, in the period under review, a 'flight from cash' has not often been important; it is the mark of true hyper-inflation, and hyper-inflation has, in this generation, been rare. It seems that, in all economies in which there is no direct control of expenditure, there is usually some correlation between income velocity and price movements, but that the former is not very sensitive to the latter.

It appears to reach its most sensitive in certain countries (Syria, Iran, Turkey, Iraq) where it may be supposed that a large part of the monetary stock is in the hands of a mercantile class, accustomed to taking note of price movements. It seems to have become even more sensitive in China, when hyper-inflation (even if a rather sluggish variety of hyper-inflation) was under way, perhaps because the use of the money by the peasantry had by then been largely abandoned, leaving hold-ings of it concentrated with price-sensitive traders to an even greater extent than in the Middle East. This high sensitivity did not, however, appear in China until after a long and severe inflationary experience.

Some immediate adjustment of velocity to rate of price change—though of a low degree of sensitivity—is to be found in hyper-inflation in countries where money is in more general use. The general 'flight from cash' in such countries, however, is hard to start; there is no evidence that it has ever started until prices have doubled in six months or less. Once started, it proceeds at quite a rapid rate in relation to the speed at which prices have been rising over the preceding two or three years, the rate of increase of velocity falling well below the annual rate of price increase over this preceding period only in the most explosive hyper-inflations. After these hyper-inflationary experiences, velocity seems to fall quickly to twice the pre-inflation level, or rather less, but may remain thus far above its old value for a considerable number of years.

A further impression left by this inquiry is that price control —even where, as in Iraq, Egypt, and India, it does not succeed in preventing a very considerable price inflation, and is gener-ally judged ineffective—may nevertheless impose sufficient restraint on spending to increase monetary liquidity, whereas in neighbouring countries which experience a similar price infla-tion in the absence of control, there is a very appreciable 'flight from cash'. Under wartime conditions, indeed, it is the presence or absence of price control, good or bad, rather than the pres-ence or absence of attempts to control the supply of money or the size of the public deficit, that determines whether price infla-tion shall reach the stage of self-reinforcement through a 'flight from cash' which leads, if unchecked, to hyper-inflation.

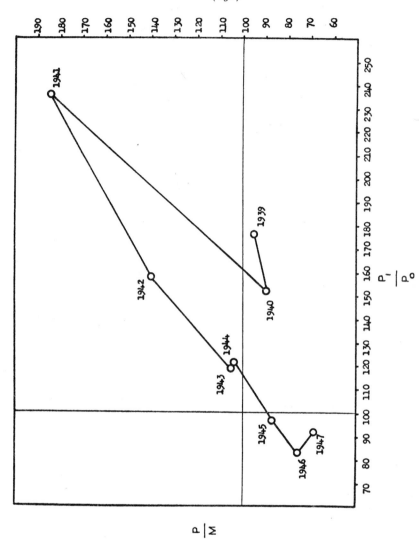

DIAGRAM 39. Rate of price change and ratio of price level to money stock, 1939–47. Syria and Lebanon.

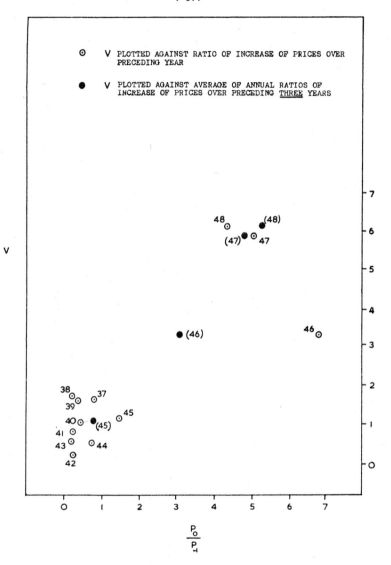

DIAGRAM 24. Price increase and income velocity, 1937–48: Japan.

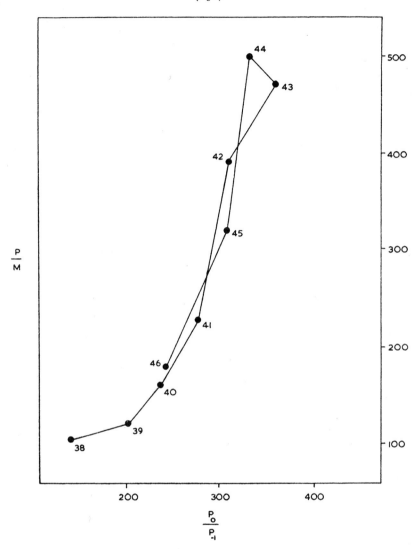

DIAGRAM 25. Rate of price change and ratio of price level to money stock, 1938–46: China.

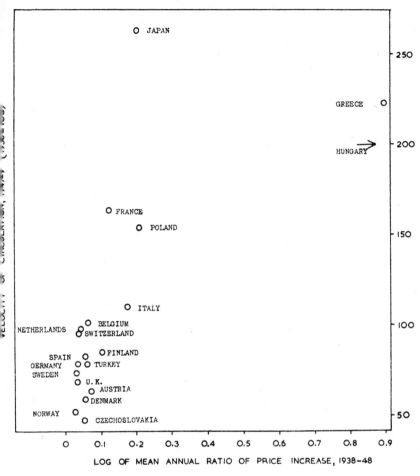

DIAGRAM 26. Logarithmic price index 1948 (1938 = 100) and income velocity 1947–9 (1938 = 100).

9

Inflation and Interest Rates

DESPITE the existence of much controversy about the determination and the effects of rates of interest, economists of all schools of thought would probably agree that the period here under discussion was for most of its length, at least, one in which these rates played unusually little part in governing the course of events. During the war, the amount of non-consumption expenditure in the principal countries was governed by central decisions based upon military considerations rather than by any weighing of prospective rates of return against the cost of borrowing; in the reconversion and (in a smaller degree) the post-war boom, such expenditure was limited for a considerable time by lack of equipment and basic raw materials, and in some cases by direct governmental control. Willingness to save, moreover, was strongly influenced by forces of unusual strength likely to outweigh and conceal any effect which interest rates exerted, or might have exerted—savings campaigns, patriotism, rationing, and price control on the one hand, speculative flights from assets of fixed money value and desires to make good wartime backlog of consumption on the other. Even those who would claim most for the importance and efficiency of interest rates either as instruments of policy or as cogs in an automatic market mechanism would expect to find relatively few illustrations of their doctrines between 1939 and 1948.

Nevertheless, it would clearly be wrong to assume, without further examination, that interest changes played no important causal part in this period, and, even if such an assumption proved on further examination to be justified, it would still remain to be seen whether they have symptomatic importance as indicators of attitudes towards money or of expectations with regard to prices.

Interest Rates as Symptoms

This last question may perhaps be considered first: if the

market price of any security (say a particular type of government bond) is formed by the ordinary competitive process, then its yield is presumably such as will just induce each holder to hold as much as he does, rather than holding one unit less and using the price of that unit for any one, or any combination of the available alternative purposes—expenditure on consumable goods, investment in some other type of interest-bearing security, or holding in the form of money. If one concentrates attention on the last-mentioned alternative (money holding) it can be seen that the yield of a security ought just to measure, for each holder of it, the benefits he would enjoy in various forms if he had held the price of one of his units of the security concerned in liquid form instead of investing it as he in fact has done. In other words, it should measure the extra convenience of holding the marginal unit of money which actually is held, rather than investing it in the kind of bond under consideration.

Now, this degree of convenience is likely to be governed by many circumstances. In the first place, it depends on the amount of money the holder possesses and the extent of his need for money to facilitate his transactions—whether these transactions are clearly foreseen or are merely possibilities against which it is worth holding cash so that lucrative opportunities may not be missed. In the second place, it is likely to depend on the amount of the bond under discussion that is held; the more of it the holder possesses, the greater will become the marginal disutility of the risk attached to that particular bond (the marginal utility of the income yield may also fall, but this effect is less likely to be important). Thirdly, both the marginal utility of income yield and the marginal riskiness of the bond in question will depend on the holdings of other types of interest-bearing asset. Fourthly, it will depend on the individual's beliefs about the future course of asset prices (or interest rates) and of the purchasing power of money, and the degree of confidence with which those beliefs are held.

In anything like hyper-inflation, the last-mentioned factor becomes all important, because expectations of further inflation become general. Cash holdings are drastically reduced in relation to the total money value of transactions. (This 'flight from cash' can be separately examined and is so examined in Chapter 8.) Moreover, since the purchasing power of the

income from fixed-interest assets is expected to fall rapidly, their
price is reduced to such an extent that their yield tends to
approach the rate per annum at which the price level is expected
to rise—so that the prospective yields from investing in bonds
and in goods approach equality. The United Nations *Report on
Inflationary and Deflationary Tendencies, 1946–48*,[1] points out that
in China the black market rate of interest did in fact rise to
rough equality with the actual rate of increase of prices. The
data there quoted are as follows:

	Rate of Increase of wholesale prices	Black Market Rate of Interest
	(Per cent. per annum)	
1940 . . .	158	22
1941 . . .	177	32
1942 . . .	180	30
1943 . . .	202	136
1944 . . .	224	197
1945 . . .	253	270
1946 . . .	151	185

From this it appears that it required four years or more of
price increase amounting to a doubling or trebling of prices
each year to make the conviction that this process would
continue so strong as to be fully reflected in interest rates. By
1945, indeed, they reflected an expectation that prices would
rise at more than the current rate; expectations do not, however, seem to have been linked by a simple functional relation
to the rate at which prices were increasing, though they responded to the reduction of this rate in 1946. In Hungary, also,
it required much experience of price inflation to raise interest
rates abnormally. Both the yield of Government bonds and
the commercial bill rate, indeed, were actually lower in early
1944 than in 1939, despite the fact that wholesale prices had
trebled in the interim. According to '*Études et Conjoncture*'[2] the
rate for day-to-day money rose to 5 or 6 per cent. a day by early
April 1946. At that time, however, the cost of living index was
rising at some 10 per cent. a day. By mid-July, according to
the same source, this interest rate was 35–40 per cent. a day,

---

[1] U.N. Dept. of Economic Affairs, *Inflationary and Deflationary Tendencies, 1946–48*
(New York, 1949), p. 48.

[2] December 1946 to January 1947.

but cost of living was then rising at about 140 per cent. a day.
Mr. Varga[1] reports that in the last days of inflation the day-to-
day interest rate rose to 100 per cent., but it seems that it did
not catch up with the rate of increase of prices. Similarly in
early 1942 (according to the *Report of the National Bank of Greece,
1941–5*) the Greek black market rate of discount on bills and
cheques rose to 40 per cent. per annum; this, however, was
accompanied by a rate of increase of the cost of living of about
800 per cent. per annum. No later data on black market rates
are available: the commercial banks during 1945 (after the
first currency reform) lent at an effective rate (including commission) of only 15–20 per cent., while prices were rising at
some 900 per cent. per annum. In some countries, such as Italy,
France, and Japan (up to the end of hostilities), in which there
was a very high rate of price increase stopping short of hyper-
inflation, yields of bonds were actually lower in the most inflationary years than before the war. Nevertheless, the sharp rise
of interest rates to abnormal heights serves as a sensitive index
of the onset of hyper-inflation.

The contention of Irving Fisher that rates of interest should
show a positive correlation with recent rates of price increase
thus receives no confirmation from experience in these inflationary times, save in the most extreme cases. The reason is clear:
in all ordinary circumstances there can be no general expectation of price increase except momentarily. In a flexible price
system, prices at every moment will be such as to discount the
general expectations of the future. If expectations of price
increase persist for any appreciable length of time, prices during
that time must rise at a rate limited only by contracts or by
monetary stringency.

The clear and obvious empirical relation in most countries
and most times has been a positive correlation between the level
of interest rates and the *level* of prices—the famous 'Gibson
Paradox'. It is over the fairly long run—the period of ten years
or more—that this relation most strikingly holds, and various
explanations of it are possible. It may be, for instance, that the
supply of money (in the sense of the total amount in existence)
is imperfectly responsive to, and varies less than, the needs of
the active circulation, after one has allowed for *very* long-term

[1] *Neue Zuercher Zeitung*, 7 Jan. 1947.

trends, such as the gradually increasing quantity of money in relation to income as the economy develops. In that case a rise of prices (and hence of money income) would normally mean a shortage of money other than that required for the active circulation, and thus a rise in the marginal rate of return required to induce investors to hold bonds. Keynes's explanation in the *Treatise on Money*[1] is that, if the 'natural rate' or equilibrium rate of interest is falling, the market rate, lagging behind, will be mainly above it, so that prices will tend to fall also. Market interest rates and prices will thus tend to move together in the same direction as 'natural rate', and Keynes believed that the last-named would tend to exhibit long-term movements extending over decades, since the total stock of capital equipment is not quickly alterable.[2]

Whatever explanation of the 'Gibson Paradox' one favours, however, it seems just to say, with Keynes, that it was 'one of the most completely established facts within the whole field of quantitative economics', holding in a most striking manner (so far as United Kingdom data are concerned) for the whole period 1791–1939.[3] Very striking, therefore, is the fact that in the period 1939–46 the correlation is, for most countries, negative. The great price movement of these years is the only major one in history which has been accompanied by an interest-movement in the opposite direction.

The explanation of this which most readily comes to mind is that the 'disequilibrium systems'—the expansion of private income coupled with varying degrees of direct control of private expenditure—which went with a certain amount of price increase, produced great increases in liquidity which depressed the marginal rate of return at which the community was willing to hold securities, even though the total volume of securities held also increased.

The connexion between reduction in interest rates and in-

[1] London, Macmillan, 1930, vol. ii, pp. 198–208.

[2] Since the marginal efficiency of capital—or rather, the expected marginal efficiency—depends on the *balance* between invention and investment, as well as on less truly relevant factors which affect anticipations generally, this seems highly doubtful, but it is not relevant to pursue the point here. The present writer has considered the consequences of linking the 'natural rate' to the rate of change of prices (*Oxford Studies in the Price Mechanism*, ch. i, pt. iv).

[3] See J. M. Keynes, *Treatise on Money*, and A. J. Brown in *Oxford Economic Papers*, No. 2, 1939, for details of the correlation between the two series.

crease in liquidity can, indeed, be shown in a number of ways. One method is to correlate, for a number of countries together, the net changes in liquidity over the decade 1938–48, with the net change in their respective interest rates, thereby showing that, where liquidity had increased most, interest rate had, on the whole, decreased most. Liquidity may be conveniently measured by the ratio of total money supply (i.e. coin, notes, and deposits transferable by cheque) to national income (the factor generally known as 'Cambridge K'), preferably in an index form, taking the 1938 value as the unit. The most appropriate interest rate for this purpose is the yield of Government bonds, again taking the 1938 value as the unit. Of the fourteen countries for which data are readily available, liquidity, as defined, fell over the period concerned only in two (Belgium and Switzerland), and these were among the four countries out of the fourteen (the others being the Netherlands and Sweden) in which the yield of Government bonds rose. Sweden is the most notable of the exceptions, for there interest rose appreciably, despite a considerable increase in liquidity; this may be attributed, however, to the abnormal depression of interest rates by the capital inflow of the base year, 1938.

In the language of regression analysis differences between the changes in liquidity in these countries may be regarded as explaining slightly more than half the differences between their interest changes (the correlation coefficient between the two variables, measured logarithmically, is -0.716). The mean elasticity of interest rate with respect to 'Cambridge K' (i.e. the mean percentage by which the index of interest rate changes when 'Cambridge K' changes by 1 per cent.) may be estimated at about 0.4.

What about the other half of the variations in experience as to interest rates, which is not explained in terms of differences in liquidity change? It would appear reasonable to suppose that they might be largely accounted for by differences in the extent to which total debt holdings expanded in relation to income. Unfortunately, an attempt to verify this on the assumption that total holdings of non-governmental debt in 1938 were proportional to national income, shows little promise; the introduction of the debt index (ratio of debt holding to national income in 1948 taking the 1938 ratio as the unit of measurement) improves the total correlation only very little, and over 43 per cent. of the international differences in interest rate changes remain unaccounted for. Nevertheless the calculation shows the importance of change in liquidity as an explanatory variable, even if other such variables remain untraced.

Another method of investigating the relation between liquidity and interest rates in the inflationary period is, of course, to consider year-to-year changes in one country at a time. This method has been adopted for other periods by the present writer (*Oxford Economic Papers*, No. 2, 1939), by M. Kalecki[1] and by J. Tobin.[2] In the United Kingdom and the United States alike, the degree of liquidity (or the mean velocity of circulation of money, which is inversely related to it) is quite strongly correlated for the inter-war years with either the long-term or the short-term rate of interest.[3] In the war and post-war years, however, the relation is not well maintained. If the long-term interest rate in the United Kingdom, for instance, is plotted against 'Cambridge K', a close relation is found to exist over the period 1929–39, the elasticity of interest rate in relation to K being about 4. From then onwards, the schedule is displaced to the right, slowly up to 1942, then very rapidly up to 1944. The data for 1944–9 form another good line, far to the right of that for 1929–39, with an elasticity of unity, or slightly less.

If the data for the whole period 1929–49 are regarded as forming a single schedule (though the correlation coefficient between the logarithmically-measured values of K and interest rate is only −0·665), the mean elasticity of this schedule proves to be slightly over one-half; for the inflationary period 1938–48 alone it would be about one-third, which is not greatly different from

---

[1] 'Short-term rate of Interest and the Velocity of Cash Circulation', *Review of Economic Statistics*, vol. xxiii, no. 2, May 1941, and *Studies in Economic Dynamics*, Essay 2.

[2] 'Monetary Velocity and Monetary Policy—a rejoinder', *Review of Economic Statistics*, vol. xxx, no. 4, Nov. 1948.

[3] Which of these rates is the more relevant is a matter of controversy. The present writer's first work on the subject, referred to above, was done with the long-term rate; Kalecki's with the bill rate. For most holders of cash, bonds are probably the most immediate alternative among fixed-interest investments, though for some of the big institutional holders, bills or other short-dated assets occupy this position. It can be demonstrated that for the United States between 1919 and 1944, the bond yield and the bill rate were almost exactly equally well correlated with monetary liquidity.

the value obtained by an international comparison of experience over this period. It is clear, however, as has been suggested above, that this is not a valid interpretation; the schedule clearly moved during the inflationary years under the influence of some other variable. Once more the variable which seems most likely to provide an explanation is the size of total debt holdings,[1] measured in relation to national income. In this case again, this variable does not help appreciably; its insertion raises the total correlation for the whole period 1929–49 from −0·665 to only −0·695. The United States data, however, seem to be different in this respect; Dr. A. M. Khusro of the University of Leeds has found that whereas the correlation between the volume of idle money[2] in the United States and the long-term rate of interest between 1921 and 1946 was only −0·719, the substitution of the ratio of idle money to total debt for idle money *simpliciter* raises the correlation to −0·890.

Two modifications of the method of investigation hitherto generally used in this field seem, however, to be called for. The first, which is of a fundamental nature, has been suggested by W. T. Newlyn. He points out that the yield of a security which concerns the investor, when he is choosing between that security and cash, is its yield net of taxation. To calculate this satisfactorily is difficult, because different holders of securities are, of course, subject to very different rates of taxation on the income they yield, and information about the distribution of security holdings between different income groups is lacking. Dr. Khusro has developed a method of estimating an average of the marginal rates of tax on British Government securities,[3] weighting this average by the total incomes received in the various income groups subject to surtax. The assumption that Government securities are distributed in the same proportion as total income would no doubt lead to an underestimate

[1] Total debt-holding was for this purpose roughly estimated as internal long-term national debt *plus* local authority debt, *plus* fixed liabilities of railway companies, *plus* estimated British holding of foreign bonds, *plus* one-third of issued capital of joint-stock companies.

[2] Idle money is defined for this purpose as time deposits *plus* the excess of total demand deposits over the amount required to carry the national income of the year at the highest average income-velocity for those deposits which is encountered during the period investigated.

[3] 'An Investigation of Liquidity Preference', *Yorkshire Bulletin of Economic and Social Research*, vol. iv, no. 1, Feb. 1952.

of the average rate of tax; the assumption also made that all such securities are held by persons receiving more than £2,000 a year works, however, in the opposite direction. For the war years, some underestimate of the rate required will result from failure to take account of holdings by firms subject to excess profits tax. Nevertheless, the calculation certainly gives a net rate of interest which is far more relevant to the discussion of idle money holdings than is the gross yield. The difference is enormous—Dr. Khusro's figure for the net yield of $2\frac{1}{2}$ per cent. Consols in 1946, for instance, is 0·67 per cent., whereas the gross yield was 2·60 per cent.

The second modification relates to the standard velocity used in calculating the amount of active money from the statistics of national income, in order to obtain an estimate of idle money. To take simply the highest average velocity recorded in the period for current accounts is clearly arbitrary. It is better to allow a standard velocity to emerge from the calculation itself, and this can be done as follows:

The relation assumed to exist between (net) interest rate and the ratio of idle money (M_2) to total liquid assets other than money (A) can be written in the form:

$$r = a - b\frac{M_2}{A}.$$

But, if M is the total amount of money in existence, active money is equal to $M - M_2$; it is also, however, by definition equal to KY, where K is the inverse of the standard income velocity of active money, and Y is the national income. Using these relations, the above equation can be transformed into:

$$r = a - b.\frac{M}{A} + bK.\frac{Y}{A}.$$

Thus, a multiple regression analysis of the time-series of r, M/A, and Y/A yields the two partial regression coefficients b and bK, the ratio of the first of these to the second giving the standard velocity of active money which best accords with this form of analysis. Dr. Khusro has found by this means a standard velocity for the United Kingdom of 6·71 per annum. Using this to estimate the amount of idle money, M_2, he finds that M_2/A for the years 1926–48 shows a correlation of −0·853 with the net rate of interest. The relation between the two variables is shown in scatter-diagram form in Diagram 27 (p. 226). From this it seems that the liquidity preference schedule may be plausibly represented as a straight line showing a fall of about 0·30 in the net rate of interest for every increase of 0·01 in the ratio of idle money to liquid non-monetary assets, or a mean elasticity of net interest rate in relation to the idle money/liquid assets ratio of about −2·8. An inspection of the scatter diagram makes it clear, however, that the schedule moved about considerably during the period to which it refers. It was high in the late nineteen-twenties, fell after 1930, and remained low until 1935; thereafter it was high until after the outbreak of war. From a low level in 1941–4, it rose to a high one in 1948.

There are many factors to which these apparent movements of the schedule might be attributed. One such is the rate of dividends being earned on ordinary shares. When this is high, there will be a tendency to sell bonds in order to buy these shares, which will pull up the bond yield even though there has been no change in the ratio of idle money to liquid assets. This helps to account for the low level of interest rate (in relation to the value which the schedule would suggest) between 1932 and 1935, its high level from 1936 to 1939, its lowness in the early war years, and its gradual rise to 1948. The very sharp falling away of dividends from a high peak in the years 1926–8 is not reflected, but neither was it reflected in the prices of equities, which rose in those years, apparently owing to sheer optimism, despite falling rates of dividend and almost constant bond prices.[1] One might, therefore, say that equity dividends explain the apparent movements of the schedule well. Dr. Khusro has shown that their inclusion in the equation raises the multiple correlation coefficient to 0·96.

Another factor to which appeal may be made is the state of expectations concerning bond prices. It can be shown that the deviations of net interest rate from its regression line on the idle money/liquid assets ratio are closely correlated with the changes in prices of Consols over the preceding three years. Dr. Khusro has found that, when this change is inserted (instead of equity dividends) as a second explanatory variable in the regressions

---

[1] For a discussion of dividends and expectations concerning them see I. M. Sahni, 'A Study of Share-Prices, 1918–1947', *Yorkshire Bulletin of Economic and Social Research*, vol. iii, no. 1, Feb. 1951.

equation, the multiple correlation coefficient is raised to 0·934. It is reasonable to suppose that, when bond prices have been rising, confidence in their continuing to do so, or, at least, in their not falling, will attract sufficient additional buyers to raise the price above what, in the existing state of supply of liquid assets and idle money, it would otherwise be, and this possible explanation clearly fits the facts quite well.

It is not necessary, of course, to choose between the two explanations just suggested for the departure of interest rate from the values given by the calculated schedule. There are, no doubt, two sets of factors affecting any price at most times—external factors, such as changes in costs of production and in the supply or quality of competing or complementary commodities, and what have sometimes been called autoregressive factors, that is to say, those depending on the past record of the price itself. The rate of interest need be no exception to this. Moreover, a high level of equity dividends is very closely associated with a bond price which has been falling for obvious reasons—when profits are high, there is a tendency to switch from bonds to equities, and both the alternative second explanatory variables may be regarded as showing different aspects of this process.

This study seems to indicate that, during the inflationary period, the long-term interest rate in the United Kingdom has not been subjected to any important influences of different kinds from those operating on it in the preceding decade or more. It reflected the opposing influences of the increase in idle money due to controls of expenditure, and of the great increase in the public debt; it reflected also the influence of confidence based upon the previous behaviour of bond prices and/or the influence of changes in dividends. All these were reflected, in proportion to their strength, to about the same extent as before the war. There is no evidence that in the United Kingdom the rate of interest was ever affected appreciably by any expectations which might be regarded as characteristic of a period of inflation. Dr. Khusro has shown that the same is true of the United States; it probably holds for other advanced economies which underwent generally similar experiences.

It may be argued, indeed, that in the United Kingdom in particular, there was little opportunity for interest rates to be affected by expectations of inflation. Income receivers accumulated funds because their opportunities for spending on consumable goods and services were curtailed, mainly by rationing and price control. If they were apprehensive of price inflation, their best hedge might seem, at first sight, to be investment in real property or in equities. The money yield of real property was, however, largely limited by rent control, direct taxation, and, later on, by the provisions of the Town and Country Planning Act, and in many cases there was fear of war damage so that, while land and house values did, in fact, rise much more than general prices, the scope for a switch to these assets as a precaution against a fall in the value of money, though by no means negligible, was limited. Equities were even more drastically affected by taxation, the Excess Profits Tax in particular; so that they became, in effect, fixed interest securities for the time being. Their prices actually fell in the United Kingdom by some 24 per cent. between 1938 and 1940, and even at their peak in 1947 were only some 18 per cent. above the 1937 level; in the United States the peak value of 1946 was only 21 per cent. above the previous peak of 1937.[1] In a number of countries—France, Italy, the Netherlands, Germany—share prices rose more markedly, in fact appreciably more than wholesale commodity prices, at some point during the war. To find out whether investment in these shares as an anti-inflationary hedge had abnormally reduced their current yield, one would, of course, need to know the course of dividends, which is not readily available, but it seems likely that this was the case, especially in Germany, where dividends were fairly effectively prevented from rising. After the end of hostilities, however, share prices nearly everywhere stood lower in relation to general commodity prices and incomes than before the war. (The main exceptions are Argentina, where a runaway stock market boom developed after 1946, and Mexico, where stock prices were very high in 1945.) Taxation and uncertainties as to earnings have rendered equities an imperfect hedge against a fall in the value of money, and savings were thus kept to a large extent in money or in bonds, even by investors who feared such a fall, because they saw no reasonably accessible line of escape from it.

---

[1] The references here are to annual averages, not to the highest or lowest daily quotations.

This reflection suggests that there may have been some enduring expectations of a further increase of prices of goods and services in economies which were rigidly controlled in wartime, without there being any of the symptoms by which, in hyperinflation, one can detect such a state of affairs. People may have expected prices to rise, while price controls prevented the immediate adjustment which would normally have followed from such a general belief; similarly, the prices of bonds may have been maintained despite a fairly general belief that the purchasing power of money would fall, by the practical difficulty for most people of finding a hedge against the expected inflation. If such a situation existed, it would deserve the name 'suppressed inflation' far more fully than the position to which that name is usually applied—a position characterized merely by the limitation of spending, and not necessarily by a general belief that prices will be significantly higher in the foreseeable future.

The Effects of Low Interest Rates

How far interest rates themselves affected the course of inflation is in principle a harder question to investigate, but one to which it seems possible in some cases to give a fairly confident answer on general grounds. Interest rates affect inflationary processes presumably through private investment, in the main, though there may be subsidiary effects through the burden of interest on the public debt, which, if taxation is increased to meet it, may weaken the will to produce, and if taxation is not increased, must increase the size of the public deficit.

So far as private investment is concerned, it is clear that the rates of interest prevailing in the principal economies of the world would have been grossly inadequate to check it if its sponsors had entertained anything like correct expectations as to the future course of prices. The rate of price increase in all these economies (except Germany), right up to the end of the inflationary period, was never much less than the current long-term rate of interest, and mostly much greater. The real rate of return, in Irving Fisher's sense, on loans of considerable duration (up to 12 years at the time of writing) has proved to be negative; that is to say the principal of a loan with the interest accruing during almost any period in the inflationary years has had a smaller purchasing power over goods and services at the end of that period than the principal alone at the beginning. If the average current rate of price increase over the years 1939–48 had been expected by borrowers to continue indefinitely, a rate of interest of perhaps 10 per cent. would have been required to restrain demand for loans in the United Kingdom or the United States, since the value of money was depreciating at some 6 or 7 per cent. per annum.

That the prices of long-term securities were kept up in these circumstances must be ascribed to one or other of the two circumstances which have already been mentioned—the practical difficulty of securing an adequate hedge against inflation, or the absence of any general belief that existing prices were too low to take account of the future possibilities of an increase. In so far as expectations of price increase, as well as the propensity to buy goods for use, were prevented by price controls from exerting their normal effect in producing an immediate price rise, and at the same time the yield of bonds was kept down by lack of inflation-proof repositories for capital, the rate of interest was clearly inadequate to restrain private demand for loans or for capital goods, and these must have been restrained by direct controls. If, on the other hand, there was nothing to prevent prices of goods from being adjusted in accordance with the general expectations of the market, there was no reason—short of hyper-inflation—for the bond yield to be abnormally high, or for a moderate rate to be abnormally ineffective in restraining borrowing or real investment.

For the war period—and for the whole period of low interest in some countries, such as the United Kingdom—it is certainly safe to conclude that private borrowing was restrained almost entirely by direct controls, either on the act of borrowing itself, or on possible uses of borrowed funds. For economies where such controls were less in evidence, such as the United States after the war, or the Latin American countries throughout, the answer is less clear. In the United States after 1945 the expectation of a long-continued price rise was certainly not general; there was, indeed, a rapid fluctuation of opinion as to the immediate future of prices, and for much of the time an underlying belief that a general fall could not be long delayed. While this might mean that the equilibrium rates of interest may not have been, on the average, greatly different from the low ruling market rates, it is not clear that investment decisions were responsive to such moderate changes in interest rates as took place.

In the economies subjected to relatively little internal direct control, the availability of investment goods—mainly from abroad—was a powerful influence. When such goods were not obtainable (largely because of war conditions in the main supplying countries) there was an increase in liquidity; when investment goods became available, a decrease. This is well shown by J. K. Horsefield's investigation of inflation in Latin America (International Monetary Fund, *Staff Papers*),[1] which shows that the average liquidity index (virtually 'Cambridge K') for twelve Latin American countries rose by 1944 to a level 23 per cent. above that of 1941, and sank by 1947 to less than the 1941 value. The fall of liquidity coincided with the growth of imports and of private investment.

This is, indeed, similar to what happened in many other countries. The accumulation of liquid assets during the war was in varying degrees the result of direct controls on consumption, but everywhere to some extent also the result of non-availability of durable goods, coupled with the anticipation of greater availability later on. Enterprises in the United Kingdom and the United States also accumulated their depreciation and other reserves in liquid form; partly in bank deposits, partly in Government securities. The impossibility of buying investment goods for the time being may or may not have increased the propensity to hold cash at a given rate of interest; it certainly increased the willingness to hold Government securities at a given price. With post-war improvements in the supply of capital goods, and the possibility of securing permission to buy them, some dishoarding of bank deposits was a possible consequence—certainly the liquidation of security holdings was to be expected. This would, normally, have produced a considerable rise in yields, and such an effect was, in fact, observed.

In the United Kingdom and the United States, however, the yields of Government bonds in the low interest period were subject to some rather special influences, more directly connected with monetary policy. Official policy—Mr. Dalton's cheap money policy in the United Kingdom—aimed, primarily,

[1] Vol. 1, no. 2, Sept. 1950.

at easing the burden of Government debt. (The importance of this objective, in relation to anti-inflationary policy, will be discussed below.) In the United States the great fall in yields which began somewhat earlier than in the United Kingdom (from late 1944) appears to have been rather less a deliberate result of official action. According to one analysis, it was the delayed result of confidence in the future lowness and steadiness of interest rates engendered by the success of the Federal Reserve System in holding yields constant throughout the war, a confidence which produced a double effect, since the banks, also, bought securities, thereby augmenting the means in the hands of the public for security purchases. For a brief time, therefore, the great safety ascribed to the market value of bonds made them appear a very close substitute for money, and the revision of this estimate of bonds in the years 1946–8 may have been responsible, as much as actual liquidation for the purpose of buying durable goods, or exhaustion of idle bank deposits, for the subsequent rise in yields. The Federal Reserve Banks appear to have assisted in forming this more cautious attitude of the public towards bond prices by ceasing to attempt to maintain yields at as steady a level as during the war. In the United Kingdom, however, there is little evidence of a changed attitude towards bonds—of any shift of the liquidity-preference schedule to the right—after the Government had failed in 1947 to maintain the low interest rates for which it had striven in the preceding two years. The relation of the bond rate to the quantity of idle money, the quantity of debt, and the level of equity dividends remained throughout the period of low interest rates almost exactly what it had been in the nineteen-twenties and nineteen-thirties.

The lowness of short-term interest rates was in some countries even more conspicuous in the war and the first three or four post-war years than that of the long-term rates. This was especially true of the United Kingdom, where the Treasury Bill and day-to-day money rates alike stood at 1 per cent. from shortly after the beginning of the war, and at half that figure from late 1945 to late 1951, and of the United States, where the Treasury Bill rate, though higher than the almost vanishingly low level of the late nineteen-thirties, did not rise above 0·5 per cent. until 1947. Official discount rates, too, were kept low—

in the United Kingdom at the conventional minimum of 2 per cent. from 1939 to 1951, in New York at 1 per cent. from 1937 to 1948, with an interval at half that value from 1942 to 1946. The level of short-term rates is, of course, generally more susceptible to control than that of long-term rates, since the market is smaller and more specialized, and the very low rates in the United Kingdom, for instance, were maintained without difficulty by keeping down the supply of Treasury Bills, threatening the banks with the non-lucrative Treasury Deposit Receipts as the only interest-bearing, liquid, alternative form of asset, and making money available to any extent required for the taking up of the issue.

The inflationary effect of these low short-term rates, in themselves, can hardly have been considerable. The normal influence of short-term rates is exerted mainly upon manufacturers and traders who wish to borrow in order to finance commodity stocks, or upon consumers who require temporary financial accommodation. The widespread control of expenditure and the allocation of raw materials during the war and the immediate post-war years clearly rendered the conditions of supply of short-term credit unimportant; indeed, in the particular case of bank advances, demand was so low during this time in the United Kingdom and the United States that the total outstanding actually fell in the former country, rose only a little in the latter during the war, and in the succeeding three or four years remained in both far below its pre-war ratio to the national income. Accumulated bank deposits and cash were sufficient to satisfy much of the public's need for purchasing power in the circumstances of the time. When bank credit again began to be sought after, as in the United States after 1946, it is unlikely that the low interest rates in themselves were important. In the face of price increases and large uncertainties about the course of prices, the difference between high and low short-term rates could not have been a major factor affecting the decisions of most traders, especially as the increases in stocks in this period seem to have been necessary to bring stocks up to the normal relation to the volume of sales—a normal relation which they did not at any point greatly exceed.

It was not everywhere that short-term rates were so conspicuously low as in the United Kingdom and the United

States. In France, Belgium, and the Netherlands they were not especially low during the first half of the war; but in none of the principal countries, except Japan and the countries which experienced hyper-inflation, did short-term rates rule higher in the later war and early post-war years than in the pre-war quinquennium. It seems reasonable to conclude that, in general, short-term rates exerted little influence in this period on the course of events in countries where expenditure was subject to effective controls, because those controls, not difficulty in providing finance, were the limiting factor; while in countries which approached true hyper-inflation, the state of individual traders' expectations was such that no ordinary interest rate policy would have acted as an appreciable brake on purchases. The intermediate condition, in which ordinary variations in short-term interest rates might have exerted an appreciable effect on the policies of traders, because they were widely dependent upon short-term borrowings, and at the same time uninfluenced by expectations of price change or profit margins so large as to outweigh interest variations, probably occurred only very rarely, if at all, in this period. Perhaps it is not a very common condition even in less troubled times. Belgium, where the rate of interest was never really low, and the incentive to private investment never really high, is perhaps the country where interest rate was most effective.

This discussion seems to confirm the presumption mentioned at the outset—that the low level of interest rates during much of the inflationary period had very little direct effect upon private investment; they could not, in the presence of direct controls on expenditure or (occasionally) of credit-rationing policy, appreciably stimulate entrepreneurial activity. On the other hand, the existence of these low rates of interest certainly exerted some effect—varying from country to country—on the budgetary position, through the interest bill on the national debt.

The Budgetary Effect of Low Interest

Reductions in the average rates of interest paid on Government obligations in 1947 (or one of the preceding years) in comparison with the corresponding years after the First World War are certainly impressive. For the United Kingdom, for instance, the reduction was some 55 per cent., for the United

States 50 per cent., for Canada 48 per cent., for Australia 37 per cent., and for Czechoslovakia and the Netherlands 35 per cent. For those countries in which debt interest was highest in relation to national income—the United Kingdom, where it was 5·7 per cent. of it in 1947, Australia where it was 5·0 per cent., the Netherlands where it was 4·3 per cent., or Canada where it was 4·2 per cent.—it was a matter of some importance that the yield of the debt was less than it had been in, say, 1920. Had it been as high as in that year, the United Kingdom, for instance, would have had to raise an additional sum in taxation equal to some 7 per cent. of the national income (some £620 million) in order to avoid a larger budget deficit than that actually experienced. The raising of so much extra taxation would certainly have discouraged production in some degree, and so produced an indirect inflationary effect; failure to raise it would have had directly inflationary consequences. The difference would not have been as sensational as appears at first sight; income from debt interest is, of course, taxable; and taxable (in view of the economic position of its recipients) at a high average rate. Much more than half of any increase in debt interest in the United Kingdom would certainly have come back automatically to the exchequer without any increase in rates of taxation. Nevertheless, the circumstance that the average rate of interest on debt was so much less after the Second World War than after the first certainly assisted very materially in keeping down the inflationary influence of public finance.

In most countries not so far mentioned in this connexion, the interest on public debt after the war was too small in relation to national income to make a considerable contribution to inflation through budget deficits or otherwise. In the United States interest on public debt was only 2·5 per cent. of net national income in 1947; in Switzerland and Sweden only 2 per cent., in France and Denmark under 1 per cent. Broadly speaking, the governments which were most successful in curbing inflation in face of the pressure imposed by a total war effort emerged with a large public debt (in real terms) but, because their success in holding down private expenditure created high liquidity, were able to borrow at low rates of interest. Those which were less successful in checking inflation were obliged to borrow at higher rates, but the interest bill they thus accumu-

lated lost much of its weight as prices rose. The claims of the
rentier at no time became as great as they were in, for instance,
1922, when interest on Government debt rose to nearly 8 per
cent. of national income in the United Kingdom and perhaps
something like the same proportion in France. Despite the
generally more successful control of price inflation, the Second
World War was no less disastrous to rentiers, as a class, than the
first.

The Revival of Interest Policy

Everywhere, except in the rare cases where price inflation was
unrestrained, the phase of low interest, which had accompanied
high liquidity generally in the later war and early post-war
years, was succeeded by a rising of interest rates. This, as has
already been mentioned, was to be expected, in so far as governmental restrictions on expenditure were removed, or long-
cherished expectations of a greater availability of goods were
realized, or as world price levels rose owing to abolition of
controls elsewhere, so that the total expenditure of money rose,
and the increased need for active balances ate into the previously
accumulated stocks of idle funds, or holders of securities sold
them to buy currently-produced goods and services.

In a few countries—Portugal, Colombia, Belgium, and
Brazil—bond yields began to rise even before the end of the war,
in the Belgian case, understandably enough, with the currency
reform. In the United Kingdom, as has already been mentioned, they rose from the beginning of 1947, as money income
increased and the policy of disinflation replaced that which put
cheap money first; in the United States from 1946 (though the
rise there was slight). For most countries, indeed, the minimum
occurred in the first year or two after the end of the war, though
in a few it came later—1948 in Norway and South Africa, 1949
in Australia and New Zealand.

Apart from the modifications of cheap-money policy in the
United States and the United Kingdom, which have been
referred to, however, the raising of the long-term rate was not
often the object of deliberate state policy until after the outbreak of the Korean War. Short-term rates, being more directly
under official control, were occasionally used in efforts to
counter the post-war boom—notably in Belgium, France, and

Italy—though it seems probable that the quantitative restriction of credit which accompanied this policy was more important than the rise in the cost of borrowing. In any case, however, official policy was not so drastic as to raise the whole structure of short-term rates—and long-term rates, too—in any serious degree until after the Korean War had begun.

It is in any case likely that the Korean War would have exerted a very widespread effect in raising interest rates, quite apart from deliberate acts of monetary policy directed to that end. Unlike even the earliest phase of the Second World War, it did not involve such large budgetary burdens as to lead to deficit financing on a great scale, nor did it cause controls of expenditure to be greatly strengthened. On the other hand, it did bring about a very great temporary increase in commodity prices, followed in most countries by a considerable consequential increase in costs of living and wage rates. In some countries, notably the United States, real output rose. In general, therefore, the effect was to increase money incomes without bringing about a proportionate increase in the quantity of money, and consequently to increase the pressure of demand on the total monetary stock. This effect manifested itself in most countries in the second half of 1950 and during 1951.

If liquidity is measured, roughly, by the ratio of money supply to national income ('Cambridge K') for a number of countries, it must be admitted that the changes in liquidity between the end of 1949 and the end of 1951 so measured are very poorly correlated with the changes in either bond yield or short-term rates. Italy and Sweden, for instance, experienced rises both in liquidity and in interest rates, and France one of the largest increases in interest rates with no change in liquidity, while Belgium, Norway, and the Netherlands experienced very large reductions in liquidity with only small increases in interest rates. Clearly, there were wide differences between countries in regard to the way in which the attitude to securities and money changed in this period. Nevertheless, for a number of countries—the United States, the United Kingdom, Canada, Australia, South Africa, Denmark, and Switzerland—for which the relevant data are available, these two years witnessed increases of one-third to two-thirds of 1 per cent. in the bond yield accompanying a reduction in the ratio of money supply to national income of from 2 to 6 per cent. (of income).

At the same time, there were changes in official policy towards interest rates. The earlier modification of the extreme cheap money policies in the United States and the United Kingdom have already been referred to; after the beginning of the Korean War, much more substantial and widespread measures were taken. In the United States the degree of continuous support to the market for Government bonds was greatly reduced in March 1951, with the result that the yield showed considerably greater month-to-month variations, and a net rise of from a quarter to a half of 1 per cent. thereafter. In August 1950 the official New York discount rate had been raised by 0·25 per cent. In the United Kingdom the Bank Rate was raised to 2·5 per cent. in November 1951, and to 4 per cent. in March 1952, the Treasury Bill rate was allowed to rise to over 2 per cent., and the effective rates for bank overdrafts and public works loans were raised. During late 1950 or 1951, also, there were substantial rises of official discount rates in Austria, Germany, Canada, Bolivia, Belgium, Finland, France, India, Japan, the Netherlands, South Africa, and Sweden.

The principal motive for this widespread raising of interest rates, in so far as it was a deliberate act of policy, was, of course, a general desire to check the renewed price inflation of the time, powerfully reinforced in most European countries, as well as in South Africa, by concern at the balance of payments difficulties created by the violent fluctuation of primary commodity prices. Why interest policy was so much more widely resorted to for the purpose of checking inflation in this period than in the two previous bursts of inflation—the war and the post-war boom—is, however, a more complex question. To a large extent, the answer is connected with differences in the scope and effectiveness of non-monetary controls, especially price control, and in the budgetary situation. In the war, investment was limited by physical controls, and since these controls, along with price control, limited consumers' spending, there remained no task of limitation for interest rates to perform. Liquidity was raised and interest lowered as a by-product of comprehensive limitation of spending. In the post-war boom, these non-monetary controls of expenditure remained important in a number of countries, particularly the United Kingdom, though they were gradually being abandoned, or weakened, and the period 1948–50 witnessed an acceleration of the process. There was little disposition to reverse this trend in order to deal with an inflationary situation not connected with full-scale conversion of the economy to war purposes. The most relevant budgetary difference between the Korean War period and the earlier bursts of inflation was that, in the former, while expenditure was rising, there was reluctance to promote inflation by resorting to borrowing to finance the limited defence expenditure which was planned, while at the same time taxation was widely held to have reached the highest level compatible with the preservation of economic incentives in peacetime. Thus, it was not thought possible to raise taxation or run deficits without seriously adverse consequences, as in total war, nor to use budgetary surpluses as a disinflationary measure, as had been widely done in the post-war boom. The monetary weapon was one which could, at any rate, be used against inflation without obviously harmful consequences. Little net new government borrowing was going on in any important country, so that the budgetary effect of allowing or causing interest rates to rise was limited to the additional interest charges on short-term debt: for the United Kingdom, where this was a particularly important matter, an extra charge of some £50 or £60 million a year.

Moreover, there had been a certain change of intellectual fashion since the immediately post-war years. At that time, economic opinion in both the United States and the United Kingdom had been strongly influenced by the doctrine that interest rates, regarded as elements in cost, were not very important in the calculations of business men, since the period over which most physical capital is amortized is short, and since the existence of uncertainty concerning the yield of new investment, increasing sharply with the futurity of the yield in question, reinforces this consideration. Non-academic opinion had been influenced also by a less rational view, adverse to the use of interest rate for the control of the level of income, which gained its support, probably, from the twin considerations that high interest rates had been condemned for their deflationary effects in the late nineteen-twenties and early nineteen-thirties, while low interest rates had (especially in the United States) appeared ineffectual for promoting activity in the later nineteen-thirties. Moreover, interest rates had been unimportant as instruments of policy during the war.

Like most intellectual fashions, especially those which are widely followed somewhat unreflectively, with a disregard for even quite obvious qualifications which should hedge the doctrines concerned, this one was succeeded by a move in some quarters towards the opposite view. In many continental European countries, also, the disparagement of interest rates as instruments for the control of investment and income had never been fashionable. Thus, there was fairly widespread readiness to accept higher interest rates as anti-inflationary measures after mid-1950, though certain countries—notably Australia—were resistant to this tendency.

How far interest policy was effective in combating inflation in this period it is impossible to say with precision; too many parallel influences were at work. The evidence suggests, however, that little can be attributed to it. Fixed investment was not appreciably curtailed in any of the important countries except in certain instances where direct controls or shortage of materials due to the priority given to rearmament are mainly responsible. The United Kingdom, which between 1945 and 1951 experienced the steepest major rise of long-term rates it had ever witnessed in peacetime, clearly failed to benefit, or suffer, from any considerable diminution of the incentive to invest. The slump in consumers' goods industries which accompanied (or in some countries slightly preceded) the interest increases is traceable to a reaction from excessive speculative or precautionary buying in late 1950 and early 1951, and recovery from it was apparent in mid-1952, even in countries (like the United Kingdom) where interest rates were then higher than they had been for twenty years. Indeed, since in the countries where interest rates were raised to a high level the most interest-sensitive kinds of long-term investment, such as building, were generally under direct encouragement or control by the state, it is little wonder that no clear effect of higher interest on long-term investment as a whole can be discerned.

So far as short-term investment is concerned, it is possible to detect reductions of imports as, for instance, into Germany in the spring of 1951, following a stiffening of monetary policy, but slightly preceding the coming into effect of more severe quantitative import restrictions. Since, however, in such cases the monetary action in question involved direct restriction of credit, as well as an increase of its price, this experience does not necessarily indicate interest change as an effective instrument for reducing traders' demand. There remains, indeed, the strong presumption that it will not be effective for this purpose at a time when traders are influenced by expectations of considerable price movements, or of an impending tightening of quantitative import restrictions. On the other hand, it is sometimes argued that reductions in the prices of Government securities may have been effective in bringing about the reduction of bank credit, since they must have made banks reluctant to sell securities at a loss in order to make advances to customers. It is clear that reductions in the values of their principal assets render banks less able to lend; but so long as customers' loan rates rise in step with, and remain above, the yields of Government securities, banks are not likely to become more reluctant to shift from the less lucrative to the more lucrative type of asset, unless they differ from the market as a whole in being more optimistic about the future price of Government securities.

It is possible that the direct effects of rises in interest rates upon expectations in this period were of some importance, as they more probably had been in the Italian monetary action at the end of 1947. A raising of interest rates is regarded in many quarters as a gesture marking the inception of a more stringent monetary policy, even when the effective limitation of credit is carried out by more sparing allocation to borrowers without any necessity of direct action in regard to rates of interest. It is true that more sparing allocation of credit is itself likely to raise rates, especially the yields of marketable securities, as such securities are sold by frustrated would-be borrowers, but that is an effect of the quantitative control of credit, not an instance of the use of interest rates to restrict borrowing.

In general, therefore, the raising of interest rates at a certain stage in the process of world-wide inflation has not provided any tangible evidence that interest rates are effective instruments for the control of the inflationary process. The presumption remains that, when there are reasons for expecting substantial price movements, or when stocks of goods are out of line with expected sales, as is most often the case in an inflationary period, interest is of little account as a cost, though interest movements may exert some direct effect upon expectations. It seems that the most substantial effects of monetary policy were those connected directly with the supply of spending power. The discussion of this demands a new chapter.

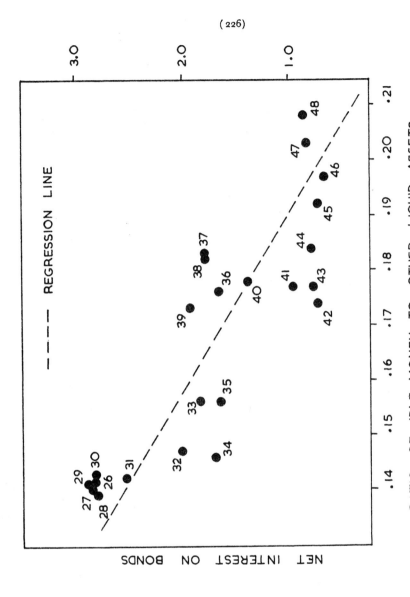

RATIO OF IDLE MONEY TO OTHER LIQUID ASSETS

NET INTEREST ON BONDS

- - - - REGRESSION LINE

DIAGRAM 27. Ratio of idle money to other liquid assets and net interest on bonds, 1926–48:

10

Liquidity, Expenditure, and Output

Even though interest rates may have been unimportant in the mechanism of inflation—except, perhaps, in some countries through their influence on the size of the government's total interest bill—it does not follow that the general monetary condition, with which interest rates are closely connected, can be so easily dismissed. Indeed, the existence of a high level of liquidity, which has characterized most countries during most of the inflationary period, has probably a far better claim than the existence of low interest rates, which generally goes with it, to be regarded as a circumstance favouring income inflation. This thesis was suggested by replies to the Oxford Economists' Research Group in 1938 (see J. E. Meade and P. W. S. Andrews, *Oxford Economic Papers*, No. 1)[1] and has been supported by more recent United States evidence. Entrepreneurs' decisions to incur capital expenditure seem to be strongly influenced in many instances by their possession of liquid resources—a fact to which the imperfection of the new capital market, and the considerations pointed out by M. Kalecki[2] in enunciating his 'principle of increasing risk', no doubt contribute. The possession of liquid resources is probably an important influence also on the consumer's decision to buy durable goods, or, indeed, to indulge in other expenditure of a non-recurring kind. Liquidity is also asserted to have exercised an effect—in extreme cases a very important one—on the will to work or to organize production.

The Inflationary Effects of Liquidity

Where governmental control of expenditure is comprehensive and efficient, a high liquidity on the part of entrepreneurs and

---

[1] 'Summary of Replies to Questions on Effects of Interest Rates', *Oxford Economic Papers*, No. 1, Oct. 1938.
[2] *Essays in the Theory of Economic Fluctuations* (London, Allen & Unwin, 1939).

consumers will, naturally, be unable to influence their expenditure to any great extent—though it may influence their will to earn. It will, however, make the abandonment of direct controls hazardous. Where controls of expenditure are weak, or weakening, on the other hand, a high level of liquidity may well play an important part in bringing about income inflation.

It is, therefore, important to know what for this purpose constitutes a liquid position—what kinds of asset are to be reckoned in assessing it. There can be no doubt, in ordinary circumstances, of the supreme liquidity of money, which can be used in direct payment for goods and services, or the only slightly smaller liquidity of savings certificates and other quickly redeemable assets. Any form of personal wealth, however, is saleable with more or less difficulty and inconvenience and therefore, to its owner, is an indirect means of buying commodities. Which one distinguishes from the general body of privately-owned wealth as particularly liable to be regarded as liquid reserves is necessarily arbitrary. Short-term assets and bonds are, however, perhaps those which it is most reasonable so to distinguish. Most of these are liquid in the sense that the market for them is highly organized, and selling costs are not very great. The holder of assets, therefore, will make little distinction between his holdings of cash and of short-term assets and bonds, but probably a more radical distinction between his holdings of either of these and his holdings of equities or real property, in assessing his reserves available for expenditure in an inflationary period. The liquidity position of the community in so far as it affects the extent to which people will be tempted to spend, therefore, depends on the amount of bills and bonds in existence, almost as much as on the amount of money. It also depends, though to a much smaller extent, on the holdings of other, less liquid, kinds of asset.

The extent to which the community as a whole can obtain additional purchasing power by internal sales of non-monetary assets is, however, another matter. Every sale entails a purchase. If the seller acquires money which he can then spend on goods and services, the buyer has to part with this same money, which he thereby loses the power of so spending. The sale of the security is, therefore, inflationary—in the sense of tending to increase expenditure on goods and services—only in so far as the buyers of the assets concerned were less likely than the sellers to spend on goods and services. In other words, the existence of a quantity of non-monetary assets constitutes an inflationary threat in so far as there exist holders of idle money who can be persuaded to use it for asset purchases, thereby transferring it to active circulation.

The temptation which normally induces an investor to buy securities instead of holding idle money is a fall in the price (i.e. an increase in the yield) of the security. When a movement towards the realization of securities for financing expenditure sets in, security prices fall. The first effect of this is to diminish the amount of money which can be obtained by realization; the price fall clearly has, indeed, to be such as to limit the amount of money obtainable by realization to the amount which holders of idle funds can be induced to give up. The desire to realize securities will also be diminished by the fall in their price, if the holders think there is any prospect of a subsequent recovery. In some circumstances they may not believe this, but may take the incipient fall in security prices as a signal to realize before they fall further. In this case the rush to realize will be great, but the fall in their prices will be correspondingly drastic.

If the holders of idle money form the same beliefs as the security holders about the future of security prices, the volume of sales, arising from speculative motives, is likely to be small; if both think prices are going to recover, security holders will be unwilling to sell, while if both think they are going to fall further, money holders will be unwilling to buy. The amount of securities realized for speculative reasons and the price obtained for them will both be high only if security holders' estimates of the future level of security prices fall relatively to the estimates formed by holders of idle money. This would suggest that opinion had become more homogeneous, since people who are already holding securities are likely to have acquired them (in preference to money) because they have been relatively optimistic about their prices, while those who have, in the past, kept money instead of securities have presumably been more pessimistic than the average about security prices. Such a change of mind may, of course, happen; but it is hard to point to any systematic cause which is likely to bring it about. In assessing the inflationary potential of a situation, it must simply be treated as a possible accident, to which a certain degree of probability must be assigned. Beyond this, all that can be said is that more money will be obtained by intending spenders through realization of their non-monetary assets if security prices are well maintained (or if they are expected to be well maintained) than if they fall heavily. This analysis of the conditions governing the voluntary realization of securities and its effect upon their prices should not be allowed to obscure the fact that all security markets receive a more or less constant stream of selling orders which are not in this sense voluntary—largely realizations of estates to pay death duties. This, however, does not affect the essential points about the relation between liquidity and expenditure.

These considerations may perhaps serve to make clearer the inflationary nature of high liquidity. In so far as there was an abnormally large amount of idle money in existence after the war, it meant both that the holders of that money were in a position to overspend their incomes, and were likely to be tempted to do so when controls permitted, and that holders of liquid securities were likely to be able to obtain a large amount of money for expenditure on goods and services by realizing their securities. In so far as there were abnormally large holdings of liquid securities, it was probable that a great many people would be tempted to indulge in heavy spending by the strength of their liquid reserves, though how far their realization of their securities for this purpose would increase the total amount of expenditure on goods and services in the community would depend on the amount of idle money in existence and the nature of expectations with regard to bond prices. An abnormally large amount of liquid securities would also increase the ease with which new credit could be raised, provided that the banks' policies and the state of their reserves allowed this.

The Liquidity Position

It is therefore necessary, in assessing the changes in liquidity during the inflationary period, to look not only at the position in regard to money, but at that in regard to other liquid assets as well. This is attempted for a number of countries in Tables I and II. In the former of these the change in the money value of the national income is first shown in index number form between 1938 and three later years—1946 (or occasionally some other year, chosen as having been the year of greatest liquidity), 1948, and 1951. Next, the corresponding changes in the amounts of means of payment (cash and deposits on current account) are similarly shown; then changes in the total amount of money, including deposit accounts, but excluding blocked accounts; then changes in the last-mentioned total *plus* the total amount of internal public debt outside the banks; and, finally, changes in this *plus* other liquid assets. The inclusion of non-governmental debt may be questioned, since its existence implies a corresponding liability, which might tend to inhibit spending by the debtors, just as it encourages and facilitates it on the part of creditors. It seems unlikely, however, that the expansionary influence of such assets will be completely offset in this way—in times of high confidence at least—and an attempt is made to include them here.

The estimation of these other liquid assets is, in most cases, a task which would require considerable research, and might even then prove to be impossible to accomplish with precision. For the United States, estimates of total debt exist, and from these it is possible to construct the relevant total for 1938—debts of corporations, consumers' credit, and the surrender value of insurance policies. It seems legitimate for the purpose of a very rough estimate to assess the corresponding figure for other countries on the basis of national income, bearing in mind the probable variation from country to country in the relation between the two. The change in the par value of non-governmental debt between 1938 and the later years can, again, be easily obtained with accuracy only for the United States. For the United Kingdom the change must have been very small, the increase in company debt and surrender value of insurance policies being mainly offset by the decline in holdings of foreign bonds. For other countries some guess may be made at the general order of magnitude of the change; in every case it can only have been small in relation to the changes in amounts of other liquid assets for which more accurate data are available, so that the crudity of this particular estimate should not invalidate the final estimate of the order of change in all liquid assets together.

Strictly speaking, debt should, no doubt, be valued at its

market price for this purpose, rather than at par. This refinement, however, has been omitted from the present estimates. In so far as a good deal of the debt in question is short-term, the importance of this omission is reduced to an extent which only a detailed estimate would reveal. The results may, therefore, be taken as a guide in the following discussion, though it is clear that their reliability declines a great deal in the more inclusive right-hand columns of the tables.

In Table II, the amounts of the total liquid assets, variously defined in the ways explained above, have been related to the national income for the appropriate year, the ratio which existed in 1938 again being taken as 100. From this, the following facts emerge.

First, the end of the war was a time of very high liquidity in general, no matter how liquidity is measured. If regard is had only to means of payment, every country for which data are given here was substantially more liquid than before the war, with the exception of France. In some of the German-occupied countries—Belgium, Norway, and the Netherlands—the quantity of means of payment was several times as great in relation to national income as before the war; but some other countries which had operated effective controls on expenditure—the United Kingdom, Australia, and New Zealand—were twice as liquid in this sense as in 1938, or not much less. Japan, just before the end of the war, and the United States, shortly after it, showed the same effect, though in a smaller degree; while in some of the other countries—Sweden, Argentina, and Switzerland—the moderately enhanced degree of monetary liquidity is to be attributed, perhaps, mainly to the difficulty of finding imports on which to spend, coupled with an expectation that it would be easier to do this later on.

By 1948 the degree of monetary liquidity had nearly everywhere diminished. In the countries which had been most liquid a few years earlier—Norway, Belgium, Germany, the Netherlands—there had in the meantime been monetary reforms of one kind or another, involving the blocking or extinction of part of the money supply. On the other hand, the increase of money income had, in most cases, been the main agent in this process. In France and Japan it had chiefly been responsible for bringing holdings of the means of payment down to a substantially lower level in relation to income (and, presumably, to transactions) than had ruled before the war. In Switzerland and the United States, with restrictions on expenditure mainly removed, liquidity in this sense was back almost exactly to the pre-war level. On the whole, nevertheless, the picture in 1948 was still one of higher holdings of the means of payment in relation to income than before the war. Norway, Denmark, New Zealand, Australia, Argentina, Sweden, Austria, and the United Kingdom, with quite widely varying degrees of restriction on expenditure in force, all display this change in a marked degree. Even Italy, for all her recent experience of severe inflation, had larger stocks of the means of payment, in relation to income, in 1948 than ten years earlier.

The diminution of monetary liquidity continued in most countries between 1948 and 1951; the only country among those included in the table in which there was a considerable increase being Australia, though there was little change in the ratio of means of payment to national income in Switzerland or Argentina. For the most part, the decreases in monetary liquidity in the sense in which the term is here used were brought about by increases in the money value of the national income rather than by reductions in the absolute amount of means of payment, though, again, there were exceptions—the reduction of the very large surplus of money in Norway continued, and there were smaller reductions in Denmark and the Netherlands, despite very substantial income increases. The result of these changes was that monetary liquidity was, by 1951, less than before the war in the United States, Italy, the Netherlands, and Denmark, as well as in Germany, Japan, France, and Belgium, where it had already fallen below the pre-war level in 1948. In Austria and Switzerland liquidity in this sense was only a little above pre-war; in Sweden moderately above. On the other hand, the United Kingdom, New Zealand, Argentina, Norway, and Australia might be classed together as being (in ascending order) very substantially more liquid in regard to means of payment than in 1938. It is, no doubt, significant that these countries include the two (the United Kingdom and Norway) which retained the greatest measure of rationing, and the three which had recently undergone the most pronounced booms, arising mainly from large increases in demand for their exports

—that is to say, the countries in which expenditure was still most subject to direct checks, and those in which the incomes of consumers were increasing most rapidly, such additional income being apt to seek an outlet largely in expenditure on imports which were still somewhat scarce.

Although much attention has been given to the amount of means of payment in surveys of the monetary situation, however, it is clear that this quantity is for many purposes less significant than the total amount of money, including deposit accounts (time deposits). In some countries the latter are unimportant, or non-existent; but in many the transfer of funds between them and current account is a matter of very considerable importance. In general, the distribution of funds between these two categories is probably sensitive to interest rates; certainly such sensitivity can be demonstrated for the United Kingdom in the inter-war years. It is not surprising, therefore, that, in a period of generally falling interest rates, time deposits have nearly everywhere increased less than demand deposits. For the period between 1938 and the end of the war, this was the case in all the countries included in the table except Switzerland and Belgium, in both of which time deposits are quantitatively unimportant. The relative decline of demand deposits was most striking in Norway, Denmark, and New Zealand, where the falls in interest rates over the relevant period were among the largest. In Norway, indeed, liquidity, which appears to have been almost sextupled during the war, if one looks at the supply of means of payment, was only doubled if one includes time deposits as well. Nevertheless, every one of the countries investigated seems to have been more liquid (in this total monetary sense) at the end of the war than in 1938.

For the whole decade 1938-48, also, the picture is much modified if one includes time deposits in the reckoning. In regard to total money, Italian liquidity was less in 1948 than ten years earlier; in Sweden and the Netherlands almost down to the pre-war level, and in the United States below it. In a number of countries, however—the United Kingdom, Norway, New Zealand, Denmark, and Argentina—total money was about one-third or one-quarter greater in relation to national income than ten years before. By 1951 the total money supply was substantially higher than before the war, in relation to national income, only (among the countries covered in the Tables) in the United Kingdom and (to a smaller extent) in Norway. In all the countries under discussion it again showed a smaller proportionate increase than that part of it which could be regarded as immediately available as a means of payment. Where means of payment were becoming scarce in relation to income, there was, of course, pressure to hold bank deposits in the most liquid form, ready for transactions, while where monetary liquidity was still high there was (until the very end of the period) still very little incentive in the form of interest to tempt funds from current into deposit accounts.

Taking the amount of public debt held outside banks into the reckoning has sharply divergent effects in different countries. Those which were involved in prolonged deficit spending—the United Kingdom, the United States, Germany, Japan, Australia, and New Zealand—had their liquidity greatly increased during the war by the accumulation of debt; but those which began with substantial public debts, not greatly increased during the war, and underwent heavy price inflation—Belgium, France, the Netherlands—had their liquidity reduced as income grew faster than debt. The continued growth of income after the war, and the reduction (in most cases) of public deficits as a proportion of income, brought about a marked diminution of liquidity, regarded as the ratio of money and public debt to national income, between the end of the war and 1948. Nevertheless, liquidity so measured was, in 1948, very markedly higher than ten years earlier in every country listed except France, Japan, and Italy, where severe inflation had dwarfed the formerly large public debt, and Western Germany, where monetary reform had wiped out nine-tenths of it. The income inflation of 1948–51, usually unaccompanied by substantial growth of public debt, served, however, to bring about very considerable reductions in the ratio of money *plus* public debt to national income in all the countries except Italy and France, which were still running appreciable deficits.

Taking other liquid assets very tentatively into account in assessing total liquidity has everywhere the effect of diminishing the wartime increase, and, indeed, the increase over the whole period. Non-governmental debt nowhere increased during the war as much, proportionately, as money income. The margins of error in these estimates are large; it seems, however, that at the end of the war, liquidity in this global sense must have been about double pre-war in Belgium and the Netherlands (before monetary reform) and considerably, but less remarkably, in excess in the United Kingdom, Norway, Japan, and Australia. By 1948, however, the scene was very much changed. In the countries which underwent large post-war inflations— France, Italy, and Japan—total liquidity so assessed was, not surprisingly, only one-third or one-fifth of pre-war, and in Germany the currency reform had reduced it to perhaps half of what it had been in 1938. In all the other countries, however, it stood remarkably close to the pre-war level, with a general tendency to be, on the whole, somewhat below it. By 1951 it was below pre-war in every one of the countries here investigated. It could no longer be said that expenditure was augmented, or production hindered, in any of these countries by an excess of liquid claims in this broadest sense.

Can the liquidity positions assessed in these various ways be connected as causes with the course of events in the economies? In order to do so, it is probably necessary to pay attention both to total liquid assets and to the quantity of money. It is plain that, at the end of the war, nearly all the economies considered had unusually high levels of monetary liquidity, or of total liquidity, or of both. The one exception is France. This highly liquid condition (where not subsequently removed by monetary reforms, as in Belgium) certainly served to facilitate price inflation in many countries in the following two or three years. The example of France, where there was very heavy price inflation despite an initial position of sub-normal liquidity, shows, however, that high liquidity is not a necessary condition for such a process; indeed, the moderate or low level of liquidity in France was probably itself a symptom of a state of expectations favourable to inflation, which the imperfectly suppressed inflation of the war period had created.

By 1948 monetary liquidity was still generally above pre-war, but total liquidity generally below. Can one connect this state of affairs with the widespread halt of price inflation in that year, or soon afterwards? The countries where there was a definite recession of economic activity—the United States, Belgium, Germany, and Italy—certainly show both monetary and total liquidity below the pre-war level, while the countries which were still, by both tests taken together, on the whole above the pre-war level of liquidity—the United Kingdom, Norway, Australia, New Zealand—had no recession of activity and continued to experience some price inflation. One has, however, still to note that France and Japan were sufficiently under the influence of an attitude towards money induced by hyper-inflation, or a near approach to it, to be very illiquid without any check to economic activity; though in both open inflation was being brought to an end. By 1951, as already noted, total liquidity was everywhere below pre-war, and monetary liquidity more often below than above; though it was far above in Australia and appreciably above in the United Kingdom. Excess liquidity, except in Australia, can hardly have been an important influence by this time. Clearly, however, to connect the state of liquidity at all closely with the inflationary or deflationary tendencies of the time, a much more detailed exa-mination of its mode of influence on the economy would be needed.

Liquidity and Expenditure

In so far as the liquidity position is abnormal, it may be expected to influence both personal expenditure on consumers' goods and services and private investment expenditure. The latter has, in most countries, been so much influenced by other factors (especially public control, shortage of capital goods, and expectations concerning prices) that it would not appear to be profitable to trace a systematic relation between it and the liquidity position. In the more extreme cases of shortage of liquidity, however, the effects on certain kinds of investment have been clearly decisive. Thus, the cessation of open inflation in Italy and France in 1947 and 1948 respectively, and the recessions of activity in Belgium and Germany in 1948 seem to have been ascribable in some degree to credit policy, operating in situations where liquidity was so low that bank credit was more than usually important. Credit restrictions were very widely effective in some degree in 1951, when liquidity in most countries had sunk to, or below, normal pre-war levels.

The activity which seems to have been hit hardest by credit restrictions in France and Italy in 1947-8 and to have turned the scale against continued inflation by its cessation was the accumulation of stocks of commodities. Statistics are, unfortunately, not available for the later years, but it seems that inventories were being accumulated rapidly in France in 1946 and less rapidly in 1947. In view of the great rise in prices in 1947–8, the financial burden even of maintaining stocks in those years must have been heavy. Bank credits to the economy almost quadrupled between the end of 1945 and the end of 1947, chiefly under the head of 'loans and advances'. Meanwhile, the control of credit had been centralized and tightened; in 1947 the granting of further credit for the purchase of real estate, equities, and interests in existing business was prohibited, and in September 1948 the general supply of credit was limited by putting a ceiling on the commercial banks' ability to raise reserves by rediscounting with the Bank of France, and fixing minimum ratios in terms of cash, short-term securities, and long-term public securities. With the total supply of liquid assets in the economy already little more than a quarter of its pre-war size, both in purchasing power and in relation to the national income, this restriction seems to have been effective in bringing about a certain unloading of stocks on to the market, and a reversal of the general expectations of price increase which had developed in the preceding years.

In Italy the course of events was similar, though earlier; a restriction of credit reversing expectations at the end of 1947. There total liquid assets had become fully as small both in purchasing power and in relation to national income as was the case in France, and the degree of control which the banks were able to exercise over stock-holdings in particular was unusually great. In Belgium, too, credit stringency has been important. Both total and monetary liquidity were, apparently, not much less than before the war, but idle money seems to have been held in hoards from which it was not easily to be dislodged; and after the wartime backlogs of consumers' demand were mainly worked off, the incentive to invest was not sufficient to tempt industrialists to borrow extensively at the banks' rate for advances of 6·5 per cent. The German situation, after the monetary reform of mid-1948, was another one in which a general background of illiquidity contributed to the effectiveness of a restrictive monetary policy. Both total liquid assets (including the remains of the Reich debt) and total money alone at the end of 1948 were perhaps only half as great, in relation to national income, as they had been ten years earlier; so that the restriction of new credits and the raising of banks' reserve requirements in October of that year had a powerful effect.

The less liquid situation existing generally during the Korean War was clearly a factor making for the effectiveness of the further reductions in liquidity which were imposed in many countries at that time by direct restrictions of credit. Measures of this kind were taken with some vigour in the United Kingdom in 1951–2, as they had been in the Netherlands in the spring of 1951, and with varying degrees of severity at about the same time in Germany, France, Austria, Belgium, and Denmark. The immediate occasion of these restrictions in most cases was a debit balance in the external payments, due to worsening terms of trade and, in some cases, to an increase in the volume of imports in order to raise commodity stocks in the countries concerned. Where the accumulation of stocks of imported goods was an important source of the disequilibrium, and where the government was not sponsoring this accumulation, credit restriction appears to have had considerable immediate, short-term effect. Some relation between credit restriction and improvement in the balance of payments is suggested by experience in, at least, Germany, Belgium, and the Netherlands during 1951, though it is not possible in all cases to disentangle the effect of credit restriction from that of direct measures of import curtailment.

With some exceptions, therefore, the connexion between liquidity and investment activity until near the end of the period under discussion is very loose, as one would expect from the number and power of the other factors bearing upon investment. On the other hand, with personal expenditure (for the post-war years, at all events) one might hope to find some closer relation. The task, however, is far from simple. To look simply at the percentage of personal income (after direct taxation) which is saved helps little, since this proportion also is affected by many factors, most notably rationing, and the size of the consumers' stocks, and the current availability of durable and semi-durable goods. It is also affected by the level of income, since the proportion of income that is saved is not necessarily—

perhaps not even probably—the same at different levels of income per head.

In many countries the rise of incomes, coupled with post-war shortages and restrictions, served to bring about a large increase in the percentage of personal expendable income saved. Thus, in the United States net saving of this kind was some 6·5 per cent. of expendable income in both 1946 and 1948 (to be contrasted with 1·5 per cent. in the recession year 1938), though it fell to less than 3 per cent. in 1947, when the largest part of the wartime backlogs was being wiped off. In Canada, New Zealand, and Australia the proportions of private expendable incomes saved have been still more consistently (and in Australia, until 1948, increasingly) higher than before the war. In France, the Netherlands, Norway, and the United Kingdom, where real income immediately after the war was less than before it, and where there were, also, very large backlogs of consumers' demand, the proportion of expendable income saved fell, after the war, below the 1938 level, though not to the same extent or at the same time. In Norway there was net personal dissaving from 1946 onwards, gradually decreasing as conditions improved and backlogs were wiped out. In the Netherlands the net savings of persons and corporations (the statistics do not permit the separation of the two groups) were higher than pre-war in 1946, presumably owing to controls and shortages, but became negative in 1948. In the United Kingdom personal saving and provision for stock appreciation was low in every post-war year; it seems to have risen somewhat from 1947 to 1950. In France the acceleration of price inflation may well have contributed to the discouragement of saving; it is surprising that it did not exercise a bigger effect in this direction. Total liquidity was decreasing in most of the countries mentioned throughout the post-war years; this should have made for an increase in saving, but such an effect is not regularly apparent. Nor is the change of liquidity as compared with pre-war correlated negatively, as one might expect, with changes in the average propensity to save.

Any effect of total liquidity on saving is hard to trace in this way, and the same is true if the effect of income changes is allowed for by considering deviations of the level of consumers' expenditure from the consumption function, as was done in

Chapter 3. Liquidity is, no doubt, a necessary condition for dissaving, since to overspend income it is necessary to have some reserves to draw upon, but it does not seem to be closely connected in any simple way with deviations from the income consumption schedule. To say that is not to deny that some systematic influence of total liquidity on consumption exists; it seems, however, that changes in the degree in which expenditure was controlled, in the size of consumers' stocks, and (in France, perhaps, particularly) in expectations of price change were sufficiently powerful influences to mask it. They are also, unfortunately, insufficiently measurable (or insufficiently measured) to permit their influence to be eliminated and any systematic influence of liquidity detected.

Liquidity and Incentives

The second major effect which has been imputed to liquidity is an effect on the will to work, or to bring about production. The crude statement of this effect is that, where people are already holding more money, or more liquid assets in general, than they normally would, having regard to the current volume of transactions, they are unlikely to be very willing to bestir themselves in order to add to their already excessive liquid stocks. This, however, is not a convincing statement, and the nature of the incentive to earn money income requires a little more discussion.

The reason why people take part in production, beyond the point where their thus taking part ceases to be in itself preferable to leisure, is presumably that the extra unpleasantness of doing so (as compared with enjoying leisure) is counterbalanced by the prospect of extra well-being and enjoyment to be derived from the extra money income earned. In a society where everyone could control his hours and intensity of work as he liked, it would be legitimate to presume an equality between the pleasantness for each person of avoiding a small amount of the work which he does (and enjoying a little more leisure instead) and the pleasure anticipated from the goods and services obtainable with the earnings from that small amount of work. In modern industrial society most people are not free to control their hours and intensity of work; the hours are apt to be prescribed—they can work eight hours a day or not at all—

and intensity of work may be a product of the decision of a group or team, or of the manager who sets the speed of the machines, or, in part, of the discipline which the management is able to enforce, rather than a matter of individual decision. Nevertheless, the strength of the incentive to produce can still affect production in a number of ways: through the size of the active labour force, the amount of absenteeism, the attitude taken by workers through their organizations towards overtime or the extra earning power obtainable by better methods and labour-saving machinery (which they will set against a natural conservatism and their fears of depriving themselves or their fellows of work), the attitude towards possible loss of earnings through dismissal for insufficiently quick or careful work, the strength of the demand for shorter working hours (where shorter hours mean less pay), the amount of trouble that the employer is willing to take to increase output or find markets, or the risk he is prepared to run in investing to provide himself with an uncertain future income. Within the money economy the purchasing power of the reward for extra effort can in all these ways exert an appreciable effect on the amount of effort expended in production.

The attractiveness of the monetary reward for extra effort will depend, in general, on three factors: how large the reward is after deduction of any taxation, &c. which may be levied upon it; the rate at which it is expected that it can be exchanged for goods and services of various degrees of futurity; and the amount of goods and services which the person concerned is already in a position to enjoy, without expending the extra unit of effort. The smaller the extra monetary reward (after taxation), the smaller the range and the higher the prices of the goods and services for which it can be employed, and the greater the supply of goods and services already available, without the extra earning, the less the inducing power of the reward will be.

A high level of liquidity, in itself, clearly has relatively little bearing on the inducing power of the money rewards offered for extra effort. If by a high level of liquidity is meant the existence of a large amount of highly marketable or redeemable assets, measured in terms of purchasing power, then all that is implied is that people are in a better position for going without the fruits of extra effort than would be the case if their assets were illiquid. This may be quite important, but, equally, the quantity of *liquid* assets may be less important in making people think they can manage without extra earnings than the quantity of *all* assets which they possess, whether liquid or not. In any case, although during the inflationary period the quantity of money (measured by its total purchasing power) was allowed to increase in many countries, it was only in a very few that there was a large and sustained increase in the total amount (similarly measured) even of those assets whose liquidity must be considered not far inferior to that of money.

What has a clear bearing on the incentive to produce is not so much an increase in the quantity of money, still less of all liquid assets; but a great reduction in the extra real benefits which extra money earnings would command. The increase in rates of taxation, and, more particularly, the increase in the steepness and range of progressive tax scales, contributed to this, but that is another matter; the relevant point here is that, under a comprehensive system of rationing and price control, earnings additional to those required to buy the standard rations could procure few extra real benefits, except in a more or less indefinite future. The existence of a black market, or a legal free market, could mitigate this position to a varying extent; but the high prices ruling in such markets made the purchasing power of marginal incomes very low, and the satisfaction of basic wants by the standard rations tended to render the utility of non-rationed goods low also.

That a high proportion of marginal income had inevitably to be saved would have reduced its value greatly even in a population which was accustomed to saving, and which had faith in the future value of the currency. Every community, however, contains plenty of people who are distrustful of any use of money except its immediate expenditure, while in Germany in particular it is unlikely that there was ever much faith in the long-term future value of money after capitulation, despite the high degree of success with which the prices of rationed goods continued to be controlled. In these circumstances—that is to say, with extra money receipts (beyond a certain point) of very little use for buying current goods and services, and with little belief in the utility of keeping money as a store of value—it was inevitable that there should be a decline in the acceptability of

R

money, which, like all general declines in confidence, became self-reinforcing. After this point was reached in Germany and (in a smaller degree) in Austria, it became, perhaps, inappropriate to speak of the situation as one of excessive liquidity; money, of which there was an excess, had largely lost its liquidity, and had become less liquid (that is to say, less generally acceptable) than many kinds of goods, such as cigarettes or coffee. Payment in money clearly had little power to tempt people to work in these conditions. Those who had no monetary reserves had to work for sufficient money to buy their rations; food additional to rations could be much more easily obtained by bartering household goods (where these could in any way be spared) than by accumulating the money necessary to buy it at the exceedingly high black-market prices which ruled. There was also a very strong incentive for industrial workers to pilfer manufactured goods, material, or fuel of kinds that could be bartered for food at the farms. People who had large holdings of money and/or goods for barter, whether legally or illegally obtained, could for a considerable time fare as well as those in regular work, by devoting their time to seeking bargains—to doing the work which a properly functioning monetary system, by virtue of the universal acceptability of money, very largely eliminates. Moreover, there was little incentive for entrepreneurs, in agriculture, manufacturing, or distribution, to market their goods through legal channels.

In this extreme state of affairs, which was reached in Germany and in a lesser degree in Austria, and perhaps approached in the Soviet Union, the root of the trouble was, to repeat, the low value set upon additional money earnings. The large stock of money (and other liquid assets) in existence was partly a symptom and partly a cause of this. It was a symptom in so far as it arose from the long-established restrictions on the spending of earnings above a certain low level, but a cause in so far as its existence prevented these restrictions from being relaxed without price inflation. In addition, it was a cause in that it lowered the acceptability of money still further than it would have been lowered by limitation of expenditure in the absence of the accumulation of liquid assets which, in fact, had followed from it.

Great changes in liquidity (however measured) can, no doubt, come about without there being any increase of restrictions on spending the income earned; in this case it is unlikely that they will exert much influence on the will to work. People may, for instance, voluntarily increase their savings and invest them in liquid securities for patriotic reasons, as they did to a considerable extent during the war, and from that development no substantial diminution in the incentive to work is to be expected. In the event, however, the relatively few great increases in total liquidity which took place in the inflationary period were associated with very stringent constraints on spending, so that, though increased liquidity is not necessarily connected with a situation in which the incentive to produce is weakened, it was, in fact, associated with such situations in the period under review.

The principal cases—Germany, Austria, and the Soviet Union—have already been mentioned. In all these cases the strength of the deterrent to production is to be measured by the extent of the improvement in output when monetary and other reforms were carried out. In the Soviet Union the reforms of December 1947 attacked the trouble at all points simultaneously. Restraints on spending (in the shape of rationing) were removed altogether; the multiple price system which had meant that the essential needs met by rations were satisfied at low prices, while other wants were satisfied at much higher prices (thus diminishing the marginal utility of earnings after rations had been provided for) was also abolished; reserves of purchasing power which would have made it impossible to abolish rationing without grave risk of a temporary, but possibly disastrous, maldistribution of necessities, were mopped up by a 90 per cent. levy on cash holdings, and levies of varying severity on holdings of state bonds and bank deposits.

Industrial production certainly made a spectacular advance after these reforms; it was 27 per cent. higher in 1948 than in 1947. How much of this can, in fact, be attributed to the reforms—as opposed to normal post-war recovery and the general buoyancy of industrial output in a rapidly industrializing country—is not so clear. Output in 1947 (the year before the reform) had been 22 per cent. greater than in 1946, and the improvement between 1948 and 1949 was still 20 per cent. Some of this later improvement may, of course, have been a delayed result of the reform; it is impossible to assess it from a mere inspection of the available statistics.

The West German reforms are easier to assess, since more information is available about them. The currency reform of June 1948, whereby virtually nine-tenths of all liquid assets were written off, preceded the abolition of rationing of most commodities by some months, though it was closely followed by the removal of price control. The effects might, therefore, be expected to be more widely dispersed in time than in the U.S.S.R. At the same time, since the demonetization of money had gone very far in Germany, the scope for improvement due to the restoration of monetary incentives was very great. In fact the level of industrial production, which had been only 33 per cent. of 1938 in 1947, rose by 22 per cent. between the first and second halves of 1947, by 14 per cent. in the next half-year, then (immediately after the monetary reform) by 43 per cent. In the next half-year (i.e. between late 1948 and early 1949) the rise was 20 per cent.; between the first and second halves of 1949 (when deflationary pressure was predominant) only 13 per cent., and in the next half-year 11 per cent. There are strong indications, therefore, that in West Germany the currency reform itself—not the abolition of rationing of butter, tobacco, sweets, soap, and textiles during 1949, or of bread, meat, and coffee in March 1950—was responsible for the biggest spurt in production, and that this spurt was very great indeed—nearly 50 per cent. in six months. The immediate operation of it seems to have been due to the sudden bringing out for sale through the ordinary channels of a great variety of consumers' goods previously held in stock or disposed of sparingly or illegally. The spectacular increase was in output per head of those in work. Employment in industry increased only about 7 per cent. in the half-year that included the reform, an increase no greater than that in the corresponding interval a year earlier; and in 1949 it increased hardly at all. Indeed, the effect of the reform would have been more spectacular still if credit restriction in the year following it had not been so severe as to produce (in addition to the structural unemployment inevitable in Germany at that time) a good deal of general unemployment.

Germany and the Soviet Union were not the only countries in which high levels of liquidity at some time necessitated controls or threatened the economy with price inflation, and where measures were taken at some time to remove liquid assets. In Austria there were two currency reforms; one in November 1945 when the Reichsmark currency was exchanged for Austrian schillings, of which only a limited quantity were left unblocked, and a second in December 1947, preceded (in July) by an upward revision (by 50–60 per cent.) of all controlled wages and prices. The effect of this second reform on production was almost as drastic as that of the German reform six months later. The Belgian reform of 1944 took the form of an issue of new currency in amounts designed to bear the pre-war relation to the current national income, and the blocking of the very large amount of purchasing power represented by the remainder of the old currency. The Czechoslovak reform of a year later was of the same nature, except that it was accompanied (as the Austrian reform of 1947 was preceded) by a planned, or permitted, increase in prices. Both of these reforms were apparently effective in removing a very large excess of liquid assets which would have rendered either drastic controls of expenditure or severe price inflation inevitable if it had remained in existence; they, therefore, probably saved the countries in question either from something approaching hyper-inflation or from the demonetization of money which occurred in Germany and Austria. They came, however, too soon after the war, and are illuminated by insufficient data on production, for it to be possible to trace their effects on the incentive to produce directly, as can be done in some measure with the later reforms in other countries. The same is true of the much milder blocking operations which took place in 1945 in Denmark, the Netherlands, and Norway.

Can it be said that there is any general relation between the degree of liquidity (or the change in liquidity since before the war) and the level, or rate of improvement, of production? Apart from the extreme cases, where liquidity was first very greatly increased, and then very greatly diminished, with dramatic effects on output, no such relation seems to be traceable. Liquidity was greatest, as were restrictions on expenditure, at the end of the war, when output was limited largely, or mainly, by bottlenecks—shortages of particular materials or fuels, of transport services, or of manpower in particular occupations—

which varied in severity from one country to another, and largely masked any differences due to the failure of monetary incentives. The speed with which these bottlenecks were widened no doubt bore some relation to the efficacy of monetary incentives, but this relation is, again, hard to trace because of the varying, and not satisfactorily measurable, severity of the difficulties which had to be overcome. By the time that bottlenecks due to war-time mobilization and destruction had ceased to be the factors limiting output in the main economies (that is to say, by late 1947 or early 1948), the differences in liquidity, broadly inter-preted, were much reduced, except in the outstanding cases of Germany and those countries where there was, or had been, very severe price inflation. In so far as liquidity differences still existed, it does not seem that the level or rate of increase of productivity was correlated with them, or, indeed, with the severity of restrictions on expenditure. The United Kingdom, where liquidity was higher than before the war, and where there were still severe limitations on expenditure, had made a better recovery in output per person employed than Belgium, where there was lower liquidity and relatively little restriction, and, until 1949, was making faster progress in output per head; but this was not true of Norway, in many ways situated like the United Kingdom. France, where liquidity was very low and where rationing was mainly abolished during 1949, made very rapid progress, but reached the pre-war level of output per head only in that year. The rate of new investment was, in any case, probably as powerful a factor making for improvement of output per head as monetary incentive, and probably varied as much from country to country. The factors determining output and its rate of increase are too complex to allow the influence of high liquidity coupled with a low marginal utility of money income to be disentangled from the rest, save in the most extreme cases. It may at least be concluded from this, however, that, while high liquidity is a feature of a situation in which the incentive to produce for money is weakened by limitations on expenditure, the degree of weakening is no more than moderate unless the situation is such that the liquidity which constitutes part of it is very great indeed.

TABLE I. *Indices of Income and Assets (1938 = 100)*

	Year	National income	Means of payment	Total money (excluding blocked accounts, but including time deposits)	Total money plus public debt outside the banks	Total liquid assets (money and bonds)
U.K.	1946	175	302	256	307	225
	1948	208	312	268	298	223
	1951	240	326	277	308	233
U.S.A. . . .	1946	265	345	308	407	282
	1948	335	350	315	408	290
	1951	410	390	347	434	312
France . . .	1946	670	695	690	446	340
	1948	1,550	1,130	1,120	595	430
	1951	2,850	1,920	1,925	1,200	825
Germany . . .	1944	111	600	575	650	400?
Western Germany .	1948	67	48	30	52	35?
	1951	110	96	62	91	58?
Italy	1948	4,300	5,020	3,500	1,850	1,280
	1951	5,900	5,660	5,310	2,870	2,070
Japan	1944	300	..	438	552	415
	1948	10,000	8,200	4,500	2,900	1,800
	1951	26,300	14,600	10,400	6,800	4,450
Belgium . . .	1943	84	310	312	278	184
	1948	375	367	364	440	267
	1951	453	410	406	466	320
Netherlands . .	1944	80	355	..	205	163
	1948	260	289	..	340	240
	1951	345	287	..	. 360	255
Denmark . . .	1945	195	337	233	220	161
	1948	257	276	234	290	194
	1951	341	268	252	290	200
Norway . . .	1944	140	836	285	280	200
	1948	245	800	325	352	250
	1951	325	520	347	370	267
Sweden . . .	1946	177	260	202	259	175
	1948	211	287	218	253	187
	1951	303	342	300	313	215
Switzerland . .	1946	172	194	200	272	194
	1948	202	208	203	267	203
	1951	225	238	228	269	207
Austria (1937 = 100) .	1948	365	494	..	644	300
	1951	810	807	..	1,140	435
Australia . . .	1946	170	370	..	603	250
	1948	248	460	..	710	250
	1951	400	785	..	945	335
New Zealand . .	1946	189	345	229	298	193
	1948	215	397	297	325	210
	1951	345	513	370	345	228
Argentina . . .	1945	170	238	210	216	180
	1947	293	453	362	360	250
	1951	820	1,280	854	690	430

TABLE II. *Indices of Liquidity: Ratios of Assets to National Income*
(*1938 = 100*)

	Year	Means of payment	Total money (excluding blocked accounts, but including time deposits)	Total money plus public debt outside banks	Total liquid assets (money and bonds)
U.K.	1946	172	146	175	128
	1948	150	129	143	107
	1951	136	115	128	97
U.S.A.	1946	130	116	154	106
	1948	104	94	122	87
	1951	95	85	106	76
France	1946	104	103	66	51
	1948	73	72	38	28
	1951	67	67	42	29
Germany	1944	540	515	580	360?
Western Germany .	⎰ 1948	72	45	78	52?
	⎱ 1951	87	56	82	53?
Italy	1948	117	81	43	30
	1951	96	90	49	35
Japan	1944	..	146	184	138
	1948	82	45	29	18
	1951	55	40	26	17
Belgium	1943	370	372	331	219
	1948	98	97	118	71
	1951	91	90	103	71
Netherlands .	1944	443	..	256	203
	1948	111	..	131	92
	1951	83	..	104	74
Denmark	1945	173	120	113	83
	1948	107	91	113	75
	1951	79	74	85	59
Norway	1944	597	204	200	143
	1948	327	133	144	102
	1951	160	107	114	82
Sweden	1946	147	114	146	99
	1948	136	103	120	87
	1951	113	99	103	71
Switzerland .	1946	113	116	158	113
	1948	103	100	132	100
	1951	106	101	120	92
Austria (1937 = 100)	1948	135	..	177	82
	1951	100	..	140	54
Australia	1946	218	..	355	147
	1948	185	..	286	101
	1951	196	..	236	84
New Zealand	1946	183	121	158	102
	1948	185	138	151	98
	1951	149	107	100	66
Argentina	1945	140	123	127	106
	1947	155	123	123	85
	1951	156	103	84	52

11

International Aspects of Inflation

The International Spread of Inflation

IN spite of great international differences, which have been discussed in their various aspects in the preceding chapters, the inflation of the years 1939–51 was, in a broad sense, world-wide —no country escaped it. In many of the countries most dependent upon international trade, moreover, the degrees of inflation experienced were not very different, though the stresses from which in the first place inflation arose—notably the stresses of war—bore very diversely upon them. How did inflation spread between countries? Two of the main mechanisms have already been described in earlier chapters, but it will, perhaps, be useful to consider the whole question rather more systematically here.

A generation ago it would have been thought appropriate to attribute the international propagation of inflation to changes in balances of international payments leading to international flows of gold or foreign exchange, leading in turn to the expansion of credit and of money incomes and prices in the receiving countries. It could hardly be agreed now that this was by any means the whole story of the way in which international adjustments came about in, say, the years before the First World War (though it was certainly an important part of the story); with the great separation which has come to exist between changes in the foreign assets and in the domestic (or the total) assets of all the main central banking systems, this line of explanation has become wholly inappropriate. How far and how quickly credit policies have affected internal price levels in recent years is itself a debatable matter, as has already been seen; but credit policies have, in any case during most of the inflationary period, borne little relation to the sizes of the respective countries' international monetary reserves.

The more recent line of explanation, also depending upon changes in balances of payments, has been more direct. The countries in which inflation originated, through (say) budget deficits, bought more imports: other countries thus acquired favourable balances of payments which were thought of, not as occasioning inflows of monetary reserves (though they might well do so), but as constituting direct net additions to the total purchasing power for those countries' goods and services. So far as the war years are concerned, this approach to the spread of inflation has already been discussed in Chapter 3, where it was shown that it is far from explaining the whole of that spread. Latin-American prices, for instance, rose very considerably in the early months of the war, despite the falling off of European buying, and before United States buying had increased at all heavily; that is to say, at a time when the improvement of the foreign exchange position was a very small factor. Again, they rose substantially during the post-war boom (1946–8) at a time when foreign exchange reserves were being lost by nearly every Latin American country. At that time, no doubt, fixed investment was going on at a great rate in many of these countries and so generating internal inflationary pressure; this, however, is unlikely to furnish the whole explanation of the price increase.

In order to complete the explanation, indeed, we have to consider what happens within a country when the prices both of its imports and of its exports are raised by external agencies, even if their volumes are changed in such a way that no change is produced in its balance of payments. This problem has already been discussed in Chapter 5. It was pointed out there that the immediate result is likely to be that the importers will make losses and the exporters will make profits, and that the increased cost of imports and, perhaps, the increased internal prices of goods which are exportable, will percolate through the economy until the internal and external price levels are brought back to their old relation. This can come about without any change in the balance of payments at all, though, in practice, some alteration (most probably an improvement) is likely to come about in a country's balance of payments if the general price level in the rest of the world rises. A rise in a country's price level will, of course, normally require an increase in the quantity of active money, the basis for which would be supplied by an increase of its external assets if a favourable balance of payments accompanied the process of adjustment; but even in the absence of such a favourable balance, the necessary money may well be supplied internally by drafts upon idle funds or by the expansionary activity of a banking system which is accustomed to provide working capital in proportion to the 'needs of trade', regarding an increase in the current values of the goods financed as providing it with security for additional advances.

The most obvious mechanism by which external price changes can percolate through an economy is a system of pricing goods in general (in the first instance imported goods) in accordance with cost and of adjusting wages and other factor prices, directly or indirectly, to changes in costs of living. This piece of machinery, however, is clearly supplemented in practice by another, which tends to equalize throughout the world those prices which are formed immediately by the interplay of supply and demand in a market rather than by the policies of producers or sellers. It is, perhaps, most natural to picture this mechanism as involving heavy international movements of goods, brought about by the search for arbitrage. In so far as this picture is correct, balances of payments are, obviously, disturbed—the low-price country has a favourable balance as a result of speculative movements of goods from it to the high-price countries, and its price level is raised, not only through the increasing scarcity of the goods which are thus exported, but through the inflow of purchasing power. In so far, however, as there are genuine world markets for the goods in question (as there are for many primary commodities), large international movements of goods are not necessary to effect price equalization. The short-run demand schedules for commodities can hardly be regarded as stationary; they move about in accordance with changes in the expectations of the people in the market as to the course of prices in the future. If consumption of, say, wool in the United Kingdom is stimulated (and looks as if it is going to remain for some time at a higher level than in the immediate past), an upward movement of wool prices either in the United Kingdom or in Australia will not be delayed until physical stocks in the country in question are visibly reduced—the expectations and attitudes of dealers in all wool markets will be affected by the news and the expectation of better trade, and prices will harden at once throughout the world. Balances of payments will, of course, be affected eventually by the higher price of wool and (if the higher rate of consumption does, in fact, persist) by the drawing down of stocks in the producing countries, where holdings of money will be correspondingly augmented. The price of wool to domestic consumers in the producing countries, as well as for export, will, however, have been raised before these events. Moreover, it will still be raised even if, through an adventitious increase in imports or some other agency, all change in the balance of payments is avoided. And, unless the supply of money for purposes of active trade in these countries is completely rigid, the rise in the price of wool (or whatever other commodities are involved) will extend to finished goods. From there, in many circumstances, it will extend to wage rates.

What all this amounts to is that inflation spreads internationally by three methods: by international net transfers of purchasing power; by rises in costs of imports which were subsequently passed on into the prices of finished goods and, ultimately, of domestic factors of production; and by simultaneous movements of the prices of internationally tradeable goods in different countries. These three methods normally come into operation when there is an increase in real effective demand, leading to a price increase, in any part of the world. On the other hand, if there is merely an increase in factor prices leading to an increase in the prices of products in some part of the world, without any increase in real income (as, for instance, when full employment already exists there), or if prices are raised through the abandonment of price control in some area, then the mechanism may be expected to work somewhat differently. There is then no increase in aggregate real demand in the world, such as would justify expectations of higher prices in the commodity markets, though there is a presumption that demand will be deflected from the products of the inflating country to those of the rest of the world, which (if the inflating country is economically important) may exert an appreciable effect. There will also, as in the case where real demand is increased in the inflating country, be an inflationary effect elsewhere arising from the raising of the cost-determined prices of its exports.

The distinctions which have just been made between different mechanisms by which inflation may spread internationally are useful in analysing events at various stages in the period under review. It has already been pointed out that the price increases in some overseas countries (notably those of Latin America) in the early months of the war are more readily attributable to general changes in market expectations than to any net inflow of purchasing power or of monetary reserves. At the same time, the price increase in the United Kingdom and her European allies was to a large extent 'imported' rather than generated by the increase in internal demand or internal factor prices. The rise in real cost of imports, due to raised shipping and insurance rates caused by war risk, was apparently responsible for at least as large a part of the increase in British commodity prices, for instance, as was the demand-induced or expectation-induced increase in the f.o.b. prices of the same commodities. Devaluation of the sterling area currencies was responsible, through immediate adjustments in market quotations rather than through changes in demand and the impact of new purchasing power, for a further large part of the increase, but must, at the same time, have exercised an appreciable effect in limiting the inflationary impact of the war on, for instance, the Americas. In the middle and later years of the war, much more of the international spread of inflation is to be traced to the international flow of purchasing power. It was in these years that the United Kingdom was disinvesting abroad at an annual rate of over £600 million, while the United States in 1943 and 1944 made net imports of goods and services (excluding lend-lease exports) at an annual rate of more than $2,000 million, and Germany, from within the narrower confines of the area under her control, was making net exactions at a rate perhaps approaching £2,000 million a year. The pouring of about £1,000 million a year mainly into the rest of the New World by the United States and the United Kingdom alone was calculated to exert a powerful inflationary influence.

In the post-war boom, however, as has already been pointed out in regard to certain countries, almost the whole of the trading world outside North America had large deficits on current account. Although internal inflationary influences in many of the countries in question cannot be denied, it is equally impossible to deny the inflationary influence of the rise in the prices of dollar goods (and similar goods from other sources) consequent upon the removal of United States (and to some extent Canadian) price control. In the countries whose products were in any considerable degree in competition with North American primary products, in particular, inflation was induced by the immediate rise in the prices of those products consequent upon the unchaining of pent-up demand in North America. This increase in prices was financed, in general, either by new bank credit or, in some cases, by drawing upon purchasing power hitherto idle. Rather more slowly, it was induced in the countries importing North American goods, or goods competing with North American goods (that is to say, in nearly all countries) by the increased cost of imports, which, similarly financed, worked its way through their economies. In those countries where price control was still important (as it was in the United Kingdom, for instance), the extent to which price inflation was due to this rise in the world prices of goods imported was especially great in comparison with the extent to which it could be attributed to excessive domestic demand or other causes.

In the Korean War crisis of 1950-1, the mechanism by which inflation spread was different from that which operated three or four years earlier to the extent, largely, that price control was a much less important factor in the situation. The initiating cause was, of course, different: in large part it was stockpiling (mainly by the United States Government) but in large part, also, it was simply expectation of prolonged scarcity induced by fear of large-scale war. Both the stockpiling and the expectation-induced rise in the prices of primary products caused the countries exporting them to enjoy large surpluses on current account, which, in their mainly uncontrolled and fully employed economies, produced varying measures of inflation in the prices of finished goods, followed, as a rule, by inflation of factor prices. At the same time, the inflated prices of primary commodities brought about general increases in the costs of living and, through them, in wage rates, in the importing countries, despite the substantial deficits which many of these countries sustained in their balances of payments on current account.

The Role of Exchange Rates

It is not hard to see that an alteration in the external value of a country's currency should operate upon price levels in the rest of the world in exactly the same way as would a change in the general level of its factor prices, unaccompanied in the first instance by any change in its real income. A rise in the external value of its currency, for instance, will exercise an immediate effect in raising the market prices abroad of those primary commodities in which it does an important amount of international trade. A little later, the increased prices of the commodities so affected will push up the prices of finished goods into which they enter. Meanwhile, foreign goods will have been substituted to some extent for those of the country in question both within it and in the outside world, with the result, in all probability, that it will have acquired a net debit in its balance of external payments; that is to say, there will be a net withdrawal of purchasing power from the country itself and a net injection of it into other areas.

Changes in external values of currencies are thus important in promoting or combating inflationary tendencies in portions of the world economy, though for the world economy as a whole they are unlikely to produce any large net effects in either direction. In this respect they differ from changes in national or local price levels without exchange adjustment, which obviously constitute net changes in the general level of world prices—both in the sense that they affect any world average of national or regional price indices, and also in the more important sense that they tend to induce movements in the same direction in other countries. The local or regional importance of changes in external values of currencies in the inflationary period can now be briefly examined.

The effects of the devaluation of the sterling area currencies in September 1939 have already been remarked upon. It is, however, difficult to assess them at all precisely, because of the other important changes which occurred at about the same time—the increase in costs of transporting imports into the countries which devalued, and the changes in expectations consequent upon the outbreak of war. Wholesale prices in the United States, for instance, rose about 5 per cent. between August and November 1939, the cheapening of goods imported from the sterling area by the 14 per cent. devaluation of sterling notwithstanding. The impact of this cheapening on the general

wholesale price level of the huge and largely self-sufficient
American market would, in any case, not be very great, but
in the event it was completely swamped by the expectation-
induced rise in demand. In Canada, where the currency was
devalued by 10 per cent. in relation to the United States dollar,
the wholesale price index rose in the same period by some 11 per
cent.—that is to say, by appreciably less than the sum of the
United States price increase and the devaluation; possibly
because the Canadian economy was so much more dependent
than that of the United States upon trade with areas whose
currencies had been devalued still more, and in particular upon
export trade with which the war interfered. In Australia, New
Zealand, and South Africa the rise in wholesale prices was as
small as in the United States, or smaller, despite the devaluation
of their currencies by 14 per cent. Australian and New Zealand
prices, in particular, were subject to control or to the consequences of inter-governmental contracts even at this early
stage: nevertheless, uncontrolled prices also rose little—a reflection, no doubt, of the fact that the interference (or threatened
interference) of the war with the disposal of exports counterbalanced the increase in costs of dollar imports. The sharp rise
(17 per cent.) in the wholesale price index in Argentina seems
to have been attributable mainly to scarcity, or anticipated
scarcity, of imported materials and manufactured goods, normally obtained largely from Europe—the home-produced foodstuffs did not rise, or actually fell in price, owing to the closing
of some main export outlets for them.

When one takes account of the dependence of the United
Kingdom on its various main sources of imports, it seems reasonable to conjecture that, without any devaluation of sterling or
any rise in costs of shipping and insurance, the prices of British
imports would not have risen more than 5 or 10 per cent. in
these early months of war, and that the effect of devaluation
alone was to raise their prices by perhaps 5 or 7 per cent. The
full effect of freight and insurance increases would not be apparent so soon; a little later its contribution was probably greater
than that of either of the two factors just mentioned. It is
noteworthy that in Switzerland, where the currency was not
devalued at all, and in Sweden, in which it was devalued by
only some 5 per cent. in terms of the United States dollar, the

immediate price increase in the early period of the war was no less than in the United Kingdom—in Switzerland, indeed, considerably greater. The part which devaluation played in raising the price levels of the sterling area countries in 1939, therefore, seems to have been considerably less than that of other factors.

The events of 1949 provide a much better opportunity for observing the effects of devaluation upon prices, since the devaluation was not in this instance overshadowed by other influences. For this period, moreover, indices of unit value are available for the imports and exports of a considerable number of countries, so that it is relatively easy to study the effect of devaluation upon the prices of 'foreign trade goods', as well as upon those of commodities in general. The experiment was tried of plotting the ratios in which the price indices of imports into a number of countries changed between the second quarter of 1949 (the last before devaluation) and the second quarter of 1950 against the ratios of change in the United States dollar values of the corresponding countries' currencies. For the twenty countries for which the necessary data were available[1] there proved to be quite a high correlation between devaluation and change of import prices; a Pearsonian coefficient of -0.825 was obtained. Imperfection in the correlation is due, of course (apart from errors of measurement), to the different movements in dollar prices of different commodities, which entered to varying extents into the imports (or, rather, the import-price indices) of the different countries, and to the different sources from which their imports were predominantly drawn. The eight countries included (the United Kingdom, Norway, Sweden, Denmark, the Netherlands, Ireland, India, and Ceylon), which devalued their currencies by 30 per cent., experienced increases ranging from 5 to 15 per cent. in their import prices, the importers of primary products encountering larger increases than those of manufactures, though this may have been largely due to the fact that the importers of manufactures, India, Ceylon, and Ireland, took a very high proportion of their imports from the rest of the sterling area. The experiences of the

[1] Austria, Finland, the United Kingdom, Norway, Denmark, Sweden, France, the Netherlands, Ireland, India, Ceylon, Western Germany, Canada, Indochina, Switzerland, the United States, Belgium, Italy, Spain, and Turkey.

countries which devalued less than this, or not at all, were more diverse. In the United States, the price index of imports rose very slightly, despite the considerable proportion of them coming from devaluing countries; Belgium, Italy, Spain, Turkey, and Switzerland, with their higher dependence upon suppliers which had devalued more than they did, experienced considerable price reductions—in the case of Turkey, whose currency was not devalued, a reduction of nearly one-quarter. The general experience of this period was that relative changes in the values of currencies were reflected within six or nine months to the extent of some 60 or 70 per cent. in the relative prices of imports.

One would expect the international average level of import prices (in some sense) to be unaffected by devaluation of some currencies in relation to others, the countries which had devalued most finding their import prices raised in terms of their national currencies, and those which had devalued least finding them lowered. In fact, the months after devaluation were months of expanding demand in a number of important economies (in the main, those which had not devalued, because internal recessions of effective demand had recently increased rather than decreased their international reserves, and which were now recovering), so that the general trend of world prices was slightly upward. But that, it must be repeated, was a result of expanding total activity, and its connexion with devaluation, if any, was indirect.

The impact of devaluation upon relative export prices may be examined in a similar way. If world markets for exported goods were perfect (that is to say, if goods of the same class exported from different countries were perfect substitutes for each other), and if the devaluing and the non-devaluing countries (considered as two single groups) exported goods of the same types, then the export prices of devaluing and non-devaluing countries measured in a common currency (e.g. dollars) could never diverge. To say this is, clearly, the same as saying that, if measured in national currencies, prices of exports would rise in devaluing countries and fall in non-devaluing countries in such a way as to diverge to the precise extent of the devaluation. Exports and imports are, of course, the same goods looked at from different points of view, and this immediate (or almost immediate) equalization of export prices measured in any one currency, or full divergence of their prices measured in national currencies, would involve the equalization of import prices measured in any one currency, or the full divergence after devaluation of import prices measured in national currencies. Since it has been shown that in the six or nine months after the devaluation of 1949 only about two-thirds of this full divergence of national import price levels took place, it is clear that the equalization of export price levels, measured in dollars, must also have been incomplete. This, however (to repeat), can be tested directly: it can be done by plotting the changes in the dollar price levels of the exports of a number of countries between the second quarter of 1949 and the second quarter of 1950 against the corresponding changes in exchange rates. Again, the correlation between the two is imperfect; indeed, it is more so—the Pearsonian coefficient is only +·589 for the twenty countries studied. This can, probably, be attributed to the fact that, for a number of the countries concerned, exports are more narrowly specialized than imports, so that changes in the terms of trade between different types of goods are more likely to affect the relation between the average prices of the exports of two countries taken at random than to affect the relation between the average prices of their more varied imports. For all the countries taken together, it appears that relative changes in values of currencies were reflected as to about one-half in the relative dollar prices of their exports—that is to say, the average 'effectiveness' of the devaluation (in the sense defined by J. J. Polak and Dr. T. C. Chang)[1] was about one-half; rather more for the industrial countries, rather less for others.

This conclusion may appear to be at variance with that which was reached from the study of import prices—that relative changes in currency values were reflected in the (national

[1] International Monetary Fund, *Staff Papers*, vol. i, no. 1, Feb. 1950. It may perhaps be noted that this definition of 'effectiveness', which makes it always equal to zero if world markets for exports are perfect, is open to some objection. A devaluation which does not lower the price of the devaluing country's exports in relation to those of its competitors may still raise profit margins in the exporting industry in the devaluing country relatively both to those in home-market industries there and to competing industries elsewhere. In this case it is likely to be highly 'effective' in altering balances of payments in favour of the devaluing countries, despite the absence of a differential of selling price in their favour.

currency) prices of imports to the extent of about two-thirds. If the dollar prices of the international goods imported by the various countries in question, after changes in the relative values of currencies, moved back two-thirds of the way towards their relative position before devaluation (as this implies), how can it be that the relative changes in export prices were as much as half of the relative changes in currency values? The answer to this question must be sought in the imperfections of the world markets, and in the limited nature of the samples of international goods to which the available price statistics apply. We do not possess statistics for all countries, and the import and export price statistics do not refer to the same sample of goods. The available import price statistics probably relate more to primary commodities, in which there are genuine world markets, than do the export price statistics. The conclusion, at all events, seems to be that the devaluation of 1949 raised import prices to the devaluing countries by the greater part of the proportion in which the average prices of foreign currencies (appropriately weighted according to their trading importance) had risen, and raised also the home currency prices of exports, in the case of industrial countries by considerably less than half, and in primary producing countries by considerably more than half that proportion.

Foreign Exchanges and Hyper-Inflation

The effect of currency depreciation or devaluation in stimulating inflation may, in special circumstances, assume very great importance for a country; in the German inflation of the early nineteen-twenties, for instance, once public confidence in the value of money was thoroughly undermined, wage rates were fixed from week to week on the basis of the current (or even the expected) dollar exchange rate. Thus, the labour costs of production of German goods, in terms of dollars and other foreign currency, could not be cheapened by depreciation of the mark on the foreign exchanges. On those exchanges, the demand for marks was less than the supply of them, so that they did in fact depreciate; and, since this depreciation could not cheapen German goods to the foreigner, it could not help to redress the balance between the supply of and demand for marks. It therefore went on indefinitely, taking the German wage level and the whole price structure with it.

The essential conditions on which the working of this powerful inflationary mechanism depended were, first, the existence of a free foreign exchange market, in which the value of the mark was determined by supply and demand, and, secondly, the attribution of sufficient importance to this market by trade unionists and others within Germany to make them take its mark–dollar exchange rate as the basis of their wage demand.

Conditions corresponding to these have existed in hardly any country at any time during the inflations since 1939. From early in the Second World War—if not before—nearly all the principal countries adopted some form of exchange control; governments or central banks were constituted the only legal buyers and sellers of foreign currencies, and fixed their own prices. International trade and capital movements, moreover, on which the supply of and demand for currencies in the international market mainly depend, were subject to rigorous additional measures of direct control. Thus, exchange rates were very far from being sensitive to the fundamental disequilibrium between one country's prices or incomes and those prevailing elsewhere. Moreover, although black foreign exchange markets existed, the amount of business transacted in them was usually small in relation to the total volume of international transactions; prices in them were important only to relatively small groups of people, and were affected by all kinds of conditions and regulations in such a way as to render them quite unrepresentative of the equilibrium rates of exchange that would have ruled in completely free foreign exchange markets. Thus, while movements in these black market rates certainly reflect to a large extent the changes in speculators' expectations with regard to the future of prices, &c., there were few cases in the period under review where they can have exerted, in their turn, an important effect on the process of inflation within a country. Perhaps the one important case in which they did exercise such an influence was that of Italy, between March 1946, when exporters were allowed to dispose of half their foreign exchange receipts in a free market, and the reforms of November 1947, which so abated the internal inflationary forces that expectations with regard to both the internal and the external values of the lira were completely changed.

If the external value of the currency is to be regarded as setting the pace for the development of internal price inflation, the market price of foreign currency must, presumably, rise ahead (even if only very slightly ahead) of internal prices generally—unless there is reason to suppose that internal prices and wage rates are being deliberately adjusted to *anticipate* the fall in the external value of the currency. Bresciani-Turroni has shown[1] that in Germany prices of foreign goods (or of imports) converted into marks at the market rate of exchange rose at the end of 1919 to as much as three times the current prices of German goods, and thereafter were seldom less than one-and-a-half times as great as current German prices until hyper-inflation entered its last phase in the summer of 1923. Then the practice of fixing wage rates and prices in anticipation of the rise in the exchange rate, or rather of the index of mark prices of foreign goods, enabled German internal prices generally to keep up with the rise in the German price of the dollar (or of foreign goods).

In certain cases, something of the same kind can be seen in the more recent inflations. In Hungary, for instance, from the time when internal price data became available again in September 1945, they show internal retail prices less than half as high as United States wholesale prices converted into pengoes at the black market rate of exchange. This state of affairs seems to have continued until the last month of hyper-inflation (July 1946), when, despite the fact that the cost of living continued to rise by some 150 per cent. a day and that the official price of the dollar in terms of tax pengoes likewise continued to rise, the black market rate of exchange suffered a sharp reversal, presumably reflecting expectations of currency reform. In the third week of the month the pengoe equivalent (at black market rates) of United States prices was only about a thousandth of current internal prices. It seems likely, however, that this dramatic change merely reflected the highly sensitive state of expectations without itself playing any considerable part in the monetary developments of the time.

In post-war Rumania the lei price of foreign goods (converted

[1] *Economics of Inflation*, trs. by M. E. Sayers (London, Allen & Unwin, 1937).

at black market exchange rates) does not seem to have exceeded domestic prices consistently during the period of hyper-inflation. Its interest as a mirror of the state of expectations is considerably increased, however, by the fact that its relation to internal prices seems to have been connected with the latter's rate of increase. It rose to something like equality with the internal price level at the end of 1946, when the latter was doubled in three months; it fell well below it when the rate of price inflation subsequently slackened off, only to rise well above it again at the end of 1946 when prices began to double in each period of two months or less. In China the black market exchange rate was not such as to make United States goods appear dearer than Chinese until the first quarter of 1948, when, again, prices had begun to double regularly every two months or less.

France and Italy provide, however, more interesting material for study from this point of view, since both are more dependent on imports than the countries just surveyed, and probably also more 'foreign-exchange minded'. In France, however, the evidence is ambiguous. Converted at the official rate of exchange, the franc price of United States goods has never been higher, in relation to pre-war, than the internal French wholesale price index, though foreign prices did rise above French for a month or two after the devaluation of early 1948, if one performs the conversion at the legal free dollar rate of exchange then established. On the other hand, the price of American goods converted at the black market rate rose above the French domestic price in late 1945, and remained above it until May 1949, when domestic prices had been falling for some four months. The discrepancy, however, bears no clear relation to the rate at which prices were changing; when they were advancing most rapidly in late 1947, it was substantially less than had been the case in, for instance, December 1946. The French black market rate seems, indeed, to have reflected opinions based largely on political and other factors which did not visibly affect internal prices, though its persistence at a level higher than that corresponding to the internal price level throughout the three years of rapid inflation may have been a minor factor in pushing that inflation further.

In Italy, also, the price of United States goods converted into lire at the Rome free market rate of exchange remained above the price of Italian goods for a long period (see Diagram 28, p. 282). The fall in the foreign exchange rates in Italy was artificially hastened by official policy. From March 1946 (as has been mentioned above) exporters were allowed to dispose of half their foreign currency in a free market, the remaining half being taken over at the low commercial rate of 225 lire to the dollar. They therefore required higher lire prices for their dollars in the free market in order to render their transactions more worth while than would have been the case if they had been able to dispose of the whole proceeds of their export sales there; and at the same time the legalization of this large class of free market transactions in foreign exchange rendered the free prices important—large amounts of imports were bought with currency purchased at free rates. The new free market value of the lira actually fell below the illegal black market rate for some months in 1946. Bruno Foa, in his able study of this period,[1] states that the Italian public had become very fully aware of the foreign exchanges at this time, so that the psychological effect of the fall in the exchanges was a powerful one.

Between April 1946 and November 1947 the discrepancy between United States prices, converted at the black market rate, and Italian prices seems to have borne some relation to the rate of increase of the latter, rising up to the end of 1946, then falling for two months, and rising to an ultimate peak in May 1947. This peak anticipated the maximum point of wholesale prices in Italy by fully eight months; by the time that maximum point was reached, the black market rate had fallen to a level at which it remained fairly stable throughout 1948. Nevertheless, despite the stabilization of both the black market exchange rate and prices in 1948, the prices of American goods, converted at the black market rate, still stood considerably higher than those of Italian goods. The level at which the legal free rate was stabilized throughout 1948, however, was almost exactly in accordance with the relative purchasing powers of money (at wholesale) in Italy and the United States, whereas in the previous two years it had been some 20 per cent. above this purchasing-power parity. There is no way of measuring the extent to which the free and black market rates affected the

[1] *Monetary Reconstruction in Italy* (New York, King's Crown Press for the Carnegie Endowment for International Peace, 1949).

course of prices within Italy, but it is clear that, in so far as they did so, they exerted an inflationary influence from about July 1946 to about mid-1948. Thereafter, while the lira remained at a discount in the black market in relation to its purchasing-power parity against the dollar, it ceased to do so in the more important legal free market. Thus, in contrast with the experience of the early nineteen-twenties, foreign exchanges exerted little effect on the more spectacular inflations of the Second World War and its aftermath, though free or black market rates have occasional value as indicators of the course of expectations.

Exchange Rates, Purchasing-Power Parity, and Disequilibrium, 1937–48

Just as foreign exchange rates had little effect on the course of inflation in most countries during the period under survey, so also because of exchange control the course of inflation had, on the whole, little influence on foreign exchange markets, or, at all events, on foreign exchange markets of any importance. In the most spectacular cases of hyper-inflation—Greece in 1944 and Hungary in 1946—the episode was over and a new currency established without its being necessary to alter the official external price of the old currency. Elsewhere, where there was drastic currency reform without hyper-inflation, as in Belgium, Yugoslavia, and Czechoslovakia, rates were chosen for the new currencies which were somewhat, but not very much, lower than the pre-war parities of the old.

Nevertheless, by 1948 there were no important currencies in the world, except those of Canada, Sweden, Switzerland, Chile, and Salvador, which remained, even nominally, at the 1937 parity in relation to the United States dollar. The Swiss franc, the Swedish krona, and the Uruguayan peso stood at a premium in relation to their pre-war values; all other currencies except the Chilean peso, the Canadian dollar, and the colon, which were at parity, stood at discounts, which were more or less heavy, but in most cases not heavy enough to offset the changes in their internal purchasing powers in relation to that of the United States dollar.

Table VI shows for a number of countries the United States dollar value of the currency in 1948 as a percentage of its 1937 value, and, where possible, the levels, in terms of dollars, of wholesale prices, cost of living, earnings or rates in manufacturing industry, and export prices, all related to a 1937 base. Out of fifty-six countries listed (excluding the United States) the currencies of twenty-nine had depreciated in official dollar value by less than 20 per cent. (the sterling group had depreciated by 18 per cent.). Then came Spain, the Netherlands, Germany, Brazil, and Belgium with depreciations in the region of one-third; Austria, Czechoslovakia, Iran, Lebanon, Luxembourg, and Turkey with depreciations of about one-half. Beyond these again came Finland and Bulgaria (about two-thirds), France (seven-eighths), and, finally, Italy, Greece, Japan, and China with depreciations still more severe.

How far can one say in the light of these price and wage data that certain currencies were under- or over-valued in 1948? The limitations of a simple purchasing-power-parity theory in this instance are soon apparent; it provides, however, a convenient starting point for an examination of the situation. It is particularly interesting to look, in the light of these comparisons of price levels, at the situation as between the United States and the rest of the world, since it was there that the great disequilibrium in international payments most clearly lay at the end of the period under discussion.

So far as wage rates were concerned, the data are scanty and hard to compare, but the United States seems to have experienced a proportionate increase somewhat greater than the median for the countries for which information exists (the wages being, in every case, measured in dollars), and certainly greater than in the other main industrial countries except Japan, Italy, Sweden and, perhaps, Switzerland. As the Economic Commission for Europe[1] has pointed out, however, the advance in productivity in the United States between 1937 and 1948 was so much greater than in most countries as to bring dollar labour cost per unit of output down in relation to the world level—output per man-hour in United States manufacturing industry rose by some 18 per cent. between 1937 and 1948, whereas in the rest of the world as a whole it seems to have advanced very little. In United States agriculture and transport it rose even more, the overall increase in productivity being some 31 per cent.

[1] *Economic Survey of Europe in 1948*, ch. 5.

In regard to the general wholesale price index, the United States stood somewhat below the median value for the forty-eight countries for which entries are made in the Table; the United Kingdom stood some 13·5 per cent. lower. The situation was much the same in regard to cost of living indices; there also the United States stood considerably below the median for all the countries listed and the United Kingdom lower still—the official British cost of living index is misleading here, but the Central Statistical Office's price index for all goods and services consumed shows an increase (when converted into dollars) of some 48 per cent. between 1938 and 1948, which gives a figure for the latter year some 11·5 per cent. less than the United States consumers' price index in relation to the position in 1937.

When one comes to the prices of exports, data are available for thirty-two countries; the United States comes sixth from the bottom of the list (arranged in descending order of price increase) and some 25 per cent. below the median. The United Kingdom's (dollar) export price index had increased only a little more than this, and very markedly less than that of most European countries.

The question which immediately arises is how far disequilibrium in international payments in 1948 and in the post-war boom generally could be attributed to the fact that the prices of United States exports were considerably lower in relation to those of most other countries' exports than before the war? It is quite possible to investigate the relation between relative changes in the prices of goods exported from different countries and the relative changes in their volumes. One has only to plot indices of export volume in a given year, for a number of countries, against the corresponding indices of export prices; the base of all the index numbers being some convenient previous year. If the plotting is done on logarithmic scales (or if the logarithms of the indices are used) then, in the event of all the points falling near to a single negatively-inclined straight line, one could say that the exports of the different countries were equally substitutable for each other, and that the elasticity of substitution between them was given by the slope of the line in question. It is, of course, unlikely that all countries will fall on or near the same line, since their exports can be substituted for each other to widely varying extents—the agricultural exporters, for instance, are unlikely to conform to the same line as the industrial exporters, even if either group forms a line at all. The test, however, is well worth making.

The experiment may, indeed, be tried separately for each of the three years 1946, 1947, and 1948, the base-year in terms of which prices and volumes of exports are expressed being in each case 1937. Data were examined for sixteen countries for 1946, seventeen for 1947, and fourteen for 1948 (see Diagram 29, p. 283). When all the countries are considered together, the correlation between price changes and volume changes since the base year (measured logarithmically) is, as one might expect, non-significant. It is, perhaps, surprising that the correlations become significant if one omits three countries (Austria, Hungary, and the Netherlands) whose exports were abnormally low in this period for a variety of reasons, including the ruin of Germany, which had been their most important market. For 1947 and 1948, indeed, the omission of these countries renders the correlation between the price and volume changes in all the rest highly significant, the overall elasticity of substitution between their products being 1·3 for 1947 and 1·5 for 1948.

It seems more reasonable, however, to select a group of countries whose products seem likely *a priori* to be fairly closely competitive with each other—the United States, United Kingdom, Switzerland, Sweden, Czechoslovakia, and France. With this much smaller number of countries, significant correlations are obtained for 1946 and 1948, and an almost significant one for 1947. The elasticities of substitution for the three years are: 1946: 2·87, 1947: 2·53, 1948: 1·69. It is tempting to speculate on the decline in the elasticity of substitution which this implies. It seems to have been the case, however, that the countries with the smaller exports (in relation to pre-war) were handicapped in the earlier post-war years not only by the dearness of their goods, consequent upon inflation, but also by limitations of supply and delays in delivery which were not allowed to produce a full effect which scarcity might have exerted in raising price. Thus, as conditions of production improved, the relations between quantity and price probably moved nearer to equilibrium.

It is interesting in this connexion to look at some pre-war data. Professor W. A. Lewis in his book *Economic Survey 1919–39*[1] gives the indices of volume and gold price of exports in 1936–8, on a 1929 base, for the main industrial countries, namely Germany, Switzerland, France, the United Kingdom, United States, Italy, and Japan. The correlation between the logarithms of these indices proves to be highly significant, and the general elasticity of substitution to be 1·27. Whether this should be taken as suggesting that elasticity of substitution since the war has been genuinely higher than in the decade of stagnating and restricted trade preceding it, or that the dearer countries in 1948 were still exporting less than the equilibrium amounts which should have been associated with their prices, is a difficult question.

For 1947 it proves also to be worth looking at the six agricultural exporters for which data are available—Australia, Argentina, Turkey, Ceylon, Ireland, and Bulgaria. The correlation between the (logarithmically measured) changes in the volumes and dollar prices of their exports since 1937 is significant, and the general elasticity of substitution appears to have been almost exactly unity. Here, too, it seems likely that there was a departure from equilibrium, but in the opposite sense from that among the industrial countries: it was the cheaper countries which were out of line; Australian prices, in particular, being much lower than they might have been in view of the limited supplies available—they rose sharply in the following year without any marked reduction of export volume.

All this suggests that export prices were, in fact, of very considerable importance in determining the flow of exports in the three years of the post-war boom. While relative prices to a large extent determined the relative amounts of exports sent out from different countries, however, there were other quite different factors which helped to determine the amount of each country's imports. Not only did most countries limit their imports to a large extent, by direct controls; even where this was not done, it was frequently evident that the war had brought about structural changes which had affected the volume of imports more drastically than had changes in relative prices, or even changes in relative real incomes.

[1] London, Allen & Unwin, 1949.

The United States is, of course, far the most important and striking case of this. Dr. T. C. Chang[1] found that, for the interwar years, the volume of imports into the United States was very well expressed in terms of that country's real income and the ratio of import prices to its own general wholesale price index by the formula:

Imports are proportional to (real income)$^{1\cdot27}$
× (ratio of import prices to home prices)$^{-0\cdot97}$

In other words, the price elasticity of demand for imports (expressing the prices of imports in terms of United States goods) was about unity, while the real-income elasticity was slightly over 1¼. Now, between 1937 and 1948, United States real income rose by 70 per cent., while the price index of United States imports rose relatively to the wholesale price index by 14 per cent. According to Dr. Chang's formula, this should have caused the volume of imports to expand by 73 per cent. Actually, it rose by only 8 per cent.—that is to say, it was only 62 per cent. of what it might have been expected to be on the basis of pre-war experience.

To judge by balances of payments on current account, the United States dollar was most certainly under-valued in 1948; the net export surplus of goods and services amounted to 37 per cent. of the gross total exported. The fact that United States exports were perhaps 25 per cent. cheaper than those of other countries in general in relation to the pre-war position might be held to account for the fact that they were twice as great in volume as before the war (this would imply that the price elasticity of demand for them, measuring the price in terms of other countries' exports, was 2·4—a not impossible figure). If United States imports had come up to the level suggested by pre-war experience, however, the dollar gap would only have been about one-third of what it actually was, despite this cheapening of United States exports, and of certain other classes of United States goods in relation to the rest of the world.

It is pointed out above that United States factor prices, on the whole, rose rather more than those in the rest of the world (allowing for exchange rates) between 1937 and 1948. The

[1] 'International Comparison of Demand for Imports', *Review of Economic Studies*, vol. xiii (2), p. 64.

relative cheapening of United States exports was due to a relative increase in productivity. Even, however, if other countries had lowered their price levels relatively to those in North America to such an extent as to maintain their exports at the same prices relatively to United States exports as in 1937, there would still, in 1948, have been a dollar gap at least two-thirds as large as that actually recorded.

Greater self-sufficiency in the United States was thus apparently responsible for a far greater share of the world-wide dollar shortage than was the greater extent of price inflation in other parts of the world as compared with the United States. The increased degree of self-sufficiency at this time is not surprising. If one looks at the way in which the volume of United States imports varied with that country's real national income over the last generation, it becomes apparent that the volume of imports in the four years 1942–5 was some 30 per cent. less than might have been expected in view of the income levels then ruling, on the basis of the income–import relation in the years 1932–41. Such a prolonged necessity for dispensing with imports, especially at a time of great economic expansion, is certainly likely to produce structural developments consistent with increased self-sufficiency. Nevertheless, subsequent events suggest that the low level of imports in the period 1946–9 was due not only to such relatively permanent structural changes, but also in large measure to shortage of importable goods. Between the triennium 1947–9 and the triennium 1950–2, the volume of United States imports rose by no less than 24 per cent., despite a very substantial increase in their relative price as compared with United States products. This is a very large increase in relation to the simultaneous growth of 17 per cent. or so in the country's real income, and it seems reasonable to attribute it largely to the greater ease of supplies outside the United States which manifested itself also in the decay of the world-wide sellers' market.

It may be objected that scarcity of the goods which are importable into the United States should have raised their prices, thus bringing the price and quantity, considered together, into conformity with any formula, such as that of Dr. Chang, which has valid claims to represent an unchanging demand function; in other words, that the failure of the data for a subsequent period to fit such a formula is an indication of the demand conditions, as distinct from the supply conditions, having changed. This, however, is true only so long as prices are determined in the market in the same way as in the period for which the demand function was originally calculated. In the post-war years the prices of, at any rate, very many manufactured and semi-finished goods exported to the United States were probably fixed in relation to cost, or some other criterion, despite the fact that the same quantity could have been sold there at a higher price, or a larger quantity (if it had been available) at the price actually charged. Moreover, it seems likely that less strenuous and successful efforts were made to raise United States demand for imports by advertising and other arts of salesmanship at a time when supplies were in any case limited, than in the subsequent period when they became more plentiful. If this is so, then the limitation of supplies outside North America must be added to the list of reasons for international disequilibrium, other than the distortion of relative prices by inflation.

This raises the more general question whether inflation can have been responsible for the international disequilibrium of the post-war years through any mechanism other than a distortion of relative price levels not corrected by alterations of exchange rates. In a world of entirely market-determined prices and therefore of open inflations, this could hardly be so. When full employment is reached in a country, and effective demand continues to increase, equilibrium can be reached either by increasing imports or by bidding up the prices of home-produced goods; normally it will be achieved in both of these ways at once, the number of goods and the quantity of each which it pays to import (rather than to buy at home) rising as the prices of the home-made commodities rise. The worsening of the balance of payments (both from increased imports and from the absorption at home of resources formerly used for exporting) will thus be functionally related to the degree of price inflation at home, measured relatively to that abroad.

In the real world, as it existed after the war, however, matters were not so simple. Prices of very many goods were sticky in the face of rising demand, either because they were customarily fixed by the sellers in relation to cost or because they were officially controlled. In these circumstances, increases in effective demand after full employment was reached resulted, in the first instance, not in price increases, but in the quoting of distant delivery dates and the existence of unsatisfied demand, backed by liquid resources in the would-be buyers' hands. With free importation this would have meant that foreign goods were bought where they could be delivered earlier than home-made goods, even if the foreign goods were somewhat dearer; the premium which buyers were willing to pay varying, presumably, as a function of the difference between the delivery dates quoted by home and foreign suppliers. It would also have meant, presumably, a tendency to buy foreign goods which happened to be available, and to which home-produced goods or services (perhaps of quite different kinds) would have been preferred at the existing prices if they could have been freely purchased. The excess of what would be spent on home-produced goods and services at the ruling prices, if they were available in unlimited quantity, over the expenditure on them which their scarcity in fact permits, may be described as the 'inflationary gap' in the market for home-produced goods and services. In a situation where this 'inflationary gap' is preserved in being by the stickiness of prices, therefore, and where there is free importation, one may say that imports may be expected to increase as a function of the gap.

In a similar way, if exporting is entirely left to private enterprise, the existence of an 'inflationary gap' in the home market may reduce exports by rendering purchasers willing to buy export-type goods instead of others which they cannot immediately get. In the longer run, also, the apparently assured sale for almost anything in the home market may divert resources from export production to production for home, even without any change in the relative prices in the two markets, because the home market is thought to be safer, or because inflation lowers home selling costs, by rendering advertisement, &c. unnecessary.

With prices rigid, therefore, an increase in the 'inflationary gap' in the home-produced goods and services market will tend to worsen the balance of payments, without any inflation of home relatively to foreign prices. It does not follow, of course, even with free importation, that the balance of payments will worsen by the full amount of the increase in this 'inflationary gap'. Buyers who cannot get as much as they would be willing to buy of the home-produced goods on offer will not necessarily (or even probably) spend on imports or goods otherwise exportable the precise amount that they would have spent on extra home-produced goods if they could have got them. An increase in spendable incomes, when there is no increase in the amount or price of goods to be had from home production, cannot, of course, lead to increased expenditure at home, but it can lead to either increased net imports or increased saving, and normally it will lead to both. The gap is filled by both these items, in proportions which will no doubt vary with circumstances.

Moreover, importation into most countries in the period in question was very far from free. Exchange controls, import licensing, and other official measures prevented the full extent of the international disequilibrium from being realized in balances of external payments. Nevertheless, it is clearly likely that suppressed inflation in the sense of the existence of an 'inflationary gap' preserved by price control or other institutional price rigidities, in the market for home-produced goods, was a considerable source of international disequilibrium. That is to say, it largely created a situation in which buyers in many countries would have liked to import very much more (mostly from North America) at the prevailing prices than could currently be paid for. There is no obvious way of estimating the magnitude of disequilibrium due to this cause, but it was probably very large in the years 1945–8, and thereafter greatly diminished.

Finally, there is one important way in which inflation—price inflation in this instance—undeniably contributed to international disequilibrium: namely by raising the prices of goods and services in general, throughout the trading countries of the world, relatively to the stationary price of gold. R. F. Harrod[1] has shown that, had the value of gold produced in the world after the war borne the same ratio to the value of world trade as in the nineteen-thirties, the rest of the world in the years 1950–2 could have paid for its net imports from North America (then $2\frac{1}{2}$ thousand million a year) out of current

[1] I.M.F., *Staff Papers*, vol. iii, no. 1, April 1953.

gold production. In the earlier post-war years, when the deficit was much greater, it could not, of course, have been wholly met in this way, but it could certainly have been met in large part even then. Nor is the change in the general commodity value of gold responsible only for this large contribution to international disequilibrium; Mr. Harrod points out also that the great inadequacy of international monetary reserves since the war which has produced foreign exchange crises out of largely temporary disequilibria, such as that due to the United States recession in 1949 and that due to the price fluctuation during the Korean War, arises mainly from the failure of both gold stocks and new gold production to appreciate in line with other commodities. In 1951 the stock of monetary gold outside the United States was equal in value to only two months' world trade; in 1937 it had been equal to nearly six months' trade. The percentage rate of annual growth of the world's monetary gold stock, moreover, was only one-sixth as great after the war as it had been before it—a result of a slightly decreased physical output (easily accounted for by the lowness of the price) and of the disappearance in the years 1946–51 of more than half the new output into private hoards—a phenomenon which may be attributed largely to fear of inflation.

In one way and another, therefore, inflation has certainly been responsible for a great part of the international disequilibrium since the war, and for the trouble which this disequilibrium has caused, though the mechanism by which it has produced disequilibrium is probably not, in the main, the most obvious one—the raising of price levels in the rest of the world relatively to those in North America. When one turns away from considering the disequilibrium in the strict sense of the imbalance which would have existed in the absence of quantitative controls, to look at the imbalance which actually existed, one sees that the cheapness of the products of the countries which were net suppliers of the rest of the world, relatively to those which the rest of the world was able to give in incomplete exchange, so far from making this imbalance worse, played a very important part in diminishing it. United States imports had risen 10 per cent. in price as compared with exports by 1947 and no less than 42 per cent. by 1951, the basis of comparison in both cases being 1937. In so far as volumes of trade were limited by quantitative control of imports or physical availability of goods for export, this clearly made a great contribution to limiting the need for loans, aid, or drafts on reserves; it is plain, however, that as conditions eased, and market demand came to be more important in determining trade volumes between North America and the rest of the world, the relative cheapness of United States goods would appear in a very different light. The United States recession of 1949 provided the first instance after the war of market demand for imports limiting their volume, and thus revealed something of the fundamental disequilibrium in payments between the United States and the rest of the world.

Devaluation and Disequilibrium

The currency devaluations of September 1949 were essentially attempts to correct this disequilibrium. How far did they succeed in the relatively short run in which their influence on events may be assumed to have been paramount, and is there any ground on which to assess their influence in the longer run?

This is not the place for a full discussion of these questions, but a tentative judgement upon them seems, nevertheless, to be in place in this attempt to see what the relation has been between inflation and the international economic position.

A direct approach to the first question may be made by studying, for a number of countries simultaneously, the relation between the changes in their currency values and the changes in their balances of international trade over a period of a year in which the devaluation is included. A study of this kind[1] yields no statistically significant connexion between the two variables in question. Nor are statistically significant relations obtained when changes in national levels of economic activity over the period studied are taken into account. A more indirect approach, however, may be made by studying separately the ways in which prices of imports and prices of exports responded to devaluation, and then the ways in which volumes of imports and volumes of exports responded to changes in their prices. Some account has already been given of the short-run responsiveness of import prices and export prices to changes in cur-

---

[1] A. J. Brown, 'Some Aspects of International Trade Changes since Devaluation', *Yorkshire Bulletin of Social and Economic Research*, vol. iii, no. 2, July 1951.

rency values in this period. It follows from what has been said earlier in this chapter that the relative dollar prices of international goods from different countries seem, on the average, to have changed by between one-third and one-half of the proportions by which the relative values of the respective national currencies changed, the national currency prices of imports into a devaluing country changing by one-half or two-thirds of the amount by which its currency was devalued relatively to all others. It remains, then, to ask how relative import volumes and relative export volumes responded to changes in the appropriate relative prices.

So far as imports are concerned, a study of their relationship to changes in (national currency) price over a period of a year during which the devaluation occurred suggests again that there is very little response in such a short period—despite the fact that an attempt was made in this study to take account of the effects of changes in economic activity. An investigation of the relation between relative changes in (dollar) prices of exports from different countries and relative changes in their volumes was, however, much more fruitful. This study was similar to that described in the preceding section of this chapter, except that, in the present instance, the changes studied were those occurring between average data for two periods of three months, separated by a year, whereas in the former study they were changes between data for whole, and widely separated, years. In the short run of less than a year, the responsiveness of average export volume to relative export price appears to have been definite, but not very great, relative volume generally changing by no more than the proportion in which relative price had changed. This clearly means that lowering the (foreign currency) price of exports by devaluation did not, in this short period, bring in an increased amount of foreign currency, and, since import volumes were apparently little changed by devaluation, and the foreign currency prices of imports not much changed by it, these results are consistent with the independently observed fact that, within six or nine months of devaluation, no systematic relation was to be seen between the extent to which a country lowered the value of its currency and the extent to which it improved its balance of trade.

As has also been remarked in the preceding section, however, the responsiveness of relative export volumes to changes in their relative (dollar) prices seems to have been considerably greater in longer runs in the past than it appears to have been over a period of twelve months or less in the years 1949–50. If (as seems likely) the trade-diverting power of the devaluations of 1949 had not been fully realized by the summer of 1950, it follows that they probably exerted some net influence in the direction of international equilibrium after that date. By that time, however, such important influences of other kinds had come to bear upon international trade that the lingering effects of devaluation, however real, can hardly be expected to be separately visible.

Inflation and International Disequilibrium after 1949

The final stage of world-wide inflation, that associated with the Korean War and general rearmament, brought very sharp fluctuations in balances of international payments, which need not be discussed in detail here—the greater part of them was clearly due to the great variations in commodity prices which have been mentioned in Chapter 2, and to large and non-simultaneous alterations in the commodity stock positions in the principal industrial countries.

The general trend of international trade and payments, so far as it can be discerned through their short-term fluctuations, was towards balance. The total surplus in the external current transactions of the United States which had been over $6 thousand million in 1948 was running on the average at an annual rate of $2½ thousand million in the years 1950–2. The reasons for this have already been touched upon. In the first place, United States imports, especially raw materials, for which demand is price-inelastic, rose greatly in price at the time of the Korean War, and, though they subsequently fell, did not in general come down to their 1949 level—a fact broadly due, no doubt, to the expansion of industrial demand. Secondly, as has been mentioned above, the volume of United States imports (especially manufactures and semi-manufactures) rose very greatly, presumably in large part for reasons connected with increased availability. Thirdly, United States exports remained relatively cheap in general, a fact which worked in the direction of balance by virtue of the very widespread quantitative control still applied to imports from the United States, which prevented their increasing as much in volume between 1948 and 1950–2 as did imports into the United States.

Whether this approach towards balance corresponds to an approach towards equilibrium in the deeper sense is, however, open to argument. Relative national price levels certainly changed during the Korean War in a direction which was on the whole unfavourable to equilibrium; a fact only prevented from manifesting itself in balance of payments statistics by the widespread control of imports from the dollar area. The cost of living rose between 1950 and 1952 by only some 11 per cent. in the United States and Canada, but by 40 per cent. in Australia, 30 per cent. in France and Spain, and about 20 per cent. in the United Kingdom, Japan, and Sweden. Western Germany and Switzerland were the only western industrial countries of importance in which the increase in costs of living and in wages had not been substantially greater than in North America. Moreover, the productivity of labour had continued to advance more rapidly in North America than in most other areas. On the other hand, the suppressed inflation outside the United States, which had certainly contributed powerfully to the existence of disequilibrium, even though quantitative trade controls prevented it from greatly influencing balances of payments, very largely vanished. Against this, the continued rise of commodity prices in general increased the contribution to general disequilibrium which was made by the relatively low price of gold. Disequilibrium, at all events, was certainly very far from ending with the general cessation of price inflation in 1951, and to this state of affairs the inflation of the previous twelve years had, on any view, made a considerable contribution, though it had most certainly not been the only cause.

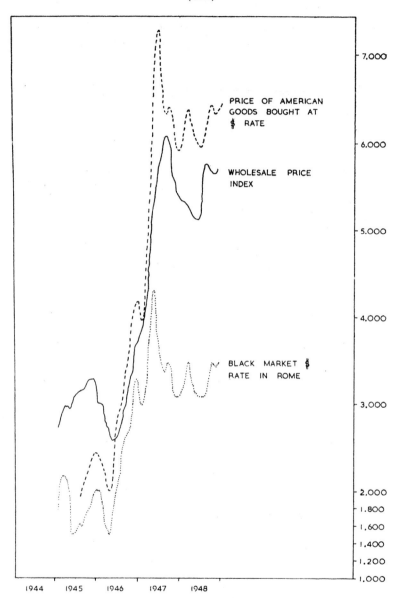

DIAGRAM 28. Internal and external prices and foreign exchanges in Italy, 1944–8.

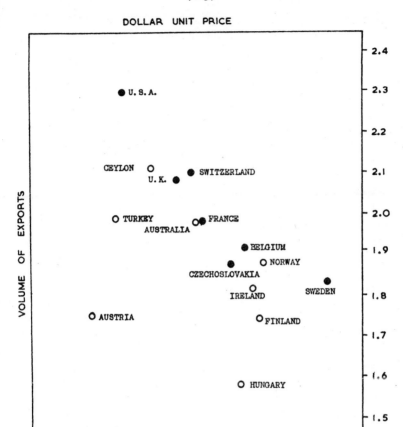

DIAGRAM 29. Logarithms of indices of dollar unit price and volume of exports from certain countries in 1948 (1937 = 100).

12

The World-wide Inflation

The Two Economies

FROM the discussions in the preceding chapters, it may now be possible to form a fairly comprehensive picture of the general nature and mechanism of the world-wide inflationary process which continued, with little interruption though with many local variations (some of them startling), from the outbreak of war in 1939 to the collapse of the Korean War boom in the spring of 1951. In order to do this, it may be helpful to emphasize the distinction, already implicit in earlier passages, between two types of economy. The first is characterized by flexible prices of finished goods—prices which are determined by the forces of the market. In such an economy it is, perhaps, most natural to assume that the prices of the factors of production are also market determined, though in practice always with a considerable lag. This (perhaps with the qualification that wages are particularly sticky, and thus especially slow to respond to changes in demand for labour, or, at least, to reductions in the demand for labour) is still the conventional picture which students of economics are shown. In it changes in the composition of output are brought about by changes in the direction of demand through the response of producers to changes in the prices their products fetch in the market; changes in total effective demand result in changes in output, possibly combined with changes in the same direction in prices, unless full employment exists, in which case increases in effective demand raise prices and also, because of the stickiness of factor prices, temporarily raise profits. A 'multiplier' analysis is applicable to the relation between non-consumption spending and total money income in such an economy whether full employment exists or not, though it may be necessary to take into account a change in the numerical value of the 'multiplier' after full employment is reached.

The second kind of economy which is to be contrasted with

this is one in which prices of finished goods are sticky and respond, not to changes in effective demand, but to changes in cost; they are fixed with reference to average total cost of production at some conventional level of plant utilization. In such an economy a change in the direction of demand away from an initial equilibrium position results, in the first place, not in price changes but simply in increased orders to manufacturers for some things and decreased orders for others, which will mean full use of capacity and plans for expansion in some industries and under-utilization and stagnation in others. To take the case in which the price mechanism plays a minimal part, let us further assume that factor prices are fixed contractually, wages perhaps with reference to the cost of living. In that case the shift in demand will not bring about any changes in the costs of production as reckoned for the purpose of fixing prices of finished goods, and these prices will, accordingly, remain constant. The use of resources will shift as a result of the change in the direction of demand, not through entrepreneurs' responses to changes in the prices of their products and workers' responses to changes in relative wage rates, but through some firms expanding, others going out of business, still others shifting from products they cannot sell to those they can sell, and workers moving from firms where they are on short time, or from which they are dismissed, to others where they can get full-time employment. Until such adjustments in supply are made, consumers will have to queue up for some products, while stocks of others will pile up or the men and the plant producing them will be partially idle.

In an economy of this kind an increase in total effective demand (that is to say, total spending on goods and services) will cause firms to expand their output if they have any idle capacity and can get additional labour and materials, and may stimulate new firms to enter industry. If plant and labour are already fully employed, stocks will run down. It will not, however, be possible for spending to go on increasing once stocks have been run down to some minimal level, except in so far as physical production is expanded through an increase in the working population or through the replacement of old plant and methods by new, leading to higher productivity of labour. A 'multiplier' relation between non-consumption spending and income may hold so long as there is not full employment of plant and labour, but once full employment is reached, money income cannot expand further (except through expansion of population or productivity), and the relation between the consumption and non-consumption components of total expenditure will depend in the short run on the nature of existing capacity and the accidents or institutional machinery which give purchasers of different kinds their places in the queue; in the longer run on the rates at which different kinds of manufacturing capacity expand, which in turn will be related to the accidents of entrepreneurial temperament and the speeds with which different kinds of plant can be delivered.

While stocks are being run down by the increased expenditure (which may be supposed to be financed by newly created money), money will be accumulating in the economy. No one will have enjoyed an increased money income, since at the time when full employment was first attained everyone was already in work and receiving an income which we have assumed not to be increased without an increase in physical production. The traders or manufacturers who formerly held stocks of goods have exchanged them for money, and, if their increased liquidity has tempted them (rather improvidently) to increase their spending, that increase will have been made possible only through someone else spending less than he would otherwise have done, and so accumulating money in excess of what he would otherwise have held.

Once stocks have finished running down, the position is very simple. In so far as any section of the community spends in excess of its current income, the rest of the community must spend less. In so far as the under-spending section chooses to hold its savings in the form of increased cash balances, the over-spenders can continue their over-spending only by creating new money, or having it created for them. Otherwise, the savings of the under-spenders may flow to the over-spenders, and will exactly finance their deficits. In such a situation, even the over-spenders (usually the government and firms investing in new plant and equipment) may not all be spending as much as they would like to, in view of the monetary resources at their disposal; that is to say, with their existing revenue and liquid reserves, they might be willing to spend more if the goods they wanted were available. They will be holding larger liquid reserves than they would have if goods were available without limit at the existing, contractual, prices. It is even more probable that the under-spenders are in this situation. In short, if any new money has been created since the arrival of full employment, and its creation has not been offset by a decision of some members of the community to hold more money instead of goods which they could have bought, it follows that some other members have been deprived of the opportunity to buy goods which, with their existing money revenue and money reserves, they would have liked to buy. It is this state of affairs that is often described as inflationary, or as constituting suppressed inflation even though there is no increase of prices.

In this second type of economy, with prices of finished goods depending on costs, and wages depending on the cost of living, price inflation can come about only through reductions of the productive efficiencies of factors, or through rises in prices of goods and services which come from outside the economy—imported raw materials or foodstuffs or, perhaps, imported equipment or capital. A rise in the prices of imported goods and services will affect the cost of living and the cost of production of manufactures to some extent directly; the rise in the cost of living will, after a lag, affect wage rates and so affect cost of production further; these rises in cost of production will affect cost of living further, and so on perhaps until all prices have risen in proportion to those of imports. In this type of economy monetary factors clearly play (or may play) a part either in the building up of a situation in which there is suppressed inflation or in the development of price inflation initiated from outside. It has been pointed out already that the creation of a measure of suppressed inflation in such an economy requires, normally, the introduction of additional money. If the monetary authorities refuse to make new money available, then it will not be possible for over-spenders, whoever they may be, to have an inflow of purchasing power in excess of their current incomes, except to the extent that other people, faced with the possibility of buying goods, prefer to accumulate and lend money instead. Clearly, suppressed inflation cannot in these circumstances develop, except by an alteration of views in some part of the community about the amount of goods which it would be reasonable to buy in any given state of income and liquid reserves.

Similarly, monetary stringency may have an influence on the course of events if price inflation is introduced into the economy from outside. Increased prices require increased active balances to carry the volume of transactions corresponding to full employment. If no new money is forthcoming, active balances can be increased only by drawing from idle balances, a process which will probably involve a rise in interest rates. This (or simply the reduced liquidity) may affect investment plans, and thus real income. In an extreme case enough money to increase active deposits in proportion to the price rise may not be available from idle deposits. Consequently stocks will have to be reduced throughout the economy, a measure involving a reduction of orders to producers which will reduce real income and perhaps employment for the time being, and may set in motion a cumulative contraction. There will, however, be wide ranges of conditions over which (say) an inexpansible supply of money will not greatly interfere with price inflation imposed from outside. If at the outset there is any substantial measure of suppressed inflation, or if, even in the absence of this, investment (including investment in stocks) is not very sensitive to interest changes, a considerable amount of price increase can take place without interruption from financial factors. Moreover, the supply of money is not normally fixed in these circumstances. An increased value of merchandise in stocks and in transit will normally call forth an increased supply of credit. Indeed, it seems that, in an economy of the kind described, in which price inflation is induced entirely by outside events, there would be little point in the authorities' pursuing a stringent monetary policy; its sole effect (if it was effective at all) would be to cause low profits and unemployment; it could not, directly or indirectly, do anything appreciable to render prosperity and low prices compatible.

The two kinds of economy which have now been briefly sketched are, of course, abstractions. No actual economy perfectly exemplifies the first, since some factor prices and prices of some finished goods are always contractual. Nor does any actual economy conform exactly to the second type—though some of the most highly organized war economies came close to doing so. Generally, some important groups of prices are to a large extent flexible and market-determined. Practically all actual national economies (and, therefore, the world economy as a whole) can, however, usefully be regarded as hybrids of the two pure types just distinguished, and an important part of the task of understanding the process of inflation consists in identifying and assessing the portions of the economy in question which conform (or more nearly conform) to one or the other of these types.

For the United Kingdom, for instance, in 1939 one might guess that far the greater part of the output of finished goods and services was already priced (in the reasonably short run, at least) in accordance with cost. A fairly high proportion of food, a good deal of clothing, furniture, and hardware was, it is true, priced in accordance with demand in the sense that a recession of demand would have caused prices to be marked down, perhaps with little regard to cost; but many even of these commodities would probably not have been marked up in price from some cost-determined level in the event of increased prosperity. On the other hand, about a sixth of expenditure in the United Kingdom was on imports, the prices of which were no doubt very largely demand-determined, but the demand which predominantly determined their prices in the short run was not that of the United Kingdom alone, but that of a world-wide trading community in which the United Kingdom was responsible for only something between a tenth and a fifth of total purchasing power. As for the price of the chief domestic factor of production—labour—it seems (as has been suggested in an earlier chapter) that its rate of increase was systematically affected by the level of demand for it, but that any really marked changes in the cost of living tended to influence it very strongly. The war rendered most prices of finished goods inflexible (or rather, cost-determined), a situation which, on the whole, persisted throughout the inflationary period.

In the United States, on the other hand, the flexibility of the prices of finished goods, up to 1942 and after 1946, at least, has been very much greater than in the United Kingdom; though the retail prices of quite a large number of manufactured goods were, to all intents and purposes, fixed by the manufacturers on a cost basis. The prices of foodstuffs and raw materials certainly were, and are, mainly market-determined, and since most of them are of internal United States origin, and United States demand is in any case so high a proportion (perhaps about one-half) of the total demand in the world trading community, these prices cannot, as in the United Kingdom, be regarded as determined mainly by something outside the economy. Wage changes, too, seem to have been rather more directly demand-determined in the United States than in the United Kingdom in periods of fluctuating employment, though there, too, the cost of living has apparently been the main determinant when employment was relatively high and steady.

In strong contrast stand the primary product exporting countries whose economic lives are so much influenced by the fact that the prices of their exports are determined by the world market as a whole. If their whole price structures are flexible, as is the case with most of the less highly developed, then export prices normally determine the level of their prices generally—except in so far as large public deficits or surpluses, or extraordinary events like heavy expenditures by occupying armies, intervene. On the other hand, some of the more highly developed primary product exporting countries have wage levels tied strictly to the cost of living, and have operated for part of the inflationary period highly efficient price controls. Such economies, however, are usually highly dependent upon the prices of their imports, as well as of their exports, and these also are, of course, outside their control.

The Course of Events

Bearing in mind the distinctions which have been made between the two main modes of price determination, and hence the two main mechanisms of inflation, one can now look more generally at the events of the twelve inflationary years.

There can be little doubt that the initial inflationary impulse in Europe during 1939–40 came from the rise in the flexible prices of primary products. This rise is to be attributed to three factors: devaluation of the most important west European currencies, increase in freights due to war risk, and changes in expectations due to the outbreak of war—expectations which became all the more important because the prices of imports into the United Kingdom, for instance, were soon largely fixed by long-term contracts. It is, perhaps, useful to emphasize the part which expectations must have played at this stage. The physical volume of imports into the main industrial countries of the world was falling in this period, apart from bursts of stock accumulation in Sweden and Switzerland in 1939. It must have been clear that, for the duration of the war, importation into Central Europe would be hampered by blockade. Nevertheless, the long-term contracts placed by the United Kingdom with primary producing countries in the early months of the war involved price increases frequently in the neighbourhood of 40 per cent. The expectations of price increase were, of course, more than justified in the event, and the raised prices at which long-term contracts were made in 1939–40 were, in the case of many commodities, more than compensated by relative cheapness in the later years. The prices of raw materials (mainly imported) and of foodstuffs thus rose ahead of wage costs, and ahead, on the whole, of retail prices.

In the United States the position was different. With some imported goods cheapened by the devaluation of sterling and other currencies at the outbreak of war, with shipping freights relatively unimportant in the prices of the materials and foodstuffs used, and without the complication of long-term bulk purchase, wholesale prices did not rise much at the outbreak of war, and began their steady climb only at the end of 1940. The advance in effective demand, meanwhile, had enabled wage rates to be significantly increased (they had not actually fallen even in the pre-war recession), and they ran ahead both of the cost of living and (until 1941–2 at least) of wholesale prices. It seems, therefore, that the United States price rise up to Pearl Harbour, if not until the end of 1942, owed as much to the direct effect of increasing effective demand on wages as to its effect on primary products. As in the United Kingdom, it also owed something to increasing profits, though these were most notable in the war industries whose products do not enter into indexes of price.

It has already been pointed out in Chapter 2 that the later half of the war was notable for stable prices both of finished products and of factors of production (with labour a partial exception) in most of the chief belligerent economies. This stability was maintained partly with the help of subsidies in

U

the face of rising import prices; the primary producing countries which were not among the main belligerents continued to sell their exports in a relatively free and flexible market. The Middle Eastern and Indian inflations of the middle and later war years were, of course, predominantly matters of demand-determined (often expectation-determined) price increase modified to only a limited extent by price rigidities of any kind.

The second great burst of price increase in the world as a whole was that which followed the abandonment of United States price control in 1946. So far as the United States economy was concerned, the first consequence of this measure was, clearly, a rise of the prices of many consumable goods (especially food) to something like a free market equilibrium level. The adjustment of wage rates which followed this, however, seems to have been mainly due to trade union demand related to the raised cost of living rather than to employers' competing demands for labour in a flexible market; the wage increases in turn raised cost-determined prices, and so a price–wage spiral —the typical mechanism of adjustment in an economy of contractual wages and cost-determined prices—came into action. So far as Europe was concerned, the price inflation of this period can be attributed mainly to a price–wage spiral set in motion by the rise of import prices consequent partly upon United States decontrol, partly upon the pressure of steadily rising demand for industrial raw materials on an inelastic supply in world markets.

The devaluations of September 1949 exercised their inflationary effects in the devaluing countries almost entirely through the mechanism of the price–wage spiral. Not only were the principal countries concerned ones in which wages respond little to changes merely of aggregate demand over so short a period, and in which prices of finished goods were still quite largely controlled, but changes in aggregate effective demand induced by the devaluations' impact upon balances of payments were relatively small, and in the most important cases were apparently offset by adjustments of public spending. In any case the inflationary effect of the devaluations was probably not very great—it had little time to mature before the much sharper impact of the Korean War.

The inflationary effect of this in all the main trading countries of the world was very similar to that of the outbreak of war in 1939 upon the economies of Western Europe. Once more, it was the great rise of flexible commodity prices, based largely on expectations, that set the process in motion. It seems that on this occasion, the wage increases in the United States, as well as those in Europe, were occasioned by previous rises in the cost of living rather than by the direct pressure of employers' demands for labour. It was, therefore, broadly true of all the main industrial trading countries of the world that increased (largely speculative) demand for primary commodities affected the prices of finished goods and of labour through costs of production and of living rather than that an increased demand for finished goods raised their prices directly and then filtered down as an increased demand for the factors of production.

The inflationary burst of 1950–1 was the only one within the period discussed here which was followed by an equally, or almost equally, sharp reversal—so far, at any rate, as commodity prices were concerned. This episode illustrates what would appear to be another general feature of the inflationary mechanism which has recently been at work in the main countries of the western world, namely, its only partial reversibility. In the short run flexible commodity prices can fall (especially as a result of expectational changes) as easily as they can rise. The same is true, no doubt, of many of the mainly cost-determined prices of finished goods—they fall with reduction of costs as readily, or almost as readily, as they rise with cost increases. With the prices of factors of production, however, and especially those of labour, the position is radically different. The money illusion operates asymmetrically. When a rise in commodity prices lowers real incomes of wage and salary earners, the fact becomes painfully apparent to them, since the effort to maintain customary standards of living very soon encounters difficulties—all the more acute if savings have been directed into the rigid channels of insurance and hire-purchase payments. The pressure for wage and salary increases, therefore, tends to be quick and insistent. On the other hand, when commodity prices and the cost of living fall, the increased well-being of receivers of fixed incomes is, perhaps, only rather slowly realized in the form of higher real consumption, and in any case brings a gratification which is considerably less acute than the pain suffered when prices rise. In these circumstances there is less reason to depart from the customary assessment of income in money terms when prices are falling than when they are rising, and reductions of money wages or salaries are stoutly opposed even when the corresponding real incomes are being raised.

The result of this asymmetry is, of course, that while upward movements of commodity prices impart (even if with some delay) an effective upward push to the whole price structure, downward movements are only partially effective in pulling it down. Fluctuations of the general level of flexible prices thus seem hard to separate from an upward trend of prices as a whole.

Clearly, however, the upward trend does not necessarily follow from the fluctuation in all circumstances. The last quarter of the nineteenth century and the twenty years between the two world wars in the twentieth century were both periods in which prices in general fluctuated vigorously, but with a falling trend. The conditions which contributed towards making this possible were, no doubt, increasing productivity and periodic unemployment of the hired factors of production. The increasing productive efficiency of the hired factors, largely due to the accumulation of technical knowledge, obviously played a considerable part in enabling the prices of products to fall while the prices of factors were either falling considerably less fast or were actually rising; the periodic depressions reduced the effective demand for hired factors to such an extent from time to time that their prices were temporarily held stationary or actually reduced. On the other hand, the period 1939-53 was notable (indeed, unique among periods of such length in modern times) for the absence of any general recession of effective demand sufficient to halt the rise of factor prices. Even in the intervals when wage and salary demands may be judged to have been least affected by current or recent increases in the cost of living, the prices of the hired factors tended to rise at a rate a little, though in some instances very little, in advance of their average physical productivities.

The Inflationary Factors and their Control

The inflation of the period which has been discussed in this book was clearly due, in the last resort, to three factors. In the first place, war and, to some extent, reconstruction gave rise to an enormous increase of demand for goods and factors of production, made effective mainly by budget deficits. This was a circumstance peculiar to the troubled times through which the world was passing, and one may hope that, in ordinary conditions of peace, all important economies will be able to avoid these long-lasting excesses of total demand—indeed, they were on the whole avoided after the fairly early years of reconstruction, despite the heavy rearmament expenditure which grew after June 1950. The excess demand, while it lasted, was dealt with not unsuccessfully by fixing prices and using physical controls to supplant the price mechanism as a distributor of factors of production and finished goods. Secondly, much shorter-lived increases in demand largely of a speculative nature, not financed by budget deficits or excessive creations of long-term credit, had the effect in 1939–40 and again in 1951–2 of drastically raising commodity prices; to this may be added the effect of increased costs of shipping and insurance in the face of the outbreak or threat of war. These are essentially temporary price-raising influences in the sense that their ceasing to exist should lower prices, not simply leave them stationary at a higher level, as the balancing of budgets after a period of deficit may be expected to do. That their influence is not entirely temporary in this sense is attributable partly to the third factor which has been important in this period—the bias in most economies towards inflation, in all times of fairly full employment, of factor prices and prices of finished goods which are based upon them.

This bias constitutes the most persistent and troublesome inflationary threat facing the western world. It can presumably be wholly suppressed by complete administrative control of wages and salaries, such as operates in the Soviet Union, or by some effective agreement limiting the increase in prices of the hired factors to the amount justified by the increase in their average physical productivity. The possibility of such agreements has been widely discussed, but so far agreed limitations have been attempted only in the Netherlands, where they succeeded wartime wage control. Their coming into being would require drastic changes in the attitudes and functions of trade unions. At the very least, the unions' functions in the field of wage bargaining would be changed largely from an industry-by-industry struggle for higher wages at the expense of the entrepreneurs and the consumers into a conscious struggle between workers in different industries for shares of a fixed, agreed, total increment. To this extent, the element of class struggle in wage negotiation would be diminished; it would, presumably, be transferred from the field of wage bargaining to the more general political field, in which economic policy governing the size of profits would become a more explicit issue than at present. Some writers have suggested that the division of the agreed increment in the wage bill between different industries might itself be done in accordance with an agreed formula, depending upon the adequacy of labour supply to each separate industry as shown by movements in rates of unemployment, those industries in which the unemployment rate fell below certain levels being given the whole, or the greater part, of the available wage increment. To the extent to which such a general agreement became effective the natural drive of employees' organizations for improved wages would presumably be still further diverted into a search for ways of increasing the ratio of wages to profits in the community as a whole; perhaps also into a more active interest in the encouragement of increased productivity in general. The political difficulties, advantages, and disadvantages of such schemes for regulating wage increases cannot, however, be discussed here; an adequate discussion would require separate and detailed consideration of the institutional factors at work in each of the principal countries. The events which have been discussed in this book merely pose the problem.

It seems that, unless the bias towards inflation of factor prices in conditions of full employment can be eliminated, it may be possible to purchase long-term stability of the price level of commodities only at the cost of recurrent periods of unemployment, in which the rise of factor prices is temporarily arrested or even reversed. This, indeed, seems to have been one of the conditions of price stability (or, for quite long periods, of price reduction) in the nineteenth century.

How hard a condition is it? The brief examination which has been undertaken in Chapter 4 of the relation between unemployment rates and price movements in recent times suggests that, in the institutional conditions now prevailing in some of the principal advanced countries in the West, it is likely to be harder than public opinion at large would tolerate. If this is so, then the countries in question are faced with a choice between some modification of their wage-determining machinery and an appreciable inflationary trend in the course of prices of finished goods and services in general.

To some extent, stabilizing the prices of primary commodities may help to prevent the upward drift of factor prices from being so rapid as to raise the prices of finished goods at an unacceptable rate. In the period under review price stabilization by subsidy was undertaken in circumstances which permitted it only partial success. It was successful in that it greatly slowed down, or even halted, the rise in prices of finished goods in the main belligerent economies during the later part of the war, and in that this result was important at the time both in preserving confidence in the value of money in the countries practising it and, perhaps, also in keeping down prices in the primary producing countries by holding the prices which they had to pay for manufactured imports. Apart from these functions, however, it served simply to prevent prices in general (both of factors and finished goods) in the subsidizing countries from rising in proportion to the prices of their imports under pressure of demand for the maintenance of real incomes. If inflation had been succeeded by deflation of primary commodity prices, as happened after the First World War, it would have become possible to remove subsidies without setting a price–wage spiral in motion, and the subsidizing policy could have been judged a total success. In the event, the post-war quinquennium brought no recession of effective demand sufficient to shake primary commodity prices downwards; on the contrary, the pressure of effective demand remained embarrassingly high in most countries; and as subsidies were abolished for budgetary reasons or to make possible the abandonment of rationing, the price–wage spiral came into operation at last. It would not be true to say that subsidies did no more than postpone an inevitable rise of prices in the countries which used them in line with the increased world market prices of their imports. In their absence inflation might have developed a momentum of its own in the countries in question owing to the growth of expectations of continued price increase, and this in turn would in some degree have reacted on world prices of primary commodities both from the side of demand and also, perhaps, by increasing their costs of production. But it is, nevertheless, clear that subsidies cannot insulate an economy from an unreversed rise in the price of its imports unless they are permanent—a condition which is likely to involve a heavy budgetary burden and to be unacceptable unless justified by some consideration apart from the general price level. The ideal opportunity for price stabilization by subsidies (as one can see after the event) was the price boom of 1950–1, which was so quickly reversed, but left more permanent inflationary consequences because of the delayed and irreversible effect of even a temporarily raised cost of living upon wage rates. On that occasion, of course, the opportunity was not taken, either because subsidies were a too recent memory to be fashionable, or because, in the absence of full economic mobilization and controls, attention was concentrated upon budgetary means of controlling effective demand.

A more drastic policy than that of subsidizing primary commodity prices country by country would be the institution of world-wide price stabilization schemes. The successful price stabilization in the latter half of the war and the first post-war years was in no small measure due to the non-competitive bulk buying and agreed allocation of raw materials and foodstuffs by the British, United States, and Canadian governments, and subsequently to allocation by the International Emergency Food Council and similar bodies. But for these substitutes for fully competitive buying, the prices of key commodities, of which there was acute shortage in the area accessible to the United Nations, such as rubber in the middle of the war, and the main foodstuffs in 1945–7, would presumably have soared to great heights. In the Korean crisis much less effective action was taken: the International Materials Conference then set up recommended the international allocation of a few key materials, and the recommendations were in three cases implemented for a time, but none of the major commodities, from which the main inflationary thrust came, were included in the list.

Apart from schemes of allocation, national or international, which are clearly called for only in times of quite exceptional shortage, commodity price fluctuations can in some degree be prevented by international control schemes of other kinds. The development of such schemes, subject to proper safeguards, was discussed along with other major international economic and monetary matters both during and after the war, but with little result, and a set of general principles in the Havana Charter for the abortive International Trade Organization remains the chief monument of these discussions, unless the present form of the International Wheat Agreement may be said to owe something to them. Agreement in this field is in any case difficult, as it is in that of wages policy, because directly conflicting interests are involved; but it may have been rendered still more difficult by a failure to realize that the gain from successful stabilization lies by no means all on the side of the producers. The importing countries may stand to lose in depression, when the prices of their imports are artificially maintained, but they stand to gain in times of boom, not only in the obvious way through their terms of trade and balances of payments, but also from an avoidance of severe inflationary thrusts such as that of 1950-1, which, under régimes of high and steady employment, exercise a powerful and irreversible effect upon their internal price levels. It would appear that efficient price stabilization can result only from schemes incorporating buffer stocks of some kind; others, like the International Wheat Agreement, are not likely to eliminate any but the very short-term fluctuations, except in so far as they in fact involve elements of stockpiling in depression or of allocation in boom through some such mechanism as guaranteed purchases and sales at stipulated prices, or in so far as the shadow of full international allocation in case of severe shortage can be perceived in the background.

The avoidance of large fluctuations in commodity prices, however, can act only as a palliative: if the circumstances are such that these fluctuations would lead to successive irreversible increases in factor prices, it is probable that factor prices will have a tendency to creep upwards by themselves, even without the stimulus of commodity price fluctuations. It is because of this tendency for an upward creep in conditions of high and steady employment that the question of wages policy must be accorded primacy among the practical problems arising from the inflationary experience of the period here discussed.

The urgency of this problem will depend upon other factors. With rapidly increasing labour productivity, or, more generally, increasing factor efficiency in production, the money rewards of factors may for long periods be able to increase at the rate which is produced by the present bargaining process in conditions of high employment without raising money costs per unit of output —or, at least, without raising them too much. Society's capacity to tolerate gradual inflation is considerable, and few problems would be raised by a steady rise of the price level over a long period by, say, 1 per cent. per annum. The record of recent years, however, does not encourage one to believe that the rate of inflation will so easily be kept down to such a low level in this way in all countries. The United States might achieve it; for the United Kingdom the prospect is far more doubtful. The dilemma which the first sustained period of full employment in the history of industrial civilization has revealed seems likely to remain with us for some time.

TABLES III–VI

TABLE III

Indices of Wholesale Prices

1 Country	*2* Dec. 1942 as % of Jan.–June 1939	*3* Aug. 1945 as % of Dec. 1942	*4* June 1946 as % of Aug. 1945	*5* Aug. 1948 as % of June 1946	*6* Aug. 1948 as % of Jan.–June 1939	*7* Aug. 1949 as % of Aug. 1948	*8* May 1950 as % of Aug. 1949	*9* May 1951 as % of May 1950
Argentina	186·5	112·6	110·5	117·9	273·5	··	··	··
Australia	136·0	103·7	99·3	123·6	173·0	109·2	115·7	123·0
Austria	··	··	··	242·0	†449·0	140·6	124·5	134·0
Belgium	··	111·2	··	151·0	390·0	94·4	100·4	131·0
Brazil	198·5	··	108·0	··	†302	109·7	105·0	140·5
Bulgaria	131·8	283·6	104·9	133·0	808·2	··	··	··
Canada	192·8	107·7	111·3	145·0	216·1	98·4	104·9	117·9
Chile	151·0	114·8	97·9	160·6	395·1	114·7	110·2	132·3
Costa Rica	145·0	127·8	184·7	116·0	219·2	97·8	113·8	125·5
Czechoslovakia	195·1	103·4	97·4	116·1	321·6	103·2	··	··
Denmark	242·1	98·4	97·0	126·7	236·9	98·1	111·8	133·2
Egypt	230·3	137·5	142·0	106·1	342·7	89·8	113·8	113·0
Finland	194·0¹	187·0	153·8	160·7	983·5	98·6	108·9	146·1
France	105·0	195·4²	··	331·0	1,930·0	108·0	107·2	135·1
W. Germany	··	··	··	··	··	112·9	101·3	125·2
Greece	··	··	··	··	25,200·0	116·0	96·5	133·1
Hungary	186·0	··	··	164·7	··	··	··	··
India	158·0¹	154·4²	108·3	143·8	358·0	101·6	101·0	116·1
Iran	378·6	122·8	87·7	122·6	500·2	95·9	82·0	112·9
Iraq	··	··	··	108·2	521·0	81·9	108·2	113·9

Ireland	169·0[1]	115·4[2]	99·5	118·5	229·9	99·1	104·2	119·6
Israel (Palestine)	292·4	111·1	103·4	118·5	398·2	87·0	90·2	104·9
Italy	150·0	2,106·0	81·4	221·5	5,700·0	85·7	95·9	121·2
Japan	128·8	293·3	275·7	1,000·0	11,467·0	138·5	108·0	151·8
Lebanon	761·0	133·9	83·6	90·8	†758·0	77·5	93·5	140·1
Mexico	119·2	175·3	112·9	111·6	263·4	101·4	109·5	128·6
Netherlands	158·0[1]	113·2[2]	139·7	112·2	280·5	104·7	110·8	129·0
New Zealand	139·3	108·4	101·3	117·1	178·1	96·7	109·7	114·2
Norway	178·1	102·8	94·5	107·2	185·5	102·8	109·3	126·9
Peru	187·5	116·8	103·7	121·9	276·7	145·6	107·0	120·5
Portugal	189·0	122·2	100·0	109·0	252·9	97·0	100·8	106·4
Spain	180·5	120·2	114·2	132·8	329·3	106·7	108·5	139·7
Sweden	178·9	99·5	95·5	116·6	198·2	99·0	103·2	136·5
Switzerland	202·8	104·0	95·3	108·3	217·7	95·0	96·0	117·2
Turkey	521·0	85·4	96·5	104·4	448·4	110·0	89·6	110·1
Union of South Africa	147·1	108·8	101·9	113·5	185·0	104·2	104·6	114·2
United Kingdom	166·1	106·0	101·1	126·9	225·9	104·0	113·0	125·0
United States	132·5	103·9	107·2	149·6	221·9	89·9	102·2	117·0
Venezuela	118·2	121·8	104·2	117·6	176·4	96·0	92·5	107·4

† Rough estimate.
[1] Average for 1942 as % of Jan.–June 1939.
[2] Aug. 1945 as % of average for 1942.

Table IV

Indices of Cost of Living

1	*2*	*3*	*4*	*5*	*6*	*7*	*8*	*9*
Country	Dec. 1942 as % of Jan.–June 1939	Aug. 1945 as % of Dec. 1942	June 1946 as % of Aug. 1945	Aug. 1948 as % of June 1946	Aug. 1948 as % of Jan.–June 1939	Aug. 1949 as % of Aug. 1948	May 1950 as % of Aug. 1949	May 1951 as % of May 1950
Argentina	111·8	119·9	108·9	..	..	..	..	129·4
Australia	123·0	100·0	101·6	114·5	143·1	109·3	107·2	119·2
Austria	..	..	..	315·3	450·0	135·6	106·5	123·0
Belgium	..	..	84·4	126·1	380·8	94·6	97·9	112·0
Bolivia	314·3	113·3	103·1	128·5	471·6	106·7	..	130·5
Brazil	141·2	132·4	109·1	182·0	371·3	96·0	108·2	113·9
Burma	..	..	..	..	289·9	144·2	73·5	96·6
Bulgaria	201·0	242·3	117·2	..	..	..	..	..
Canada	115·7	103·7	102·5	127·9	157·3	103·1	100·5	111·2
Ceylon	..	..	..	†113·4	241·4	98·0	103·9	106·3
Chile	182·0	129·7	113·1	166·7	445·1	117·9	108·0	120·0
China	..	..	..	925·0	305×10^6	..	..	..
Colombia	106·6	144·5	106·5	147·0	241·1	104·0	118·5	115·7
Costa Rica	138·2	126·7	100·6	119·6	210·5	109·8	106·0	111·8
Czechoslovakia	160·0[1]	101·9[2]	187·1	92·7	282·7	..	105·0	..
Denmark	156·6	101·5	98·7	106·3	166·9	100·0	105·0	111·0
Finland	181·8	172·7	143·6	181·4	818·1	98·9	107·8	120·8
France[3]	162·0[1]	217·9[2]	152·4	293·4	1,578·5	106·2	84·5	121·2
W. Germany	..	..	..	..	160·0[4]	100·0	99·4	105·8
Greece	8,900·0	..	1,100·0	130·0	25,221·0	125·0	96·0	126·0
Hungary	152·3	8,536·0	†31×10^{16}	130·1[5]	450·0	..	..	..
India	180·8	129·4	106·0	124·2	310·5	95·5	101·6	107·2

Indo-China	...	...	...	252·0	3,490·0	118·9	99·6	113·2
Iran	684·7	89·4	88·4	116·3	629·0	113·1	80·3	105·5
Iraq	...	...	...	123·0	†681·0	73·6	96·5	103·0
Ireland	158·2	106·8	98·2	105·9	175·8	101·1	101·5	107·3
Israel (Palestine)	128·6	111·2	102·8	134·0	357·0	94·4	94·6	107·8
Italy	166·0	1,460·2	140·3	151·7	5,160·0	102·8	96·9	111·5
Japan	122·2	165·3	1,574·0	†475·0	†15,000·0	118·0	89·2	122·4
Lebanon	365·0	157·0	91·2	92·0	481·2	90·5	96·5	109·5
Mexico	128·4	171·8	120·9	123·9	326·9	104·2	103·8	109·4
Netherlands	144·0¹	112·5²	112·3	111·0	202·0	106·4	101·6	111·7
New Zealand	115·5	100·0	100·0	108·9	125·0	108·0	104·9	113·9
Norway	149·5	105·0	101·3	99·4	158·0	103·0	101·6	117·0
Paraguay	†147·0	†145·0	113·7	185·0	447·0	125·8	169·6	128·8
Peru	136·6	136·9	107·5	173·1	347·9	118·0	107·5	109·1
Poland	...	...	152·0	116·2	12,820·0	100·0	110·5	101·1
Portugal³	146·0	125·3	108·2	94·5	187·1	100·3	101·5	104·5
Spain	160·0	115·8	130·8	125·0	289·8	106·9	103·0	111·4
Sweden	142·4	101·1	100·0	106·7	153·6	101·8	100·0	117·3
Switzerland	145·9	105·5	98·7	107·2	162·9	99·4	98·1	105·0
Turkey	340·0	102·9	94·9	99·9	331·6	112·2	94·0	96·8
Union of South Africa	120·2	109·8	102·3	110·7	149·4	102·6	103·7	107·2
United Kingdom	128·7	103·3	100·0	131·8	167·5	102·8	102·8	108·8
United States	118·8	109·4	103·8	130·8	176·6	96·6	100·0	109·6
Uruguay	108·8	131·4	103·5	117·9	170·1	106·7	93·1	115·0
Venezuela³	108·9	121·2	104·5	137·7	191·5	100·5	96·2	105·0

† Rough estimate.
¹ Average for 1942 as % of Jan.–June 1939.
² Aug. 1945 as % of average for 1942.
³ Food only.
⁴ Average for 1948 as % of Jan.–June 1939.
⁵ Aug. 1948 as % of Sept. 1946 (date of issue of new currency).

TABLE V

Indices of Quantity of Money (Currency plus Current Accounts)

1 Country	2 Dec. 1942 as % of Dec. 1938	3 Aug. 1945 as % of Dec. 1942	4 June 1946 as % of Aug. 1945	5 Aug. 1948 as % of June 1946	6 Aug. 1948 as % of Dec. 1938	7 Aug. 1949 as % of Aug. 1948	8 May 1950 as % of Aug. 1949	9 May 1951 as % of May 1950
Argentina	167	162	120	167	518[2]	132[1]	122[1]	139[1]
Australia	192	160	114	111	399	117	124	132
Austria	..	..	..	150	527	115	106	122
Belgium[5]	230	101	122	115	442	105	99	102
Bolivia	318	145	113	121	635	122	121	141
Brazil	155	238	112	115	395	115	115	132
Bulgaria	275	224	112	..	..	..	..	..
Canada	250	130	100	105	371	103	107	106
Chile	194	157	125	146	610	114	108	135
Costa Rica	222	137	90	125	367	124	112	106
Czechoslovakia[6]	..	..	164	176	487[1]	102[1]	..	..
Denmark	221	166	112	70	380	91	102	98
Egypt	324	218	102	101	640[1]	106[1]	114[1]	104[1]
Finland	420	171	104	157	1,120	108	110	124
France	327	138	135	167	1,019	110	114	115
Greece	..	..	..	..	13,080	..	138	122
India	303	196	127	99	477	91	109	108
Iran	424	373	..	106[3]	680	105	..	..
Iraq	..	..	..	..	775	104	112	98
Ireland	138	131	106	110	210	105	108	103
Israel (Palestine)	280	228	110	95	..	..	..	149[4]

Italy	319	128	410	215	4,349	123	104	112
Japan	236	104	371	348	3,170	237	112	135
Lebanon[7]	376	97	206	100	1,199	98	116	105
Mexico	299	107	224	106	481	109	114	135
Netherlands	248	105	112	125	286	100	99	94
Norway	515	100	107	120	851	98	100	103
Paraguay	..	..	..	..	664[5]	160	149	153
Peru	155	112	238	115	584	116	100	151
Portugal	276	118	144	100	436	95	100	107
Spain	..	..	..	..	265[1]	103[1]	108[1]	112[1]
Sweden	168	102	121	136	284	104	102	107
Switzerland	136	105	132	122	208	108	99	110
Turkey	248	98	140	126	438	103	110	110
Union of S. Africa	216	117	147	115	335	85	107	112
United Kingdom	190	103	136	104	300	101	99	103
United States	193	105	160	103	343	99	101	104
Uruguay	124	117	165	116	344	113	104	124
Venezuela	174	113	175	162	413	116	105	100

X

[1] Currency only.
[2] July 1948 as % of December 1938.
[3] As % of December 1946.
[4] As % of June 1950.
[5] As % of December 1939.
[6] As % of December 1937.
[7] As % of December 1935.

TABLE VI

Changes in Dollar Values of National Currencies and Prices, 1937–48
(1948 values as % of 1937)

1 Country	*2* Dollar value of Currency	*3* Wholesale Prices ($)	*4* Cost of Living ($)	*5* Wage rates or Earnings[1] ($)	*6* Unit Value of Exports ($)
Argentina[2] . .	83	184	150	205 (ME)	348
Australia . .	81	138	121	150 (HR)	231
Austria . . .	54	171	163	152 (HR)	162
Belgium . . .	68	244	265	252 (HE)	265
Bolivia . . .	41	..	274	..	262
Brazil . . .	62	210	237	..	196
Bulgaria . . .	29	217	198	..	249
Canada . . .	100	181	153	167 (WE)	187
Ceylon . . .	81	311	211	255 (WR)	251
Chile . . .	90	312	400	669 (DE)	..
China . . .	27	725	845	1,180	..
Colombia . .	90	281	255	197	..
Costa Rica . .	99	222	215	..	..
Cuba . . .	100	242	270	..	186
Czechoslovakia .	57	186	185	148 (HR)	243
Denmark . .	94	201	160	198 (HE)	264
Egypt . . .	81	258	235	..	..
El Salvador . .	100	241	215	..	269
Finland . .	34	302	284	399 (HE)	368
France . . .	12	234	234	206 (ME)	216
W. Germany .	74	138	120	103 (WE)	..
Greece . . .	2·2	550	549	..	..
Honduras . .	100	..	290	..	..
Hungary . .	28	185	136	154 (HE)	244
Iceland . . .	70	..	226	..	248
India . . .	81	279	233	..	332
Indonesia . .	69	222	..	..	..
Iran . . .	50	295	390	..	..
Iraq . . .	82	449	550	..	..
Ireland . . .	81	190	152	158 (HE)	258
Israel (Palestine) .	89	376	302	495 (DE)	..
Italy . . .	3·3	180	160	173 (HE)	235
Japan . . .	9·6	980	1,410	820 (ME)	340
Lebanon . .	57	445	284	..	..
Luxemburg . .	54	..	164	..	..
Mexico . . .	74	198	271	..	..
Netherlands . .	69	178	142	145 (HE)	279
New Zealand . .	88	158	125	136 (WR)	172
Nicaragua . .	40	137	140	..	..
Norway . . .	81	148	130	145 (HE)	255
Panama . . .	100	..	199	..	..
Paraguay . .	80	..	246	226 (DR)	..

1	2	3	4	5	6
	Dollar value of Currency	Wholesale Prices ($)	Cost of Living ($)	Wage rates or Earnings[1] ($)	Unit Value of Exports ($)
Country					
Peru . . .	61	240	205	..	..
Philippines . .	100	464	408	..	292
Poland . . .	17	..	22	..	..
Portugal . . .	89	214	170	..	..
Spain . . .	69	276	312	..	260
Sweden . . .	109	210	172	235 (HE)	260
Switzerland . .	108	225	177	201 (DR)	275
Thailand . .	23	374	284	..	..
Turkey . . .	45	205	156	..	174
Union of S. Africa .	82	149	126	..	..
United Kingdom .	82	164	142	149 (WR)	203
United States . .	100	191	167	216 (HE)	193
Uruguay . .	103	..	185	..	..
Venezuela . .	95	166	194	..	..

[1] DE = Daily Earnings.
HE = Hourly Earnings.
WE = Weekly Earnings.
ME = Monthly Earnings.
HR = Hourly Rates.
DR = Daily Rates.
WR = Weekly Rates.
[2] All data for 1947.

INDEX

PRINTED IN
GREAT BRITAIN
AT THE
UNIVERSITY PRESS
OXFORD
BY
CHARLES BATEY
PRINTER
TO THE
UNIVERSITY